Access Your Free Subscription to *NC Crimes* Online

The purchase of this supplement includes FREE access to the online version of *NC Crimes* through **March 1, 2018**. The online version features the following:

- Updated content through 2016
- Keyword searching
- Linking to cross-references
- Printable pages throughout the site
- Accessibility anywhere your electronic device can connect to the Internet
- Collapsible and expandable statutes

Follow the instructions below to begin using the online version.

- Visit **bit.ly/nccrimesonline2017** to activate your free subscription.
- Enter coupon code 2017NCCRIMES for free access (included with the purchase of this book).
- New users should complete the "New Customer Information Form" to create an account. Returning users may use their account login information from previous UNC School of Government purchases.
- You will receive an automatic e-mail from the School of Government granting you access to the online version.

Create an account today for unlimited access through **March 1, 2018**. This is a free subscription. You will not be charged.

For questions about your online subscription, contact the bookstore at **sales@sog.unc.edu**.

For information about other publications and resources from the School of Government, visit **sog.unc.edu**.

2016 Cumulative
Supplement to
NORTH CAROLINA

CRIMES

A Guidebook on the Elements of Crime

Seventh Edition

Jessica Smith

The School of Government at the University of North Carolina at Chapel Hill works to improve the lives of North Carolinians by engaging in practical scholarship that helps public officials and citizens understand and improve state and local government. Established in 1931 as the Institute of Government, the School provides educational, advisory, and research services for state and local governments. The School of Government is also home to a nationally ranked Master of Public Administration program, the North Carolina Judicial College, and specialized centers focused on community and economic development, information technology, and environmental finance.

As the largest university-based local government training, advisory, and research organization in the United States, the School of Government offers up to 200 courses, webinars, and specialized conferences for more than 12,000 public officials each year. In addition, faculty members annually publish approximately 50 books, manuals, reports, articles, bulletins, and other print and online content related to state and local government. The School also produces the *Daily Bulletin Online* each day the General Assembly is in session, reporting on activities for members of the legislature and others who need to follow the course of legislation.

Operating support for the School of Government's programs and activities comes from many sources, including state appropriations, local government membership dues, private contributions, publication sales, course fees, and service contracts.

Visit sog.unc.edu or call 919.966.5381 for more information on the School's courses, publications, programs, and services.

Michael R. Smith, Dean
Thomas H. Thornburg, Senior Associate Dean
Frayda S. Bluestein, Associate Dean for Faculty Development
Johnny Burleson, Associate Dean for Development
Michael Vollmer, Associate Dean for Administration
Linda H. Weiner, Associate Dean for Operations
Janet Holston, Director of Strategy and Innovation

FACULTY

Whitney Afonso
Trey Allen
Gregory S. Allison
David N. Ammons
Ann M. Anderson
Maureen Berner
Mark F. Botts
Anita R. Brown-Graham
Peg Carlson
Leisha DeHart-Davis
Shea Riggsbee Denning
Sara DePasquale
James C. Drennan
Richard D. Ducker
Robert L. Farb
Norma Houston
Cheryl Daniels Howell
Jeffrey A. Hughes
Willow S. Jacobson
Robert P. Joyce
Diane M. Juffras
Dona G. Lewandowski
Adam Lovelady

James M. Markham
Christopher B. McLaughlin
Kara A. Millonzi
Jill D. Moore
Jonathan Q. Morgan
Ricardo S. Morse
C. Tyler Mulligan
Kimberly L. Nelson
David W. Owens
LaToya B. Powell
William C. Rivenbark
Dale J. Roenigk
John Rubin
Jessica Smith
Meredith Smith
Carl W. Stenberg III
John B. Stephens
Charles Szypszak
Shannon H. Tufts
Vaughn Mamlin Upshaw
Aimee N. Wall
Jeffrey B. Welty
Richard B. Whisnant

Printed in the United States of America

21 20 19 18 17   3 4 5

ISBN 978-1-56011-892-3

♾ This publication is printed on permanent, acid-free paper in compliance with the North Carolina General Statutes.

♲ Printed on recycled paper

Contents

11

Crime against Nature, Incest, Indecent Exposure, and Related Offenses   73

12

Kidnapping and Related Offenses   77

13

Larceny, Possession of Stolen Goods, Embezzlement, and Related Offenses   83

Acknowledgments

Producing this annual supplement in a timely fashion is a challenging process that I wouldn't be able to accomplish without help. This year, I am especially grateful to my colleague Bob Farb, who helped identify relevant legislative changes, and to research assistant Christopher Tyner for cite checking assistance. Also thanks to the School's Publications Division—particularly Nancy Dooly and Jennifer Henderson, for careful editing, and Daniel Soileau, for technical assistance related to producing the online version of this book.

Introduction

This book supplements *North Carolina Crimes: A Guidebook on the Elements of Crime*
(UNC School of Government, 7th ed. 2012). It includes cases decided and legislation enacted
through December 31, 2016. Chapter and page numbers used throughout this supplement
refer to chapters and pages in the main edition.

Due to the very large body of case law regarding charging language that threatened to
overwhelm the book, all notes on that topic have been deleted from this supplement. Please
consult the following resources for more information. For a detailed paper on point, see
Jessica Smith, The Criminal Indictment: Fatal Defect, Fatal Variance, and Amendment,
ADMINISTRATION OF JUSTICE BULLETIN No. 2008/03, www.sog.unc.edu/publications/
bulletins/criminal-indictment-fatal-defect-fatal-variance-and-amendment. For all relevant
cases decided since 2008, see Jessica Smith, SMITH'S CRIMINAL CASE COMPENDIUM,
www.sog.unc.edu/resources/legal-summaries/criminal-case-compendium (under heading
"Criminal Procedure," subheading "Indictment & Pleading Issues").

1
States of Mind

General Intent and Specific Intent (page 4)

Add the following at the end of the first paragraph:

> ; State v. Maldonado, ___ N.C. App. ___, 772 S.E.2d 479, 483 (2015); State v. Bryant, ___ N.C. App. ___, 779 S.E.2d 508 (2015).

Add the following at the end of the third paragraph:

> ; State v. Maldonado, ___ N.C. App. ___, 772 S.E.2d 479, 483 (2015) (same; shooting into occupied property).

Wantonly (page 7)

> For another case supporting the statement in this note that this mental state is essentially the same as willfully, see *State v. Hunt*, ___ N.C. App. ___, ___ S.E.2d ___ (Nov. 1, 2016).

Criminal Negligence (page 7)

Add the following at the end of this section:

> In assault cases, the State is required to allege a theory of criminal negligence. State v. Stevens, 228 N.C. App. 352 (2013) (error in an assault on a child under 12 case where criminal negligence was not alleged in the indictment).

Strict Liability (page 9)

As a result of 2015 legislation, S.L. 2015-181, the first three bullets of this note should read as follows:

- G.S. 14-27.24 (first-degree statutory rape). State v. Anthony, 351 N.C. 611, 616 (2000) (noting that first-degree statutory rape is a strict liability crime); State v. Rose, 312 N.C. 441, 445 (1984) (noting that for first-degree statutory rape, mistake regarding the victim's age is no defense); State v. Ainsworth, 109 N.C. App. 136, 145 (1993) ("Criminal mens rea is not an element of statutory rape.").
- G.S. 14-27.29 (first-degree statutory sexual offense). *Anthony*, 351 N.C. at 616–18 (construing former G.S. 14-27.4 and noting that consent is not a defense to statutory sexual offense).
- G.S. 14-27.25 & -27.30 (respectively, statutory rape and sexual offense of a person 15 years old or younger). *Anthony*, 351 N.C. at 616–18 (construing former G.S. 14-27.7A (statutory rape or sexual offense of a person who is 13, 14, or 15 years old) and holding that consent is not a defense under that statute); State v. Browning, 177 N.C. App. 487, 491 (2006) ("Statutory rape under [former G.S.] 14-27.7A is a strict liability crime."); State v. Sines, 158 N.C. App. 79, 84 (2003) ("Statutory sexual offense and statutory rape are categorized as strict liability crimes.").

Delete the fourth bullet in this note.

Add the following paragraph to the bulleted list in this note:

- G.S. 90-95(d1)(1)c (possession of pseudoephedrine after methamphetamine conviction). State v. Miller, ___ N.C. App. ___, 783 S.E.2d 512, 516 (2015).

In the sixth paragraph, delete the citation to *State v. Haskins*.

2
Bars and Defenses

Bars to Prosecution (page 13)

Double Jeopardy (page 13)

The sixth paragraph of this note states that even when offenses are not the same, legislative intent controls whether multiple punishment may be imposed at the same trial. It goes on to indicate that some decisions analyze this issue as one of double jeopardy. For another such case, see *State v. Baldwin*, ___ N.C. App. ___, 770 S.E.2d 167, 176 (2015) (because the assault inflicting serious bodily injury statute begins with the language "[u]nless the conduct is covered under some other provision of law providing greater punishment," the trial court erred by sentencing the defendant to this Class F felony when it also sentenced the defendant for assault with a deadly weapon with intent to kill inflicting serious injury, a Class C felony).

Delete the last paragraph of this note and replace it with the following:

> For a more detailed discussion of double jeopardy, see Robert L. Farb, *Double Jeopardy and Related Issues, in* NC Superior Court Judges' Benchbook (2013), http://benchbook.sog.unc.edu/criminal/double-jeopardy.

Lack of Jurisdiction (page 16)

As a result of 2014 legislation, S.L. 2014-100, sec. 34.30(b), add the following to the list of statutes in this section:

> **§ 14-7.45. Crimes committed by use of unmanned aircraft systems.**
> All crimes committed by use of an unmanned aircraft system, as defined in G.S. 15A-300.1, while in flight over this State shall be governed by the laws of this State, and the question of whether the conduct by an unmanned aircraft system while in flight over this State constitutes a crime by the owner of the unmanned aircraft system shall be determined by the laws of this State.

Defenses That Justify (page 18)

Necessity and Duress (page 18)

> For a case where the defendant was not entitled to a jury instruction on duress, see *State v. Burrow*, ___ N.C. App. ___, 789 S.E.2d 923, 926–27 (2016) (attempted felony breaking or entering case; among other things, the defendant failed to show that his actions were caused

by a reasonable fear that he would suffer immediate death or serious bodily injury if he did not act).

Public Authority (page 19)

The G.S. 20-145 exemption from speed limits does not apply to bail bondsmen. State v. McGee, 234 N.C. App. 285, 288 (2014).

Defenses Showing Lack of Blameworthiness (page 20)

Entrapment (page 21)

The trial court erred by refusing to instruct on entrapment in a drug delivery case where an undercover officer tricked the defendant into believing that the officer was romantically interested in the defendant to persuade him to obtain cocaine, the defendant had no predisposition to commit the offense, and the criminal design originated solely with the officer. State v. Foster, 235 N.C. App. 365, 374–76 (2014).

Failure of Proof or "Negating" Defenses (page 22)

Accident (page 22)

The trial court did not err by refusing to instruct the jury on the defense of accident in a child sexual offense case where no evidence indicated that the defendant digitally penetrated the victim accidentally. State v. Clapp, 235 N.C. App. 351, 361 (2014).

For another case supporting the statement in this note that the defense of accident is not available if the defendant was engaged in misconduct at the time of the killing, see *State v. Robinson*, ___ N.C. App. ___, ___ S.E.2d ___ (Dec. 20, 2016) ("A person who, while carrying a loaded firearm, starts a physical fight and discharges the firearm injuring another person, is not entitled to a jury instruction on the defense of accident.").

3

Participants in Crimes

Principals—Acting in Concert (page 29)

Notes (page 29)

Element (1) (page 29)

The fact that a person helped plan a crime, was available to an accomplice by telephone when it was committed, or was present at the crime scene after the offense occurred does not establish constructive presence. State v. Hardison, ___ N.C. App. ___, 779 S.E.2d 505, 507–08 (2015).

For cases holding that the evidence was insufficient to establish that the defendant was actually or constructively present, see *State v. Greenlee*, 227 N.C. App. 133, 138 (2013) (obtaining property by false pretenses case arising out of sales of stolen goods to a pawn shop), and *State v. Hardison*, ___ N.C. App. ___, 779 S.E.2d 505, 507–08 (2015) (contaminating a public water system case where the defendant was never present when the accomplice broke the water lines in question).

For a case holding that the evidence was sufficient to establish that the defendant was actually or constructively present when a victim was shot, see *State v. Johnson*, ___ N.C. App. ___, ___ S.E.2d ___ (Dec. 20, 2016) (among other things, the victim's blood was found on the defendant's pants, and after the shooting, the defendant aided the shooter in a fight with the victim to gain control of the gun);

Element (3) (page 30)

The defendant need not expressly vocalize his or her assent to the criminal conduct; all that is required is an implied mutual understanding or agreement. State v. Marion, 233 N.C. App. 195, 204–05 (2014) (evidence was sufficient to support convictions for murder, burglary, and armed robbery on theories of acting in concert and aiding and abetting where, among other things, the defendant was present for discussions and aware of the group's plan to commit a robbery and remained in the vicinity of the crime scene where she helped by telling her accomplices that two of them had fled and encouraging the others to hurry up and leave).

For a case where the evidence was insufficient with respect to this element, see *State v. Holloway*, ___ N.C. App. ___, 793 S.E.2d 766, 774–75 (2016) (the State presented no evidence that the defendant had a common plan or purpose to possess the drugs or paraphernalia with his alleged accomplice, McEntire; at most, the evidence showed that the two were acquainted and the defendant was present when the drugs were found at McEntire's home; mere presence at the scene of a crime is insufficient where the State presented no evidence that the two shared any criminal intent), *temporary stay allowed*, ___ N.C. App. ___, ___ S.E.2d ___ (Dec. 20, 2016).

Extent of criminal liability (page 30)
Although the group initially planned to rob just one person at the residence, their attempted robbery of a second person found there was in pursuit of the group's common purpose. State v. Jastrow, 237 N.C. App. 325, 330 (2014).

Aiding and Abetting (page 31)

Notes (page 31)

Element (2) (page 32)
The evidence was sufficient to support convictions for murder, burglary, and armed robbery on theories of acting in concert and aiding and abetting where, among other things, the defendant was present for discussions about and aware of the group's plan to commit a robbery and remained in the vicinity of the crime scene where she helped by telling her accomplices that two of them had fled and encouraging the others to hurry up and leave. State v. Marion, 233 N.C. App. 195, 204–05 (2014).

Related Offenses Not in This Chapter (page 34)

As a result of 2012 legislation, S.L. 2012-56, the following offense should be added to this section:

Bank examiner aiding and abetting by making false or fraudulent report. G.S. 53C-8-7.

Accessory before the Fact to a Felony (page 34)

Punishment (page 34)

Replace the citation at the end of this section with the following:

G.S. 14-5.2; see State v. Larrimore, 340 N.C. 119 (1995); State v. Grainger, 367 N.C. 696, 699 (2014) (because the defendant's conviction for first-degree felony murder was not based solely on the uncorroborated testimony of a principal, the exception in G.S. 14-5.2 did not apply). A defendant is convicted of a capital felony when he or she is convicted of first-degree murder, even if the case was tried non-capitally. State v. Grainger, 224 N.C. App. 623, 630–31 (2012), *rev'd on other grounds*, 367 N.C. 696 (2014) (noting that this conclusion was central to the decision of the North Carolina Court of Appeals holding that the G.S. 14-5.2 exception applied, the Supreme Court held that the exception did not apply for a separate reason: because the conviction did not rest on uncorroborated testimony of a principal).

4
Punishment under Structured Sentencing

Felonies (page 39)

Prior Record Level (page 40)

Delete the last paragraph of this note.

Aggravating and Mitigating Factors (page 41)

As a result of 2013 legislation, S.L. 2013-284, sec. 2(b); S.L. 2013-368, sec. 14, the first sentence of the fourth paragraph in this note should read as follows:

> G.S. 15A-1340.16(d) sets out over 20 statutory aggravating factors, including, among other things, that the crime was especially heinous, atrocious, or cruel, *id.* at -1340.16(d)(7); that the victim was very young, very old, or mentally or physically infirm or handicapped, *id.* at -1340.16(d)(11); and that the defendant involved a person under the age of 16 in the commission of the crime, *id.* at -1340.16(d)(13).

Sentence Disposition (page 43)
Intermediate punishment (page 44)

2012 legislation, S.L. 2012-146, amended G.S. 15A-1343(a1), adding the following condition to those listed on page 45:

- Abstain from alcohol consumption and submit to continuous alcohol monitoring when alcohol dependency or chronic abuse has been identified by a substance abuse assessment.

Community punishment (page 45)

2012 legislation, S.L. 2012-39, repealed G.S. 15A-1382.1(b). Thus, the last paragraph of this note (page 46) should be deleted.

Restitution (page 46)

Delete the second sentence of this note.

Special Provisions (page 47)

Class A felonies (page 47)

Delete the last sentence of this note and replace it with the following:

> For a discussion of capital sentencing issues, see JEFFREY B. WELTY, NORTH CAROLINA CAPITAL CASE LAW HANDBOOK (UNC School of Government, 3d ed. 2013).

Armed habitual felon (new note)

2013 legislation, S.L. 2013-369, sec. 26, creates a new armed habitual felon status. Put simply, when a person who has been convicted of one firearm-related felony commits a second such offense, the defendant may, in the discretion of the district attorney, be charged as an armed habitual felon. If convicted, the defendant must be sentenced as a Class C felon with a minimum 120-month prison term. *See generally* G.S. 14-7.35 through -7.41 (enacted by S.L. 2013-369, sec. 26).

Firearm or deadly weapon enhancement (page 48)

2013 legislation, S.L. 2013-369, sec. 5, amended the enhancement described in this note so that punishment applies as follows:

> - If the felony is a Class A through E felony, the minimum term of imprisonment is increased by 72 months; the applicable maximum is the maximum that corresponds to the enhanced minimum.
> - If the felony is a Class F or G felony, the minimum term of imprisonment is increased by 36 months; the applicable maximum is the maximum that corresponds to the enhanced minimum.
> - If the felony is a Class H or I felony, the minimum term of imprisonment is increased by 12 months; the applicable maximum is the maximum that corresponds to the enhanced minimum.
>
> G.S. 15A-1340.16A(c) (as amended by S.L. 2013-369, sec. 5).

Conditional discharge for certain drug offenders (page 49)

As a result of 2013 legislation, S.L. 2013-210, the conditional discharge described in this note is no longer mandatory.

As a result of 2014 legislation, S.L. 2014-119, sec. 2(a), conditional discharge is now authorized for any misdemeanor or Class H or I felony that would be eligible for deferred prosecution.

Methamphetamine enhancement (page 49)

As a result of 2013 legislation, S.L. 2013-124, sec. 2, the following should be added at the end of this note:

> If a defendant is convicted of manufacturing of methamphetamine and a person under 18 years old or a disabled or elder adult
>
> - resided on the property used for the manufacture of methamphetamine or
> - was present where methamphetamine was being manufactured,
>
> the defendant's minimum sentence must be increased by 24 months. G.S. 15A-1340.16D(a1). If both a minor and a disabled or elder adult resided on the property or were present, the minimum sentence must be increased by 48 months. *Id.* The maximum sentence is the maximum that corresponds to the enhanced minimum. The terms "disabled adult" and "elder adult" are defined by cross-reference to G.S. 14-32.3(d). G.S. 15A-1340.16D(a2). The facts supporting the enhancement must be alleged in an indictment or information and proved to a jury beyond a reasonable doubt, unless the defendant pleads guilty or no contest to the issue. G.S. 15A-1340.16D(b), (c).

Domestic violence protective order enhancement (page 50)

The G.S. 50B-4.1(d) enhancement does not apply to felony convictions when the defendant also is charged with a Class A or B1 felony or under G.S. 50B-4.1(f) or (g). State v. Jacobs, ___ N.C. App. ___, 768 S.E.2d 883, 885 (2015) (trial court erred by enhancing the defendant's conviction for assault with a deadly weapon with intent to kill inflicting serious injury and attempted second-degree kidnapping where the defendant also was charged with a violation of G.S. 50B-4.1(g)).

Misdemeanors (page 50)

Sentence Disposition (page 52)

Active punishment (page 52)

2014 legislation, S.L. 2014-100, sec. 16C.1, made changes to the place of confinement for misdemeanants.

Special Provisions (page 53)

Infamous or related misdemeanor enhancement (page 53)

The evidence was sufficient to establish that the defendant obstructed justice with deceit and intent to defraud where he gave eight different statements to authorities providing an array of scenarios surrounding the victim's death and identifying four different individuals as the perpetrator and admitted that he had been untruthful to investigators. State v. Cousin, 233 N.C. App. 523, 530–31 (2014).

Conditional discharge for certain drug offenders (page 54)

As a result of 2013 legislation, S.L. 2013-210, the conditional discharge described in this note is no longer mandatory.

As a result of 2014 legislation, S.L. 2014-119, sec. 2(a), conditional discharge is now authorized for any misdemeanor or Class H or I felony that would be eligible for deferred prosecution.

Tables

Table 1 (page 55)

2013 legislation, S.L. 2013-410, sec. 3(a), amended the punishment for a Class A felony from "Life Imprisonment Without Parole or Death" to "Life Imprisonment With Parole or Without Parole, or Death."

Table 2A (page 58)

2013 legislation, S.L. 2013-101, sec. 6, made three changes to the maximum sentences grid, effective October 1, 2013, and applying to offenses committed on or after that date:

the maximum sentence for a 66-month minimum is 92 months

the maximum sentence for an 86-month minimum is 116 months

the maximum sentence for a 216-month minimum is 272 months

Tables 3 and 3A (pages 60, 62)

These forms have been updated. Updated N.C. AOC forms are available here: www.nccourts.org/Forms/FormSearch.asp.

Table 4 (page 63)

2013 legislation, S.L. 2013-360, sec. 18B.13, amended the misdemeanor sentencing grid shown in this table. Specifically, for misdemeanor offense Class 3 at prior conviction level II, the punishment should read:

> 1–15 days C if one to three prior convictions
>
> 1–15 days C/I if four prior convictions

That same legislation also enacted G.S. 15A-1340.23(d), providing that "[u]nless otherwise provided for a specific offense, the judgment for a person convicted of a Class 3 misdemeanor who has no more than three prior convictions shall consist only of a fine."

5

General Crimes

Attempt (page 67)

Notes (page 67)

Generally (page 67)

For another case on the elements of attempt, see *State v. Floyd*, ___ N.C. ___, ___ S.E.2d ___ (Dec. 21, 2016).

Evidence that the defendant committed a completed crime is sufficient to support a conviction of an attempt to commit that crime. State v. Primus, 227 N.C. App. 428, 431–32 (2013).

Element (1) (page 68)

In attempted rape cases, the State need not show that the defendant made an actual physical attempt to have intercourse. State v. Baker, ___ N.C. App. ___, 781 S.E.2d 851, 855, *rev. allowed*, ___ N.C. ___, 789 S.E.2d 2 (2016). Intent is established "if the evidence shows that defendant, at any time during the incident, had an intent to gratify his passion upon the victim, notwithstanding any resistance on her part." *Id.* (quotation omitted).

For cases where the evidence was sufficient to show an intent to engage in a sexual assault, see *State v. Marshall*, ___ N.C. App. ___, 784 S.E.2d 503, 505, 508–509 (2016) (the evidence was sufficient to establish attempted sex offense and attempted rape; after isolating the victim from her husband, one of the perpetrators said, "Maybe we should," to which the other responded, "Yeah"; an accomplice then forced the victim to perform fellatio on him; after the defendant touched the victim, saying, "Nice," the victim's husband tried to protect her and was shot; a reasonable jury could infer that the defendant intended to engage in a continuous sexual assault involving both fellatio (like his accomplice) and rape and was thwarted only because of the husband's intervention); *State v. Minyard*, 231 N.C. App. 605, 616–17 (2014) ("The act of placing one's penis on a child's buttocks provides substantive evidence of intent to commit a first degree sexual offense, specifically anal intercourse."); *State v. Miles*, 237 N.C. App. 170, 173–74 (2014) (the defendant's conduct before and after his request that the victim perform fellatio on him sufficiently established that he intended to commit a sexual offense by force and against her will).

For a case where the evidence was insufficient to show an intent to engage in a sexual assault, see *State v. Baker*, ___ N.C. App. ___, 781 S.E.2d 851, 855–56 (2016), *rev. allowed*, ___ N.C. ___, 789 S.E.2d 2 (2016) (only two events were alleged to support an attempted statutory rape charge; evidence as to the first event supported only a conviction for first-degree rape, not attempted rape; evidence as to the second event supported, at most, an indecent liberties conviction; during the second event the defendant sat next to the victim, touched her shoulder and chest, and tried to get her to lie down).

Attempted homicide (page 68)

The crime of attempted first-degree felony murder does not exist under North Carolina law. State v. Marion, 233 N.C. App. 195, 202 (2014).

For another case holding that assault with a deadly weapon with intent to kill inflicting serious injury is not a lesser-included offense of attempted first-degree murder and that a defendant may be convicted of and punished for both offenses, see *State v. Rogers*, 219 N.C. App. 296, 307–08 (2012).

Attempted assault (page 69)

Delete the text of this note and replace it with the following:

In *State v. Floyd*, ___ N.C. ___, ___ S.E.2d ___ (Dec. 21, 2016), the supreme court held that attempted assault is a crime in North Carolina; it reversed the court of appeals, which had held that attempted assault with a deadly weapon inflicting serious injury is not a recognized crime because it constituted an attempt of an attempt. *Id.* The *Floyd* court concluded that "[a]ttempted assault is not an attempt of an attempt because assault may be defined by the show-of-violence rule," a form of assault that "does not involve an attempt to cause injury to another person, but is based upon a violent act or threat that causes fear in another person."

Conspiracy (page 72)

Notes (page 72)

Element (1) (page 72)

Add the following after the second sentence of the second paragraph of this note:

Circumstantial evidence can establish the scope of the agreement. State v. Fish, 229 N.C. App. 584, 591–92 (2013) (evidence that the defendant and an accomplice stole property valued at more than $1,000 established that they had an agreement to do so).

Add the following to the end of the third paragraph of this note:

For other cases where there was sufficient evidence of an agreement to commit robbery, see *State v. Young*, ___ N.C. App. ___, 790 S.E.2d 182, 187–88 (2016) (circumstantial evidence established that the defendant and his accomplices agreed to rob a second victim; the accomplices agreed to take the first victim's car and then commit other unlawful acts, with defendant wielding the shotgun and another person driving the vehicle; the acts against the second victim occurred within minutes of and very near the acts against the first); *State v. Oliphant*, 228 N.C. App. 692, 704 (2013) (implied agreement to commit armed robbery where the defendants approached the victim from behind and one held a gun while the other reached for the victim's cell phone); and *State v. Rogers*, 227 N.C. App. 617, 623–24 (2013) (conspiracy to commit armed robbery; implied understanding to use a dangerous weapon).

For a case where there was insufficient evidence of an agreement to commit robbery, see *State v. Fleming*, ___ N.C. App. ___, 786 S.E.2d 760, 766 (2016) (the "mere fact that the crime the defendant allegedly conspired with others to commit took place does not, without more, prove the existence of a conspiracy").

Add the following to the end of the fourth paragraph of this note:

For other cases where the evidence was insufficient to establish an agreement to engage in drug offenses, see *State v. Velazquez-Perez*, 233 N.C. App. 585, 593 (2014) (among other things, there was no evidence that the driver of a vehicle owned by an alleged co-conspirator knew about drugs hidden in the vehicle), and *State v. McClaude*, 237 N.C. App. 350, 353–54 (2014) (following *Euceda-Valle*, where the evidence showed only that the drugs were found in a car driven by another person in which the defendant was a passenger).

For cases where the evidence was sufficient to show an agreement to engage in drug offenses, see *State v. Winkler*, 368 N.C. 572, 581–83 (2015) (rejecting the defendant's argument that the evidence showed only "the mere existence of a relationship between the two individuals"); *State v. Garrett*, ___ N.C. App. ___, 783 S.E.2d 780, 785 (2016) (sufficient evidence of conspiracy to sell methamphetamine where the incident arose out of a controlled buy involving the defendant and two accomplices); *State v. Torres-Gonzalez*, 227 N.C. App. 188, 195 (2013) (conspiracy to traffic in cocaine by possession where the defendant and an accomplice worked together to complete a drug sale); and *State v. Davis*, 236 N.C. App. 376, 385 (2014) (implied agreement to engage in drug trafficking by manufacture where the defendant was present at the scene and aware that his accomplice was involved in producing methamphetamine and the defendant was involved in the manufacturing process; "Where two subjects are involved together in the manufacture of methamphetamine and the methamphetamine recovered is enough to sustain trafficking charges, we hold the evidence sufficient to infer an implied agreement between the subjects to traffic in methamphetamine by manufacture and withstand a motion to dismiss.").

Withdrawal (new note)

Due process is not violated when the trial court puts the burden on the defendant to prove withdrawal from the conspiracy. Smith v. United States, 568 U.S. ___, 133 S. Ct. 714, 719 (2013).

Related Offenses Not in This Chapter (page 75)

As a result of 2015 legislation, S.L. 2015-47, delete the last offense listed in this section and replace it with the following:

> Furnishing poison, controlled substances, deadly weapons, cartridges, ammunition, or alcoholic beverages to inmates; furnishing tobacco products or mobile phones to inmates; furnishing mobile phones to delinquent juveniles. G.S. 14-258.1.

Continuing Criminal Enterprise—Non-Drug Offenses (page 75)

Statute (page 75)

2012 legislation, S.L. 2012-38, amended G.S. 14-7.20, making three changes. First, subsection (a) was amended to read:

> (a) Except as otherwise provided in subsection (a1) of this section, any person who engages in a continuing criminal enterprise shall be punished as a Class H felon and in addition shall be subject to the forfeiture prescribed in subsection (b) of this section.

Second, a new subsection, (a1), was enacted as follows:

> (a1) Any person who engages in a continuing criminal enterprise where the felony violation required by subdivision (c)(1) of this section is a violation of G.S. 14-10.1 shall be punished as a Class D felon and, in addition, shall be subject to the forfeiture prescribed in subsection (b) of this section.

Third, the first sentence of subsection (b) was amended to read:

> (b) Any person who is convicted under subsection (a) or (a1) of this section of engaging in a continuing criminal enterprise shall forfeit to the State of North Carolina:

Punishment (page 76)

Delete the first sentence of this section and replace it with the following:

> Class H felony, G.S. 14-7.20(a), except that if the offense constitutes the crime of terrorism under G.S. 14-10.1, it is punished as a Class D felony. G.S. 14-7.20(a1); *see generally* "Terrorism" in Chapter 20 in this supplement.

Accessory after the Fact to a Felony (page 76)

Notes (page 77)

Element (2) (page 77)

There was sufficient evidence of accessory after the fact to murder where the defendant made false statements to the police in an effort to shield the perpetrator's identity. State v. Cousin, 233 N.C. App. 523, 532–33 (2014) (the defendant gave eight different written statements to authorities providing an array of scenarios surrounding the victim's death and identifying four different individuals as the perpetrator; he also admitted that he had been untruthful to investigators).

Element (3) (page 78)

For a case where the evidence was sufficient to show that the defendant knew the identity of the murderer and was protecting that person from apprehension, see *Cousin*, 233 N.C. App. at 532.

For a case where the evidence was sufficient to establish that the defendant knew that a gun he hid previously was used to commit a murder, see *State v. Schiro*, 219 N.C. App. 105, 113–14 (2012).

Multiple convictions and punishments (page 78)

No double jeopardy violation occurred when the trial court sentenced the defendant for felony obstruction of justice and accessory after the fact to murder arising out of the same conduct. *Cousin*, 233 N.C. App. at 537 (reasoning that each offense contains an element not in the other).

6

Homicide

Murder (page 83)

First-Degree Murder (page 83)

Statute (page 83)

2013 and 2012 legislation, S.L. 2013-410, sec. 3(a); S.L. 2012-165, amended G.S. 14-17. The amended statute reads:

§ 14-17. Murder in the first and second degree defined; punishment.

(a) A murder which shall be perpetrated by means of a nuclear, biological, or chemical weapon of mass destruction as defined in G.S. 14-288.21, poison, lying in wait, imprisonment, starving, torture, or by any other kind of willful, deliberate, and premeditated killing, or which shall be committed in the perpetration or attempted perpetration of any arson, rape or a sex offense, robbery, kidnapping, burglary, or other felony committed or attempted with the use of a deadly weapon shall be deemed to be murder in the first degree, a Class A felony, and any person who commits such murder shall be punished with death or imprisonment in the State's prison for life without parole as the court shall determine pursuant to G.S. 15A-2000, except that any such person who was under 18 years of age at the time of the murder shall be punished in accordance with Part 2A of Article 81B of Chapter 15A of the General Statutes.

(b) A murder other than described in subsection (a) of this section or in G.S. 14-23.2 shall be deemed second degree murder. Any person who commits second degree murder shall be punished as a Class B1 felon, except that a person who commits second degree murder shall be punished as a Class B2 felon in either of the following circumstances:

(1) The malice necessary to prove second degree murder is based on an inherently dangerous act or omission, done in such a reckless and wanton manner as to manifest a mind utterly without regard for human life and social duty and deliberately bent on mischief.

(2) The murder is one that was proximately caused by the unlawful distribution of opium or any synthetic or natural salt, compound, derivative, or preparation of opium, or cocaine or other substance described in G.S. 90-90(1)d., or methamphetamine, and the ingestion of such substance caused the death of the user.

2013 legislation, S.L. 2013-47, added a new subsection, (c), to the statute as follows:

(c) For the purposes of this section, it shall constitute murder where a child is born alive but dies as a result of injuries inflicted prior to the child being born alive. The degree of murder shall be determined as described in subsections (a) and (b) of this section.

Punishment (page 84)

In *Miller v. Alabama*, ___ U.S. ___, 132 S. Ct. 2455, 2463–64 (2012), the U.S. Supreme Court held that an automatic sentence of life imprisonment without the possibility of parole for a person under 18 years old who is convicted of murder violates the Eighth Amendment. Because North Carolina law had required such a sentence for a juvenile's conviction for first-degree murder, the General Assembly enacted legislation to bring the state's law in compliance with *Miller*. S.L. 2012-148. That legislation authorizes a sentence of life imprisonment with the possibility of parole after 25 years for defendants convicted of first-degree murder who were under 18 years old at the time of the offense. G.S. 15A-1476. If a conviction is based solely on the felony murder rule, the court must impose this sentence. G.S. 15A-1477(a)(1). In other first-degree murder cases, the court must conduct a hearing to determine whether the defendant should be sentenced to life imprisonment with or without the possibility of parole. G.S. 15A-1477(a)(2).

Replace the last sentence of the second paragraph on this note with the following:

For a discussion of capital law, see Jeffrey B. Welty, North Carolina Capital Case Law Handbook (UNC School of Government, 3d ed. 2013).

The last paragraph of this note cites G.S. 15A-2005(b). 2015 legislation, S.L. 2015-247, sec. 5, amended that statute to, among other things, replace the term "mentally retarded" with "intellectual disability."

Notes (page 84)

Elements (1) and (2) (page 84)

G.S. 14-17(c) provides that it is murder when a child is born alive but dies as a result of injuries inflicted prior to the child being born alive. *See* State v. Broom, 225 N.C. App. 137, 143–44 (2013) (the trial court did not err by denying the defendant's motion to dismiss first-degree murder charges where the victim was in utero at the time of the incident but was born alive and lived for one month before dying).

Element (3)(a)(i) (page 84)

This note describes three forms of malice. Delete (1) in this note and replace it with the following:

(1) express malice, in the form of hatred, ill will, or spite, State v. Reynolds, 307 N.C. 184, 191 (1982);

Add the following after the numbered list in this note:

The second form of malice sometimes is called "depraved heart malice." State v. Lail, ___ N.C. App. ___, ___ S.E.2d ___ (Dec. 30, 2016). Although depraved heart malice is frequently used to support second-degree murder convictions based on impaired driving, it is not limited to cases involving impaired driving. *Id.* (citing cases).

Element (3)(a)(ii) (page 85)

For additional cases where the evidence was sufficient to establish premeditation and deliberation, see *State v. Hicks*, ___ N.C. App. ___, 772 S.E.2d 486, 493 (2015) (among other things, there was no provocation by the unarmed victim; the defendant shot the victim at least four times; and after the shooting the defendant immediately left the scene without aiding the victim); *State v. Mitchell*, ___ N.C. App. ___, 770 S.E.2d 740, 747 (2015) (among other things, there was no provocation by the victim; just before the shooting, the defendant said he was going to shoot a man over a trivial matter; the defendant shot the victim three times; and the victim may have been turning away or trying to escape at the time); *State v. Horskins*, 228 N.C. App. 217, 225–26 (2013) (after exchanging words in a nightclub parking lot, the defendant shot the unarmed victim, who had not reached for a weapon, had not engaged the defendant in a fight, and did not provoke the defendant's violent response; after the victim fell from the defendant's first shot, the defendant shot the victim six more times; and the defendant left the scene and attempted to hide evidence); *State v. Rogers*, 227 N.C. App. 617, 621–22 (2013) (the victim begged for his life and was shot eight times, primarily in the head and chest, and there was a lack of provocation); and *Broom*, 225 N.C. App. at 144 (the defendant was having an affair with another woman and wanted his wife to terminate her pregnancy; he became angry when his wife said that if they divorced she might move out of the state with their children; and before he shot her, the defendant placed his wife's cell phone out of her reach).

Element (3)(b) (page 86)

Add the following at the end of the first paragraph of this note:

; *State v. Grullon*, ___ N.C. App. ___, 770 S.E.2d 379, 384 (2015) (neither specific intent to kill nor deadly purpose to kill is required; the evidence was sufficient where the defendant ambushed the victim for the purpose of committing a robbery).

Add the following at the end of the second paragraph of this note:

For recent cases where the evidence was sufficient to establish lying in wait, see *State v. Gosnell*, 231 N.C. App. 106, 113 (2013), and *Grullon*, ___ N.C. App. ___ at ___, 770 S.E.2d at 384 (the defendant hid under a darkened staircase for the purpose of robbing the victim).

Element (3)(c) (page 86)

Add the following to the fourth paragraph of this note:

For another case supporting the statement in this note that felonious child abuse can support a felony murder charge, see *State v. Perry*, 229 N.C. App. 304, 318 (2013).

For another case supporting the statement in this note that discharging a firearm into occupied property can support a felony murder charge, see *State v. Juarez*, ___ N.C. App. ___, 777 S.E.2d 325, 328–30 (2015).

The sixth paragraph of this note discusses the continuous transaction doctrine. Add the following to that discussion:

There need not be a causal relationship between the underlying felony and the homicide; all that is required is that the felony and the killing occur in a single transaction. State v. Maldonado, ___ N.C. App. ___, 772 S.E.2d 479, 484 (2015). However, the felony murder rule will not apply where there is a break in the chain of events between the felony and the act causing death. *Id.* For a case where the court rejected the defendant's argument that such a break occurred, see *id.* (in a case where the felony murder charge was based on shooting into occupied property, the court rejected the defendant's argument that the victim's attempt to take his gun after he entered the house constituted a break in the chain of events that led to her later shooting death at the defendant's hand inside the property).

Replace the last sentence of the sixth paragraph of this note with the following:

For a fuller discussion of the continuous transaction doctrine, see Jeffrey B. Welty, North Carolina Capital Case Law Handbook 22–23 (UNC School of Government, 3d ed. 2013).

Delete the seventh paragraph and replace it with the following:

Although the felony and the homicide must be part of a continuous transaction, *State v. Jones*, 353 N.C. 159 (2000), suggests that when the underlying offense is an assault on a single victim who dies from injuries inflicted during the assault, the assault cannot be used as an underlying felony for purposes of the felony murder rule. *Id.* at 170 n.3 (reasoning that "[o]therwise, virtually all felonious assaults on a single victim that result in his or her death would be first-degree murders via felony murder, thereby negating lesser homicide charges such as second-degree murder and manslaughter"). However, if the transaction involves multiple assaults, only one of which caused death, the *Jones* rule does not apply. For example, in *State v. Carroll*, 356 N.C. 526 (2002), the defendant committed a nonfatal assault on the victim with a machete and then killed her by strangulation. The court held that the felony assault with a machete was a separate offense from the strangulation and properly was used as a felony to support felony murder. *Id.* at 535. Additionally, the *Jones* rule only applies when a single victim is involved; cases involving multiple victims fall outside of the rule. *Jones*, 353 N.C. at 170 n.3 (distinguishing the single victim scenario from one involving a felonious assault on one victim that results in the death of another victim); State v. Jackson, 189 N.C. App. 747, 752 n.3 (2008). Note that some pre-*Jones* cases uphold felony murder convictions based on related non-assault offenses that cause death. *See, e.g.*, State v. King, 316 N.C. 78 (1986) (felony murder based on discharging a firearm into occupied property); State v. Pierce, 346 N.C. 471, 493 (1997) (same based on felonious child abuse). It is not clear whether these cases remain good law after *Jones*.

Replace the last sentence of the eleventh paragraph with the following:

For a fuller discussion of the merger rule, see Jeffrey B. Welty, North Carolina Capital Case Law Handbook 113–14 (UNC School of Government, 3d ed. 2013).

Proximate cause (page 88)

The defendant's shooting of the victim's mother while the victim was in utero was a proximate cause of the victim's death after being born alive where the gunshot wound required the child's early delivery, which in turn caused a complicating condition that resulted in death. State v. Broom, 225 N.C. App. 137, 143 (2013).

Greater and lesser-included offenses (page 90)

Replace the first sentence of this note with the following:

Second-degree murder is a lesser-included offense of premeditated and deliberate first-degree murder, State v. Stevenson, 327 N.C. 259, 263 (1990), but not of first-degree felony murder. State v. Frazier, ___ N.C. App. ___, 790 S.E.2d 312, 317 (2016).

Delete the last sentence of this note.

Attempted first-degree murder (page 90)

The crime of attempted first-degree felony murder does not exist under North Carolina law. State v. Marion, 233 N.C. App. 195, 202 (2014).

Related Offenses Not in This Chapter (page 90)

The following offense, enhanced to a Class D felony by 2013 legislation, S.L. 2013-88, should be added to this section:

Interfering with gas, water, or electric meters and causing death. G.S. 14-151.

The last listed offense in this section should read:

"Concealing a Death" (Chapter 21).

Second-Degree Murder (page 90)

Punishment (page 91)

As a result of 2012 legislation, S.L. 2012-165, delete the text of this note and replace it with the following:

Class B1 felony, except that punishment is as a Class B2 felony when (1) the malice necessary to prove second-degree murder is based on an inherently dangerous act or omission, done in such a reckless and wanton manner as to manifest a mind utterly without regard for human life and social duty and deliberately bent on mischief [this is the second form of malice discussed in the note on Element (3)(a)(i) to "First-Degree Murder" (page 84)]; or (2) the murder was proximately caused by the unlawful distribution of opium or any synthetic or natural salt, compound, derivative, or preparation of opium, or cocaine or other substance described in G.S. 90-90(1)d., or methamphetamine, and the ingestion of such substance caused the death of the user. G.S. 14-17(b).

Notes (page 91)

Element (3) (page 91)

For another second-degree murder case involving impaired driving, see *State v. Grooms*, 230 N.C. App. 56, 68–69 (2013) (there was sufficient evidence of malice where the defendant drove impaired and killed two bicyclists; the defendant was warned of the dangers of drinking and driving and his prior incident of doing so on the same road led a passenger to fear for her life; his blood alcohol level was 0.16; the defendant knowingly consumed an illegal controlled substance that caused impairment; the defendant swerved off the road three times before the collision, giving him notice that he was driving dangerously; the defendant failed to watch the road and made a phone call right before the collision; and the defendant failed to apply his brakes before or after the collision, to call 911, or to aid the victims).

Insert the following after the first sentence of the first full paragraph on page 92:

State v. Rollins, 220 N.C. App. 443, 453–55 (2012) (the defendant drove without a license after being cited twice for that offense; the defendant took control of the vehicle from another driver by climbing over the back seat while the vehicle was moving; the defendant was evading the police because he had shoplifted items in the vehicle; the defendant drove well in excess of the speed limit, crossed a yellow line to pass, passed vehicles using a turn lane, drove through a corn field and ditch, and again crossed the center line, colliding with another vehicle while traveling 66 mph and without applying his brakes; and to avoid arrest, the defendant repeatedly struck an injured passenger as he tried to exit the vehicle and escape);

Insert the following at the end of this note:

For a case where the evidence showed that the death resulted from a mishap with a gun and that there was insufficient evidence of malice, see *State v. Hatcher*, 231 N.C. App. 114, 118–20 (2013).

Death resulting from distribution and ingestion of a controlled substance (page 92)

Where there was no evidence that the defendant intended to kill the victim by selling him methadone, the trial court did not err by instructing the jury on second-degree murder and involuntary manslaughter. State v. Barnes, 226 N.C. App. 318, 329–30 (2013) (rejecting the defendant's argument that under G.S. 14-17 he only could have been convicted of second-degree murder).

Murder of an Unborn Child (page 94)

Related Offenses Not in This Chapter (page 96)

As a result of 2015 legislation, S.L. 2015-265, sec. 2, add the following offense to this section:

Sale of remains of an unborn child. G.S. 14-46.1.

Manslaughter (page 96)

Voluntary Manslaughter (page 96)

Notes (page 96)

Elements (1) and (2) (page 96)

Although no intent to kill is required for this crime, the act that causes death must be intentional. State v. English, ___ N.C. App. ___, 772 S.E.2d 740, 745 (2015) (the evidence was sufficient to show that the defendant intentionally hit the victim with her car).

Element (3) generally (page 96)

No legally adequate provocation existed when the victim insisted, shortly after having sex with the defendant, that he allow her to use his cellphone to text another man saying that she and the defendant were no longer in a relationship and when the defendant refused, the victim taunted him. State v. Chaves, ___ N.C. App. ___, 782 S.E.2d 540, 544 (2016) (noting that "mere words, however abusive or insulting are not sufficient provocation" and that "this level of provocation must ordinarily amount to an assault or threatened assault by the victim against the perpetrator" (quotation omitted)).

Multiple convictions and punishments (page 98)

G.S. 20-141.4(c) does not bar simultaneous prosecutions for involuntary manslaughter and death by vehicle; it only bars punishment for both offenses when they arise out of the same death. State v. Elmore, 224 N.C. App. 331, 336 (2012).

Involuntary Manslaughter (page 99)

Notes (page 99)

Element (3)(a) (page 100)

Other acts that fall within this element include

- misdemeanor improper storage of a firearm, State v. Lewis, 222 N.C. App. 747, 752 (2012), and
- supplying alcohol to a person under 21, State v. Noble, 226 N.C. App. 531, 536–37 (2013) (person under 21 died from alcohol poisoning; the defendant aided and abetted the victim in the possession or consumption of alcohol in violation of G.S. 18B-302).

Element (3)(b) (page 100)

For another case where the defendant's culpably negligent act was sufficient to support a conviction of this offense, see State v. Fisher, 228 N.C. App. 463, 473–75 (2013) (the defendant attacked the victim, leaving him semiconscious; instead of taking the victim to be picked up by his parents as arranged, the defendant drove him to an isolated area and again beat him; the defendant abandoned the victim outside knowing that the temperature was in the 20s and that the victim was injured, intoxicated, and not wearing a shirt; the defendant realized that his actions put the victim in jeopardy; and after being told that the victim was missing and that officers were concerned about him, the defendant lied about the victim's whereabouts, hindering efforts to find and help the victim).

Proximate cause (page 100)

For a case where improper storage of a firearm was the proximate cause of a child's death, see Lewis, 222 N.C. App. at 752.

Death by Vehicle (page 103)

Statute (page 103)

Effective for offenses committed on or after December 1, 2012, S.L. 2012-165 amended subsection (a6) of G.S. 20-141.4 by deleting the last sentence of that subsection. That same legislation also amended subsection (b), the punishment provision, to provide:

> (b) Punishments.—Unless the conduct is covered under some other provision of law providing greater punishment, the following classifications apply to the offenses set forth in this section:
>
> (1) Repeat felony death by vehicle is a Class B2 felony.
>
> (1a) Aggravated felony death by vehicle is a Class D felony. Notwithstanding the provisions of G.S. 15A-1340.17, the court shall sentence the defendant in the aggravated range of the appropriate Prior Record Level.
>
> (2) Felony death by vehicle is a Class D felony. Notwithstanding the provisions of G.S. 15A-1340.17, intermediate punishment is authorized for a defendant who is a Prior Record Level I offender.
>
> (3) Aggravated felony serious injury by vehicle is a Class E felony.
>
> (4) Felony serious injury by vehicle is a Class F felony.
>
> (5) Misdemeanor death by vehicle is a Class A1 misdemeanor.

Felony Death by Vehicle (page 104)

Punishment (page 104)

As a result of the 2012 legislation noted above, delete the text of this section and replace it with the following:

> Class D felony. G.S. 20-141.4(b)(2). Notwithstanding G.S. 15A-1340.17, intermediate punishment is authorized for a defendant who is a Prior Record Level I offender. *Id.*

Notes (page 104)

Multiple convictions and punishments (page 104)

Delete the first paragraph of this note and replace it with the following:

> G.S. 20-141.4(b), the punishment provision for all death by vehicle offenses, provides, in part, that unless the conduct is covered under some other provision of law providing greater punishment, repeat felony death by vehicle is a Class B2 felony, aggravated felony death by vehicle is a Class D felony, felony death by vehicle is a Class D felony, and misdemeanor death by vehicle is a Class A1 misdemeanor. Thus, a defendant may not be punished for a death by vehicle offense when the defendant is convicted also for an offense carrying a greater punishment and both offenses are based on the same conduct. State v. Davis, 364 N.C. 297, 303 (2010) (the trial court erred by imposing punishment for felony death by vehicle (then a Class E felony) and second-degree murder (Class B2 felony)).

Insert the following at the end of the second paragraph of this note:

> G.S. 20-141.4(c) does not bar simultaneous prosecutions for involuntary manslaughter and death by vehicle; it only bars punishment for both offenses when they arise out of the same death. State v. Elmore, 224 N.C. App. 331, 334–36 (2012).

Related Offenses Not in This Chapter (page 105)

As a result of 2016 legislation, S.L. 2016-34, add the following to this section:

> Death by impaired boating offenses. G.S. 75A-10.3.

Aggravated Felony Death by Vehicle (page 105)

Punishment (page 105)

As a result of the 2012 legislation noted above, delete the text of this note and replace it with the following:

> Class D felony. G.S. 20-141.4(b)(1a). Notwithstanding G.S. 15A-1340.17, the defendant must be sentenced in the aggravated range. *Id.*

Repeat Felony Death by Vehicle (page 106)

Punishment (page 106)

As a result of the 2012 legislation noted above, delete the text of this note and replace it with the following:

> Class B2 felony. G.S. 20-141.4(b)(1).

Notes (page 106)

Multiple convictions and punishments (page 107)

Delete the text of this note and replace it with the following:

> See this note to "Felony Death by Vehicle," as amended by this supplement.

7
Assaults

Simple Assault (page 111)

Statute (page 111)

2012 legislation, S.L. 2012-149, enacted a new subsection, (c1), to G.S. 14-33 as follows:

> (c1) No school personnel as defined in G.S. 14-33(c)(6) who takes reasonable actions in good faith to end a fight or altercation between students shall incur any civil or criminal liability as the result of those actions.

2015 legislation, S.L. 2015-62, sec. 4(b), amended the definition of "in the presence of a minor" in G.S. 14-33(d)(2) to now read as follows:

> (2) "In the presence of a minor" means that the minor was in a position to see or hear the assault.

Notes (page 113)

Element (1) (page 113)

Add the following citation after the first sentence of this note:

> State v. Floyd, ___ N.C. ___, ___ S.E.2d ___ (Dec. 21, 2016).
> For another case defining and explaining the two forms of assault discussed in this note, see *State v. Floyd*, ___ N.C. ___, ___ S.E.2d ___ (Dec. 21, 2016). The *Floyd* court explained that its case law regarding the second form of assault—assault by show of violence—"appears to have evolved from early cases in which a person caused another to flee, leave a place sooner than desired, or otherwise alter course through the threatened use of a weapon." *Id.* (going on to discuss one of the court's earliest assault by show of violence cases, *State v. Shipman*, 81 N.C. 513 (1879)). Importantly, in *Floyd*, the North Carolina Supreme Court held that assault by show of violence "does not involve an attempt to cause injury to another person, but is based upon a violent act or threat that causes fear in another person." *Id.* It continued: "Accordingly, although North Carolina law provides one definition of assault that describes the offense in terms of 'an overt act or an attempt, or the unequivocal appearance of an attempt,' our common law also provides a second definition that does not include any reference to attempt." *Id.* The court went on to hold that "[a]ttempted assault is not an attempt of an attempt because assault may be defined by the show-of-violence rule." *Id.* It explained that "there is substantial overlap between the two definitions of assault because an overt act or attempt to do immediate physical injury to another person is likely to constitute a show of violence that causes fear and a change of behavior." *Id.* "As a result," it concluded, "relying upon the show-of-violence rule to define attempted assault does not create a significant limitation on the conduct covered by

this offense." Ultimately the *Floyd* court reversed the court of appeals, which had held that the offense of attempted assault with a deadly weapon inflicting serious injury is not a recognized crime in North Carolina because it constituted an attempt of an attempt. *Id.*

2012 legislation, S.L. 2012-149, enacted G.S. 14-33(c1), providing that no school personnel defined in G.S. 14-33(c)(6) who take reasonable actions in good faith to end a fight or altercation between students shall incur any civil or criminal liability as the result of those actions.

Attempted assault (page 114)

Delete the text of this note and replace it with the following:

In *State v. Floyd*, ___ N.C. ___, ___ S.E.2d ___ (Dec. 21, 2016), the supreme court held that attempted assault is a crime in North Carolina; it reversed the court of appeals, which had held that attempted assault with a deadly weapon inflicting serious injury is not a recognized crime because it constituted an attempt of an attempt. *Id.* The *Floyd* court concluded that "[a]ttempted assault is not an attempt of an attempt because assault may be defined by the show-of-violence rule," a form of assault that "does not involve an attempt to cause injury to another person, but is based upon a violent act or threat that causes fear in another person."

District attorney approval required for charging (new note)

As a result of 2012 legislation, S.L. 2012-149, G.S. 15A-301(b1) requires district attorney approval before a magistrate may charge a school employee defined in G.S. 14-33(c)(6) with an offense that occurred while the school employee was in the process of discharging his or her duties of employment. The new statute does not apply to traffic offenses or to offenses that occur in the presence of an officer. Additional procedures are specified if the district attorney declines to accept this authority to approve charges. Although not specifically targeted to assaults, the new statute is most likely to apply with respect to these crimes.

Multiple convictions and punishments (page 114)

The State presented substantial evidence supporting two separate assaults where the defendant attacked his wife with his hands and, when his child intervened with a baseball bat to protect his mother, the defendant grabbed the bat and used it to beat his wife; the assaults involved separate thought processes, they were distinct in time, and the victim sustained injuries on different parts of her body as a result of each assault. State v. Wilkes, 367 N.C. 116 (2013) (affirming per curiam 225 N.C. App. 233 (2013)).

For a case where the State sufficiently proved two distinct incidents of assault with a deadly weapon inflicting serious injury supporting two convictions, see *State v. Lanford*, 225 N.C. App. 189, 204 (2013) (rejecting the argument that only one offense occurred because the assaults were part of chronic and continual abuse).

Assaults Inflicting a Particular Type of Injury (page 115)

Assault Inflicting Serious Injury (page 115)

Notes (page 115)

Element (3) (page 115)

Insert the following after the first sentence of the last paragraph of this note:

State v. Anderson, 222 N.C. App. 138, 145 (2012) (the trial court did not err by instructing the jury that three gunshot wounds to the leg constituted serious injury where the victim was hospitalized for two days, had surgery to remove a bone fragment, and experienced pain at the time of trial);

Multiple convictions and punishments (page 116)

Add the following to the string cite following the fourth sentence of this note:

State v. Coakley, 238 N.C. App. 480, 491–92 (2014) (based on the "unless covered language" in G.S. 14-32.4(a) (assault inflicting serious bodily injury), the trial court erred by sentencing the defendant for both that offense and the more serious offense of assault with a deadly weapon inflicting serious injury under G.S. 14-32(b)); State v. Baldwin, ___ N.C. App. ___, 770 S.E.2d 167, 176 (2015) (same where the more serious offense was the Class C felony of assault with a deadly weapon with intent to kill inflicting serious injury); State v. Jones, 237 N.C. App. 526, 532–33 (2014) (because of the "unless the conduct is covered" language in the assault on a female statute, the trial court erred by sentencing the defendant to that offense (Class A1 misdemeanor) and habitual misdemeanor assault (Class H felony) when both convictions were based on the same conduct); State v. Jamison, 234 N.C. App. 231, 238–39 (2014) (the defendant could not be convicted and sentenced for both assault inflicting serious bodily injury and assault on a female when based on the same conduct; the "unless covered" language in the assault on a female statute reflects a legislative intent to limit a trial court's authority to impose punishment for that offense when punishment also is imposed for higher class offenses that apply to the same conduct).

The courts have noted that *State v. Hines*, discussed in this note, is distinguishable from this line of cases because the offenses at issue there (aggravated assault on a handicapped person and armed robbery) were based on distinct conduct by the defendant, not the same act. *Jones*, 237 N.C. App. at 531–32 (2014).

Delete the second to last sentence of this note.

Assault Inflicting Serious Bodily Injury (page 117)

Notes (page 118)

Element (3) (page 118)

Add the following after the last bullet in this note:

- the victim had broken bones in her face, a broken hand, and a cracked knee; she could not see properly out of her eye at the time of trial and she testified that her hand and eye "hurt all of the time," State v. Jamison, 234 N.C. App. 231, 235–36 (2014).

Assault Inflicting Physical Injury by Strangulation (page 119)

Notes (page 119)

Element (3) (page 119)

The evidence was sufficient to establish assault by strangulation where the defendant strangled the victim twice, a medical expert testified that the victim's injuries were consistent with strangulation, and photographic evidence showed bruising, abrasions, and a bite mark on and around the victim's neck. State v. Lowery, 228 N.C. App. 229, 232–33 (2013) (rejecting the defendant's arguments that the statute required "proof of physical injury beyond what is inherently caused by every act of strangulation" or extensive physical injury).

Element (4) (page 119)

The statute does not require a particular method of restricting the victim's airway, such as direct application of force to the trachea. State v. Lanford, 225 N.C. App. 189, 197 (2013). Thus, the evidence is sufficient when it shows that the defendant obstructed the victim's airway by putting his hand over her nose and mouth. *Id.*

Deadly Weapon Assaults (page 120)

Assault with a Deadly Weapon (page 120)
Notes (page 120)

Element (3) (page 120)
For a case where the trial court properly concluded that a knife was not a deadly weapon per se and left that determination to the jury, see *State v. Edgerton*, 234 N.C. App. 412, 419 (2014) (there was conflicting evidence regarding whether or not the knife was capable of producing death or great bodily harm; among other things, a witness testified that the knife was so dull that even though the defendant was "sawing" the victim's neck with it, the knife left only nicks on her neck), *rev'd on other grounds*, 368 N.C. 32 (2015).

Insert the following after the citation to *State v. Ferguson* in the fourth bullet on page 121:

; State v. Spencer, 218 N.C. App. 267, 274–75 (2012) (based on a vehicle's high rate of speed and the fact that the victim had to take affirmative action to avoid harm, a car was a deadly weapon as a matter of law);

Insert the following after the eighth bullet on page 121:

- a kitchen table chair, State v. James, 224 N.C. App. 164, 170 (2012);

Insert the following at the end of this note:

Because there was evidence that the defendant assaulted the victim with a lawn chair and not with his fists alone, the State was not required to present evidence as to the defendant's and the victim's size or condition. State v. Mills, 221 N.C. App. 409, 413 (2012).

Greater and lesser-included offenses (page 122)
Assault with a deadly weapon is a lesser-included offense of armed robbery. State v. Hinton, 361 N.C. 207, 210 (2007); State v. Richardson, 279 N.C. 621, 628 (1971).

Related Offenses Not in This Chapter (page 123)

The following offense was repealed by 2012 legislation, S.L. 2012-12, sec. 2(c), and should be removed from this section:

Transporting dangerous weapon or substance during emergency; possessing off premises; exceptions. G.S. 14-288.7.

Assault with a Deadly Weapon with Intent to Kill (page 123)
Notes (page 124)

Element (1) (page 124)
In a concurring opinion in *State v. Floyd*, ___ N.C. ___, ___ S.E.2d ___ (Dec. 21, 2016), Justice Newby stated that the court's decision in *State v. Birchfield*, 235 N.C. 410, 413 (1952), "recognized that the statutory definition of 'assault' under [G.S. 14-32] requires a completed battery."

Element (4) (page 124)
For additional assault cases where the evidence was sufficient to show an intent to kill, see *State v. Stewart*, 231 N.C. App. 134, 145–46 (2013) (after shooting and killing eight people, the defendant ignored an officer's instruction to drop his shotgun, reloaded it, and fired at the officer); *State v. Stokes*, 225 N.C. App. 483, 485 (2013) (during a robbery the defendant fired a gun beside the victim's head, and the victim thought the defendant was going to kill him); and

State v. Wilkes, 225 N.C. App. 233, 237 (2013) (the defendant hit the victim with a bat after she fell to her knees, he repeatedly struck her head until she lost consciousness, she never fought back, and the wounds could have been fatal; the circumstances of the attack, including the parties' conduct, provided additional evidence of intent to kill, including that the two had a volatile relationship and the victim had recently filed for divorce), *aff'd per curiam*, 367 N.C. 116 (2013).

Assault with a Deadly Weapon Inflicting Serious Injury (page 124)
Notes (page 125)
Element (1) (page 125)
In a concurring opinion in *State v. Floyd*, ___ N.C. ___, ___ S.E.2d ___ (Dec. 21, 2016), Justice Newby stated that the court's decision in *State v. Birchfield*, 235 N.C. 410, 413 (1952), "recognized that the statutory definition of 'assault' under [G.S. 14-32] requires a completed battery."

Assault with a Deadly Weapon with Intent to Kill Inflicting Serious Injury (page 125)
Notes (page 126)
Element (1) (page 126)
In a concurring opinion in *State v. Floyd*, ___ N.C. ___, ___ S.E.2d ___ (Dec. 21, 2016), Justice Newby stated that the court's decision in *State v. Birchfield*, 235 N.C. 410, 413 (1952), "recognized that the statutory definition of 'assault' under [G.S. 14-32] requires a completed battery."

Greater and lesser-included offenses (page 126)
Replace the first sentence of this note with the following:

Because all of the elements of (1) simple assault, (2) assault with a deadly weapon, (3) assault with a deadly weapon with intent to kill, (4) assault inflicting serious injury, and (5) assault with a deadly weapon inflicting serious injury are included in assault with a deadly weapon with intent to kill inflicting serious injury, all of those offenses are lesser-included offenses of this offense.

Multiple convictions and punishments (page 126)
Assault with a deadly weapon with intent to kill inflicting serious injury is not a lesser-included offense of attempted first-degree murder; a defendant may be convicted of and punished for both offenses. State v. Rogers, 219 N.C. App. 296, 307–09 (2012).

Assault by Pointing a Gun (page 126)
Notes (page 127)
Element (2) (page 127)
For a case with multiple victims where the court rejected the defendant's argument that the State's evidence was too vague for the jury to infer that he pointed the gun at any particular person, see *State v. Pender*, ___ N.C. App. ___, 776 S.E.2d 352, 361 (2015) (witnesses testified that the defendant waved the gun "at us" and pointed the gun "toward everybody in one room").

Related Offenses Not in This Chapter (page 127)

The following offense was repealed by 2012 legislation, S.L. 2012-12, sec. 2(c), and should be removed from this section:

Transporting dangerous weapon or substance during emergency. G.S. 14-288.7.

Discharging Barreled Weapons and Firearms (page 128)

Discharging a Barreled Weapon or Firearm into Occupied Property (page 128)

Notes (page 128)

Element (1) (page 128)

Insert the following after the first sentence of this note:

State v. Bryant, ___ N.C. App. ___, 779 S.E.2d 508, 513–14 (2015).

Element (3) (page 128)

Add the following at the end of the second paragraph of this note:

; State v. Hicks, ___ N.C. App. ___, 772 S.E.2d 486, 492 (2015) (same); State v. Mitchell, ___ N.C. App. ___, 770 S.E.2d 740, 748 (2015) (same; the evidence was sufficient where the defendant's hips, chest, and head were outside the vehicle and part of his leg and arm were inside it).

Element (4) (page 129)

Replace the second paragraph with the following:

To be guilty of this offense, a defendant must discharge the weapon "with knowledge that the building is then occupied . . . or when he has reasonable grounds to believe that the building might be occupied." State v. James, 342 N.C. 589, 596 (1996) (quoting State v. Williams, 284 N.C. 67, 73 (1973), and emphasizing the word "might" in this standard); see also State v. Everette, 361 N.C. 646, 650 (2007). For cases where there was sufficient evidence that the defendant had reasonable grounds to believe that property might be occupied, see Everette, 361 N.C. at 651 (lights were on in a restaurant in an area known to be crowded in the early morning hours, the surrounding streets were crowded, and nearby establishments remained open until the early morning); James, 342 N.C. at 597 (reasonable grounds to believe that cars were occupied when the defendant fired a semiautomatic weapon in a club's parking lot knowing that vehicles were parked there and that people who had left the club were in the parking lot); and State v. Charleston, ___ N.C. App. ___, 789 S.E.2d 513, 516 (2016) (a shooting into the victim's residence occurred in a residential neighborhood in the evening while the victim's car was parked outside her home).

Add the following text to this note:

A residence was occupied when the family was on the front porch. State v. Miles, 223 N.C. App. 160, 163–64 (2012).

Discharging a Barreled Weapon or Firearm into an Occupied Dwelling or Occupied Conveyance in Operation (page 130)

Notes (page 130)

Multiple convictions and punishments (page 130)

No violation of double jeopardy occurred when the defendant was sentenced for three counts of discharging a firearm into occupied property where each shot was "distinct in time, and each bullet hit the [house] in a different place." State v. Kirkwood, 229 N.C. App. 656, 667–68 (2013) (internal quotation marks, citations omitted).

Discharging Firearm within Occupied Building, etc. to Incite Fear (new crime)

This offense was enacted by 2013 legislation, S.L. 2013-144.

Statute

> **§ 14-34.10. Discharge firearm within enclosure to incite fear.**
> Unless covered under some other provision of law providing greater punishment, any person who willfully or wantonly discharges or attempts to discharge a firearm within any occupied building, structure, motor vehicle, or other conveyance, erection, or enclosure with the intent to incite fear in another shall be punished as a Class F felon.

Elements

A person guilty of this offense

(1) willfully or wantonly
(2) discharges or attempts to discharge a firearm
(3) within any occupied building, structure, motor vehicle, or other conveyance, erection, or enclosure
(4) with the intent to incite fear in another.

Punishment

Class F felony. G.S. 14-34.10.

Notes

Element (1). See this note to "Discharging a Barreled Weapon or Firearm into Occupied Property" in the main volume.

Element (2). See this note to "Discharging a Barreled Weapon or Firearm into Occupied Property" in the main volume. Note that unlike the other "Discharging Barreled Weapons and Firearms" offenses, this one only covers discharge of a firearm, not a barreled weapon.

Element (3). For the meaning of the term "occupied," see the note on Element (4) to "Discharging a Barreled Weapon or Firearm into Occupied Property" in the main volume. Note that this offense covers discharge of a firearm "within" the building, etc. The other "Discharging Barreled Weapons and Firearms" offenses cover discharging "into" the specified location.

Attempt. See this note to "Discharging a Barreled Weapon or Firearm into Occupied Property" in the main volume.

Multiple convictions and punishments. See this note to "Discharging a Barreled Weapon or Firearm into Occupied Property" in the main volume. This statute begins with the language: "Unless covered under some other provision of law providing greater punishment." For a discussion of the meaning of this phrase, see this note on "Assault Inflicting Serious Injury" in the main volume.

Related Offenses Not in This Chapter

See the offenses listed under "Discharging a Barreled Weapon or Firearm into Occupied Property" in the main volume.

Assault on a Female (page 133)

Notes (page 133)

Greater and lesser-included offenses (page 133)

Assault on a female is not a lesser-included offense of first-degree sexual offense. State v. Martin, 222 N.C. App. 213, 221–22 (2012).

Assaults Involving Children (page 133)

Assault in the Presence of a Minor (page 134)

Statute (page 134)

2015 legislation, S.L. 2015-62, sec. 4(b), amended G.S. 14-33(d)(2) as noted under "Simple Assault," above in this supplement.

Notes (page 135)

Element (4) (page 135)

Delete the first sentence of this note and replace it with the following:

"In the presence of a minor" means that the minor was in a position to see or hear the assault. G.S. 14-33(d)(2).

Assaults on Handicapped Persons (page 139)

Simple Assault on a Handicapped Person (page 139)

Notes (page 139)

Element (2) (page 139)

There was a sufficient factual basis to support a plea where the victim was 80 years old, crippled by arthritis in her knees, and walked with a crutch. State v. Collins, 221 N.C. App. 604, 607–08 (2012).

Assaults on Government Officers, Employees, and Similar Persons (page 141)

Assault on a Governmental Officer or Employee (page 141)
Notes (page 141)
Element (3) (page 141)

Add the following to the first paragraph of this note:

> An arresting officer was discharging the duties of his office when, after transporting the defendant to the jail and escorting him to a holding cell, the officer remained at the jail. State v. Friend, 237 N.C. App. 490, 495 (2014) (reasoning that by remaining at the jail, the officer was ensuring the safety of other officers).

Delete the third paragraph of this note and replace it with the following:

> In *State v. Friend*, 237 N.C. App. 490, 495 (2014), the court stated: "unlike the offense of resisting, delaying, or obstructing an officer, criminal liability for the offense of assaulting an officer is not limited to situations where an officer is engaging in lawful conduct in the performance or attempted performance of his or her official duties" (citation omitted).

Assault with a Firearm on a Law Enforcement Officer, Probation or Parole Officer, Member of the National Guard, or Detention Facility Employee (revised title) (page 145)

Statute (page 145)

2015 legislation, S.L. 2015-74, sec. 2, changed the title of the statute and added a new subsection, (a1), to the statute to read as follows:

> **§ 14-34.5. Assault with a firearm on a law enforcement, probation, or parole officer, or on a member of the North Carolina National Guard, or on a person employed at a State or local detention facility.**
> (a1) Any person who commits an assault with a firearm upon a member of the North Carolina National Guard while the member is in the performance of his or her duties is guilty of a Class E felony.

Elements (page 145)

As a result of the 2015 legislation noted immediately above, Element (3) should now read as follows:

> (3) on a
> (a) law enforcement officer,
> (b) probation officer,
> (c) parole officer,
> (d) member of the North Carolina National Guard, or
> (e) state or local government detention facility employee

Assault Inflicting Physical Injury on a Law Enforcement Officer, Probation or Parole Officer, Member of the National Guard, or Detention Facility Employee (revised title)

(page 146)

Statute (page 146)

2015 legislation, S.L. 2015-74, sec. 1, amended the statute to now read as follows:

> **§ 14-34.7. Certain assaults on a law enforcement, probation, or parole officer, or on a member of the North Carolina National Guard, or on a person employed at a State or local detention facility; penalty.**
>
> (a) Unless covered under some other provision of law providing greater punishment, a person is guilty of a Class F felony if the person assaults a law enforcement officer, probation officer, or parole officer while the officer is discharging or attempting to discharge his or her official duties and inflicts serious bodily injury on the officer.
>
> (a1) Unless covered under some other provision of law providing greater punishment, a person is guilty of a Class F felony if the person assaults a member of the North Carolina National Guard while he or she is discharging or attempting to discharge his or her official duties and inflicts serious bodily injury on the member.
>
> (b) Unless covered under some other provision of law providing greater punishment, a person is guilty of a Class F felony if the person assaults a person who is employed at a detention facility operated under the jurisdiction of the State or a local government while the employee is in the performance of the employee's duties and inflicts serious bodily injury on the employee.
>
> (c) Unless covered under some other provision of law providing greater punishment, a person is guilty of a Class I felony if the person does any of the following:
>
>   (1) Assaults a law enforcement officer, probation officer, or parole officer while the officer is discharging or attempting to discharge his or her official duties and inflicts physical injury on the officer.
>
>   (2) Assaults a person who is employed at a detention facility operated under the jurisdiction of the State or a local government while the employee is in the performance of the employee's duties and inflicts physical injury on the employee.
>
>   (3) Assaults a member of the North Carolina National Guard while he or she is discharging or attempting to discharge his or her official duties and inflicts physical injury on the member.
>
> For the purposes of this subsection, "physical injury" includes cuts, scrapes, bruises, or other physical injury which does not constitute serious injury.

Elements (page 147)

As a result of the 2015 legislation noted immediately above, Element (2) should now read as follows:

  (2) on a

      (a) law enforcement officer,

      (b) probation officer,

      (c) parole officer,

      (d) member of the North Carolina National Guard, or

      (e) state or local government detention facility employee

Assault Inflicting Serious Injury or Serious Bodily Injury on a Law Enforcement Officer, Probation or Parole Officer, Member of the National Guard, or Detention Facility Employee (revised title) (page 147)

Statute (page 147)

As a result of the 2015 legislation noted above, the statutory citation in this section should read as follows:

See G.S. 14-34.7(a), (a1), **and** (b).

Elements (page 147)

As a result of the 2015 legislation noted above, Element (2) should now read as follows:

(2) on a
   (a) law enforcement officer,
   (b) probation officer,
   (c) parole officer,
   (d) member of the North Carolina National Guard, or
   (e) state or local government detention facility employee.

Punishment (page 148)

The citation in this section is incorrect. The correct citation is G.S. 14-34.7.

Notes (page 148)

Element (4) (page 148)

2015 legislation, S.L. 2015-74, sec. 1, revised the title of this offense, deleting the words "serious injury" and thus calling into question the reasoning of the *Crawford* case cited in this note. If this statutory change was meant to abrogate *Crawford*, only proof of serious bodily injury would satisfy the statute.

Malicious Conduct by a Prisoner (page 148)

Notes (page 149)

Multiple convictions and punishments (page 149)

A defendant may be convicted of two counts of this offense for two acts that occurred during one incident. State v. Heavner, 227 N.C. App. 139, 146 (2013) (the defendant spit on an officer's forehead while the defendant was in a house; five minutes later he spit on the officer's arm after being taken out of the house).

Assault on an Executive, Legislative, or Court Officer (page 150)

Statute (page 150)

2014 legislation, S.L. 2014-119, sec. 6(a), amended G.S. 14-16.6(a) so that it now reads:

(a) Any person who assaults any legislative officer, executive officer, or court officer, or assaults another person as retaliation against any legislative officer, executive officer, or court officer because of the exercise of that officer's duties, or any person who makes a violent attack upon the residence, office, temporary accommodation or means of transport of any one of those officers or persons in a manner likely to endanger the officer or person, shall be guilty of a felony and shall be punished as a Class I felon.

2014 legislation, S.L. 2014-100, sec. 17.1(v), amended G.S. 14-19.9 so that it now reads:

> Any person who has been elected to any office covered by this Article but has not yet taken the oath of office shall be considered to hold the office for the purpose of this Article and G.S. 143B-919.

Elements (page 150)

As a result of the legislative change noted above, Element (2) should now read as follows:

> (2) any
>   (a) executive officer,
>   (b) legislative officer,
>   (c) court officer, *or*
>   (d) other person as retaliation against any legislative officer, executive officer, or court officer because of the exercise of that officer's duties.

Notes (page 150)

Additional conduct included within statute (page 151)

As a result of the legislative change noted above, replace the text of this note with the following:

> The statute also prohibits a violent attack on the residence, office, temporary accommodation, or means of transport of any covered officer in a manner likely to endanger the officer, as well as a similar attack on the residence, office, temporary accommodation, or means of transport of any person as retaliation against any legislative officer, executive officer, or court officer because of the exercise of that officer's duties. G.S. 14-16.6(a).

Assaults on Firefighters and Emergency and Medical Personnel (page 155)

Assault on a Firefighter or Medical Personnel Inflicting Physical Injury (revised title) (page 155)

Statute (page 155)

2015 legislation, S.L. 2015-97, amended the title of the statute and subsection (a)(3) to now read as follows:

> **§ 14-34.6. Assault or affray on a firefighter, an emergency medical technician, medical responder, and hospital personnel.**
> (a)(3) Hospital personnel and licensed healthcare providers who are providing or attempting to provide health care services to a patient in a hospital.

Elements (page 156)

As a result of the 2015 legislation noted above, Element (2)(e) should now read as follows:

> (e) hospital personnel and licensed healthcare providers who are providing or attempting to provide health care services to a patient in a hospital

Assault on a Firefighter or Medical Personnel Inflicting Serious Injury or Inflicting Physical Injury and Using a Deadly Weapon Other Than a Firearm (revised title) (page 157)

Elements (page 157)

As a result of the 2015 legislation noted above, Element (2)(e) should now read as follows:

> (e) hospital personnel and licensed healthcare providers who are providing or attempting to provide health care services to a patient in a hospital

Element (4)(b) of this offense should read:

> inflicts physical injury and uses a deadly weapon.

Assault on a Firefighter or Medical Personnel Causing Physical Injury and with a Firearm (revised title) (page 158)

Elements (page 158)

As a result of the 2015 legislation noted above, Element (2)(e) should now read as follows:

> (e) hospital personnel and licensed healthcare providers who are providing or attempting to provide health care services to a patient in a hospital

Revise Element (4) and add Element (5) as follows:

> (4) inflicts physical injury *and*
> (5) uses a firearm.

Habitual Misdemeanor Assault (page 161)

Notes (page 161)

Element (1)(a)(ii) (page 161)

Add the following citations after the first sentence of this note:

> G.S. 14-33.2; State v. Garrison, 225 N.C. App. 170, 174 (2013) (trial court erred by failing to instruct the jury that the assault under G.S. 14-33 must have inflicted physical injury).

Malicious Injury by Use of an Explosive or Incendiary (page 164)

Related Offenses Not in This Chapter (page 164)

The following offense was repealed by 2012 legislation, S.L. 2012-12, sec. 2(c), and should be removed from this section:

> Transporting dangerous weapon or substance during emergency; possessing off premises; exceptions. G.S. 14-288.7.

8

Threats, Harassment, Stalking, and Violation of Domestic Protective Orders

Communicating Threats (page 167)

Notes (page 167)

Element (4) (page 168)

For a case where the State presented sufficient evidence that a detention officer believed that the defendant—an inmate—would carry out his threats against her, see *State v. Hill*, 227 N.C. App. 371, 378–80 (2013).

Related Offenses Not in This Chapter (page 168)

The following offense, enacted by 2012 legislation, S.L. 2012-149, sec. 4, should be added to this section:

Cyberbullying of school employee by student. G.S. 14-458.2.

Threat to Kill or Inflict Serious Injury on Executive, Legislative, or Court Officers

(page 168)

Statute (page 168)

2014 legislation, S.L. 2014-119, sec. 6(b), amended G.S. 14-16.7 so that it now reads as follows:

(a) Any person who knowingly and willfully makes any threat to inflict serious bodily injury upon or to kill any legislative officer, executive officer, or court officer, or who knowingly and willfully makes any threat to inflict serious bodily injury upon or kill any other person as retaliation against any legislative officer, executive officer, or court officer because of the exercise of that officer's duties, shall be guilty of a felony and shall be punished as a Class I felon.

(b) Any person who knowingly and willfully deposits for conveyance in the mail any letter, writing, or other document containing a threat to commit an offense described in subsection (a) of this section shall be guilty of a felony and shall be punished as a Class I felon.

Elements (page 169)

As a result of the legislative change noted above, Element (5) should now read as follows:

(5) any

(a) executive officer,

(b) legislative officer,

(c) court officer, *or*

(d) any person as retaliation against any legislative officer, executive officer, or court officer because of the exercise of that officer's duties

---

Harassing Telephone Calls (page 169)

Using Threatening Language on the Telephone (page 170)

Related Offenses Not in This Chapter (page 171)

The following offense was repealed by 2015 legislation, S.L. 2015-286, sec. 1.1, and should be removed from this section:

False report of emergency. G.S. 14-401.8.

Cyberstalking (page 174)

Statute (page 174)

2015 legislation, S.L. 2015-282, added new subsections (a)(3) and (4) as follows:

(3) Electronic tracking device.—An electronic or mechanical device that permits a person to remotely determine or track the position and movement of another person.

(4) Fleet vehicle.—Any of the following: (i) one or more motor vehicles owned by a single entity and operated by employees or agents of the entity for business or government purposes, (ii) motor vehicles held for lease or rental to the general public, or (iii) motor vehicles held for sale, or used as demonstrators, test vehicles, or loaner vehicles, by motor vehicle dealers.

That same legislation added a new subsection, (b)(5), as follows:

(5) Knowingly install, place, or use an electronic tracking device without consent, or cause an electronic tracking device to be installed, placed, or used without consent, to track the location of any person. The provisions of this subdivision do not apply to the installation, placement, or use of an electronic tracking device by any of the following:

a. A law enforcement officer, judicial officer, probation or parole officer, or employee of the Division of Corrections, Department of Public Safety, when any such person is engaged in the lawful performance of official duties and in accordance with State or federal law.

b. The owner or lessee of any vehicle on which the owner or lessee installs, places, or uses an electronic tracking device, unless the owner or lessee is subject to (i) a domestic violence protective order under Chapter 50B of the General Statutes or (ii) any court order that orders the owner or lessee not to assault, threaten, harass, follow, or contact a driver or occupant of the vehicle.

c. A legal guardian for a disabled adult, as defined in G.S. 108A-101(d), or a legally authorized individual or organization designated to provide protective services to a disabled adult pursuant to G.S. 108A-105(c), when the electronic tracking device is installed, placed, or used to track the location of the disabled adult for which the person is a legal guardian or the individual or organization is designated to provide protective services.

d. The owner of fleet vehicles, when tracking such vehicles.

e. A creditor or other secured party under a retail installment agreement involving the sale of a motor vehicle or the lessor under a retail lease of a motor vehicle, and any assignee or successor in interest to that creditor, secured party, or lessor, when tracking a motor vehicle identified as security under the retail installment sales agreement or leased pursuant to a retail lease agreement, including the installation, placement, or use of an electronic tracking device to locate and remotely disable the motor vehicle, with the express written consent of the purchaser, borrower, or lessee of the motor vehicle.

f. The installation, placement, or use of an electronic tracking device authorized by an order of a State or federal court.

g. A motor vehicle manufacturer, its subsidiary, or its affiliate that installs or uses an electronic tracking device in conjunction with providing a vehicle subscription telematics service, provided that the customer subscribes or consents to that service.

h. A parent or legal guardian of a minor when the electronic tracking device is installed, placed, or used to track the location of that minor unless the parent or legal guardian is subject to a domestic violence protective order under Chapter 50B of the General Statutes or any court order that orders the parent or legal guardian not to assault, threaten, harass, follow, or contact that minor or that minor's parent, legal guardian, custodian, or caretaker as defined in G.S. 7B-101.

i. An employer, when providing a communication device to an employee or contractor for use in connection with his or her work for the employer.

j. A business, if the tracking is incident to the provision of a product or service requested by the person, except as limited in sub-subdivision k. of this subdivision.

k. A private detective or private investigator licensed under Chapter 74C of the General Statutes, provided that (i) the tracking is pursuant to authority under G.S. 74C-3(a)(8), (ii) the tracking is not otherwise contrary to law, and (iii) the person being tracked is not under the protection of a domestic violence protective order under Chapter 50B of the General Statutes or any other court order that protects against assault, threat, harassment, following, or contact.

Unauthorized Use of Electronic Tracking Device (new crime)

This offense was created by the 2015 legislation noted immediately above.

Statute

See G.S. 14-196.3(b)(5), reproduced above in this supplement.

Elements

A person guilty of this offense

(1) knowingly *and*

(2) without consent

(3) (a) installs, places, or uses an electronic tracking device *or*
     (b) causes an electronic tracking device to be installed, placed, or used
(4) to track the location of any person.

Punishment

Class 2 misdemeanor. G.S. 14-196.3(d).

Notes

Element (1). See "Knowingly" in Chapter 1 (States of Mind).

Element (3). An "electronic tracking device" refers to an electronic or mechanical device that permits a person to remotely determine or track the position and movement of another. G.S. 14-196.3(a)(3).

Exceptions. See this note to "Using Electronic Mail or Communication to Threaten or Extort" in the main volume.

G.S. 14-196.3(b)(5), reproduced above, sets out 11 exceptions to this offense, including, among others, exceptions for law enforcement officers engaged in their duties, owners of fleet vehicles, certain creditors, and private detectives and private investigators in certain circumstances.

Related Offenses Not in This Chapter

None.

Cyberbullying (page 179)

Statute (page 179)

2012 legislation, S.L. 2012-149, sec. 3, amended G.S. 14-458.1(a)(3) to read as follows:

(3) Make any statement, whether true or false, intending to immediately provoke, and that is likely to provoke, any third party to stalk or harass a minor.

That same legislation amended G.S. 14-458.1(a)(5) and (6) to read as follows:

(5) Sign up a minor for a pornographic Internet site with the intent to intimidate or torment the minor.
(6) Without authorization of the minor or the minor's parent or guardian, sign up a minor for electronic mailing lists or to receive junk electronic messages and instant messages, with the intent to intimidate or torment the minor.

Elements (page 180)

Elements (2)(c), (e), and (f) should be revised to conform to the legislative changes noted above. Element 2(c) should be revised to read:

(c) to make any statement intending to immediately provoke, and that is likely to provoke, any third party to stalk or harass a minor,

Elements (2)(e) and (f) should be revised to read:

(e) sign up a minor for a pornographic Internet site with the intent to intimidate or torment the minor, *or*
(f) without authorization of the minor or the minor's parent or guardian, sign up a minor for electronic mailing lists or to receive junk electronic messages and instant messages, with the intent to intimidate or torment the minor.

Notes (page 181)

Element (2)(a) (page 181)

2012 legislation, S.L. 2012-149, sec. 2, amended G.S. 14-453(7c) to include within the meaning of the term "profile" "a Web site user's personal page or section of a page made up of data, in text or graphical form, which displays significant, unique, or identifying information, including, but not limited to, listing acquaintances, interests, associations, activities, or personal statements."

Constitutionality (new note)

In *State v. Bishop*, 368 N.C. 869 (2016), the court held that G.S. 14-458.1(a)(1)d is unconstitutional; that portion of the cyberbullying statute criminalizes use of a computer or computer network, with the intent to intimidate or torment a minor, to post or encourage others to post on the Internet private, personal, or sexual information pertaining to a minor and is listed as Element (2)(a)(iv) in the main volume of this book. The court found that the provision restricts speech; the restriction is content based; and the statute is not narrowly tailored to the State's asserted interest in protecting children from the harms of online bullying; it thus concluded that the provision violates the First Amendment. *Id.* at 872–80.

Related Offenses Not in This Chapter (page 181)

The following offense, enacted by 2012 legislation, S.L. 2012-149, sec. 4, should be added to this section:

Cyberbullying of school employee by student. G.S. 14-458.2.

Stalking (page 182)

Misdemeanor Stalking (page 183)

Notes (page 183)

Jury instructions (new note)

When the charged conduct encompasses conduct occurring both before and after statutory amendments that changed the elements of this offense, the trial court must submit a special verdict form to the jury. State v. Williams, 226 N.C. App. 393, 401 (2013) (plain error to fail to do so).

Violation of a Domestic Violence Protective Order (page 186)

Misdemeanor Violation of a Domestic Violence Protective Order (page 187)

Notes (page 187)

Element (1) (page 187)

For a case where the evidence was insufficient to establish that the defendant knowingly violated a domestic violence protective order (DVPO), see *State v. Williams*, 226 N.C. App. 393, 406 (2013) (DVPO required the defendant to "stay away from" the victim's place of work, without identifying her workplace; there was no evidence that the defendant was aware that the victim worked at the location he visited).

Element (2) (new note)

The evidence was insufficient to establish that the defendant violated a DVPO provision that he "stay away from" the victim's workplace when he was seen at a mall parking lot when the victim was working at a salon in the mall. *Williams*, 226 N.C. App. 393 (the defendant was not in a location that would permit him to harass, communicate with, follow, or even observe the victim).

Element (2)(a) (page 187)

Add the following citation at the end of the last paragraph of this note:

State v. Poole, 228 N.C. App. 248, 259 (2013) (pursuant to legislative amendments to the statute, an ex parte DVPO is valid).

Add the following text at the end of this note:

Although a 2012 case held that a consent domestic violence protective order that lacks a finding that the defendant committed an act of domestic violence is void *ab initio*, Kenton v. Kenton, 218 N.C. App. 603 (2012), and cannot support a charge under this statute, 2013 legislation changed that rule. Specifically, S.L. 2013-237 amended G.S. 50B-3 to provide that a consent protective order may be entered without findings of fact and conclusions of law if the parties agree in writing. The statute further provides that such a consent protective order is valid and enforceable.

Repeat Violation of a Domestic Violence Protective Order (page 188)

Notes (page 189)

Multiple convictions and punishments (page 189)

Delete all text after the first sentence of this note and replace it with the following:

Thus, a defendant may not be convicted of this offense and another that is sentenced more severely when the convictions are based on the same conduct. State v. Jones, 237 N.C. App. 526, 530–32 (2014) (trial court erred by sentencing the defendant for felony violation of a domestic violence protective order (Class H felony) and interfering with a witness (Class G felony) based on the same conduct). For a discussion of this issue in the assault context, see this note under "Assault Inflicting Serious Injury" in Chapter 7 (Assaults).

Violation of a Domestic Violence Protective Order with a Deadly Weapon (page 189)

Related Offenses Not in This Chapter (page 190)

Add the following offense to this section:

Purchase or possession of firearms by person subject to domestic violence order prohibited. G.S. 14-269.8; 50B-3.1(j).

Entering Domestic Violence Safe House or Haven (page 190)

Notes (page 190)

Element (3) (page 190)

For a defendant to be guilty of this offense, the State need not show that the defendant actually entered the building housing the safe house or haven; it need only prove that the defendant entered the real property on which the building was located. State v. Williams, ___ N.C. App. ___, 784 S.E.2d 232, 234–35 (2016).

9
Abuse and Neglect

Child Abuse (page 193)

Misdemeanor Child Abuse (page 193)

Notes (page 193)

Element (2) (page 194)

For a case where the evidence was insufficient to establish that the defendant created or allowed to be created a substantial risk of physical injury to a child, see *State v. Reed*, ___ N.C. App. ___, 789 S.E.2d 703, 709–12 (after the defendant went to use the bathroom in her home for a few minutes, leaving her toddler in the care of an adult, the child fell into a backyard pool and drowned), *temporary stay allowed*, ___ N.C. ___, ___ S.E.2d ___ (Sep. 6, 2016). For a case were the evidence was sufficient on this element, see *State v. Watkins*, ___ N.C. App. ___, 785 S.E.2d 175, 178 (2016) (the defendant left a two-year-old alone in a vehicle and out of her sight line for over six minutes; one of the vehicle's windows was open, the outside temperature was 18 degrees, and weather included sleet, snow, and wind; the court relied on the harsh weather conditions, the child's young age, and his danger of being abducted or subjected to physical harm).

Child abuse reporting (page 194)

As a result of 2013 legislation, S.L. 2013-52, sec. 7, delete the text of this note and replace it with the following:

G.S. 7B-301(a) requires any person or institution suspecting that a child has been abused to report the incident to the local director of the local social services department. Any person or institution that knowingly or wantonly fails to make the required report or that knowingly or wantonly prevents another person from making a report is guilty of a Class 1 misdemeanor. G.S. 7B-301(b). Additionally, any director of social services who receives a report of a juvenile's sexual abuse in a child care facility and who knowingly fails to notify the State Bureau of Investigation is guilty of a Class 1 misdemeanor. G.S. 7B-301(c).

Multiple convictions and punishments (page 195)

For a case where the State sufficiently proved three instances of felony child abuse, see *State v. Lanford*, 225 N.C. App. 189, 204 (2013) (rejecting the argument that the fact that the assaults were part of chronic and continual abuse precluded such a holding).

Related Offenses Not in This Chapter (page 195)

Add the following offense to this list:

"Sale, Surrender, or Purchase of a Minor," below in this supplement in Chapter 12 (Kidnapping and Related Offenses).

Replace the last offense in this list with the following:

Unlawful payments related to adoption. G.S. 48-10-102.

As a result of 2016 legislation, S.L. 2016-115, add the following offense to this section:

Unlawful transfer of custody of minor child. G.S. 14-321.2.

Child Abuse—Inflicting Serious Mental or Physical Injury (page 195)

Statute (page 195)

2013 legislation, S.L. 2013-35, modified the punishments set out in G.S. 14-318.4 for felony child abuse as described below.

Another piece of 2013 legislation, S.L. 2013-52, sec. 3, added a new subsection, (a6), as follows:

> (a6) For purposes of this section, a "grossly negligent omission" in providing care to or supervision of a child includes the failure to report a child as missing to law enforcement as provided in G.S. 14-318.5(b).

Punishment (page 196)

2013 legislation, S.L. 2013-35, increased the punishment for this offense from a Class E to a Class D felony.

Notes (page 196)

Element (2) (page 196)

For another case holding that when the State proceeds under Element (2)(b), it need not prove that the defendant intended to inflict serious injury, see *State v. Frazier*, ___ N.C. App. ___, 790 S.E.2d 312, 319 (2016) (the State need only prove that the assault was intentional and that it resulted in serious injury).

Child Abuse—Willful Act or Omission Causing Serious Mental or Physical Injury (page 197)

Punishment (page 198)

2013 legislation, S.L. 2013-35, increased the punishment for this offense from a Class H to a Class G felony.

Notes (page 198)

Element (2)(b) (new note)

Failing to report the disappearance of a child as required by G.S. 14-318.5(b) constitutes a grossly negligent omission. G.S. 14-318.4(a6) (enacted by S.L. 2013-52); see "Failure to Report the Disappearance of a Child" (new crime), below in this supplement.

Child Abuse—Inflicting Serious Bodily Injury or Mental or Emotional Injury (page 198)
Punishment (page 199)

2013 legislation, S.L. 2013-35, increased the punishment for this offense from a Class C to a Class B2 felony.

Notes (page 199)
Element (3)(a) (page 199)
There was sufficient evidence of serious bodily injury where the victim experienced subarachnoid hemorrhaging. State v. Bohannon, ___ N.C. App. ___, 786 S.E.2d 781, 786 (2016).

Child Abuse—Willful Act or Omission Causing Serious Bodily Injury (page 200)
Notes (page 200)
Element (2)(b) (new note)
Failing to report the disappearance of a child as required by G.S. 14-318.5(b) constitutes a grossly negligent omission. G.S. 14-318.4(a6) (enacted by S.L. 2013-52); see "Failure to Report the Disappearance of a Child" (new crime), below in this supplement.

Child Abuse—Prostitution (page 201)
Punishment (page 201)

2013 legislation, S.L. 2013-35, increased the punishment for this offense from a Class E to a Class D felony.

Related Offenses Not in This Chapter (page 201)
Add the following offense to this list:

> "Sale, Surrender, or Purchase of a Minor," below in this supplement in Chapter 12 (Kidnapping and Related Offenses).

Replace the last offense in this list with the following:

> Unlawful payments related to adoption. G.S. 48-10-102.

Child Abuse—Sexual Act (page 202)
Punishment (page 202)

2013 legislation, S.L. 2013-35, increased the punishment for this offense from a Class E to a Class D felony.

Notes (page 202)
Element (2)(a) (page 202)
This note references G.S. 14-27.1. That statute was recodified as 14-27.20 by 2015 legislation. S.L. 2015-181, sec. 2.

> The term "sexual act" includes vaginal intercourse. State v. McClamb, 234 N.C. App. 753, 756 (2014).

Failure to Report the Disappearance of a Child (new crime)

Statute

§ 14-318.5. Failure to report the disappearance of a child to law enforcement; immunity of person reporting in good faith.

(a) The following definitions apply in this section:
- (1) Child.—Any person who is less than 16 years of age.
- (2) Disappearance of a child.—When the parent or other person providing supervision of a child does not know the location of the child and has not had contact with the child for a 24-hour period.

(b) A parent or any other person providing care to or supervision of a child who knowingly or wantonly fails to report the disappearance of a child to law enforcement is in violation of this subsection. Unless the conduct is covered under some other provision of law providing greater punishment, a violation of this subsection is punishable as a Class I felony.

(c) Any person who reasonably suspects the disappearance of a child and who reasonably suspects that the child may be in danger shall report those suspicions to law enforcement within a reasonable time. Unless the conduct is covered under some other provision of law providing greater punishment, a violation of this subsection is punishable as a Class 1 misdemeanor.

(d) This section does not apply if G.S. 110-102.1 is applicable.

(e) Notwithstanding subsection (b) or (c) of this section, if a child is absent from school, a teacher is not required to report the child's absence to law enforcement officers under this section, provided the teacher reports the child's absence from school pursuant to Article 26 of Chapter 115C of the General Statutes.

(f) The felony of failure to report the disappearance of a child as required by subsection (b) of this section is an offense additional to other civil and criminal provisions and is not intended to repeal or preclude any other sanctions or remedies.

(g) Any person who reports the disappearance of a child as required by this section is immune from any civil or criminal liability that might otherwise be incurred or imposed for that action, provided that the person was acting in good faith. In any proceeding involving liability, good faith is presumed.

Elements

A person guilty of this offense

(1) is a parent or any other person providing care to or supervision of a child *and*
(2) knowingly or wantonly
(3) fails to report
(4) the disappearance of a child
(5) to law enforcement.

Punishment

Class I felony. G.S. 14-318.5(b).

Notes

Element (1). A child is a person less than 16 years of age. G.S. 14-318.5(a)(1).

Element (4). The disappearance of a child occurs "[w]hen the parent or other person providing supervision of a child does not know the location of the child and has not had contact with the child for a 24-hour period." G.S. 14-318.5(a)(2).

Exceptions and immunity. This offense "does not apply if G.S. 110-102.1 is applicable." G.S. 14-318.5(d). G.S. 110-102.1 pertains to reports of missing or deceased children by child care providers.

If a child is absent from school, a teacher is not required to report the absence to law enforcement officers, provided the teacher reports the child's absence from school pursuant to Article 26 of Chapter 115C of the General Statutes. G.S. 14-318.5(e).

Any person who reports the disappearance of a child as required is immune from any civil or criminal liability that might result from that action, so long as the person acted in good faith, which is presumed. G.S. 14-318.5(g).

Multiple convictions and punishments. The statute provides that "[u]nless the conduct is covered under some other provision of law providing greater punishment," a violation is a Class I felony. G.S. 14-318.5(b). This may suggest that a defendant cannot be convicted of this offense and another offense providing greater punishment. See the note on this Element to "Assault Inflicting Serious Injury" in the main volume. However, this conclusion is unclear given that the statute also provides that the crime "is an offense additional to other civil and criminal provisions and is not intended to repeal or preclude any other sanctions or remedies." G.S. 14-318.5(f).

Related Offenses Not in This Chapter

"Concealing a Death" (Chapter 21)

Misdemeanor failure to report the disappearance of a child who might be in danger. G.S. 14-318.5(c).

Contributing to a Juvenile's Being Delinquent, Undisciplined, Abused, or Neglected (page 203)

Elements (page 203)

The statutory reference in Element (6)(d) is incorrect. It should read:

G.S. 7B-101(15).

Notes (page 203)

Generally (new note)

This offense does not require the defendant to be the juvenile's parent, guardian, custodian, or caretaker. State v. Stevens, 228 N.C. App. 352, 355 (2013); State v. Harris, 236 N.C. App. 388, 394 (2014) (following *Stevens*).

Element (6)(d) (page 204)

The State presented sufficient evidence of this Element where (1) the defendant took the juvenile away from the area near the juvenile's home, ignored the juvenile after he was injured, and abandoned the sleeping juvenile in a parking lot, *Stevens*, 228 N.C. App. at 357, and (2) the defendant entered the child's bedroom, tried to get her to drink liquor, squeezed her buttocks, and asked to suck on her chest. *Harris*, 236 N.C. App. at 395 (the child "was clearly placed in a location in which and subject to conditions under which she could not and did not receive proper care from her caretakers").

For a case where the evidence was insufficient as to this element, see *State v. Reed*, ___ N.C. App. ___, 789 S.E.2d 703, 716 (after the defendant went to use the bathroom in her home for a few minutes, leaving her toddler in the care of an adult, the toddler fell into a backyard pool and drowned), *temporary stay allowed*, ___ N.C. ___, ___ S.E.2d ___ (Sep. 6, 2016).

Jury instructions (new note)

The jury instructions should define the statutory terms "delinquent," "undisciplined," "abused," and "neglected." *Harris*, 236 N.C. App. at 397 n.4.

Related Offenses Not in This Chapter (page 204)

Add the following offense to this list:

> "Sale, Surrender, or Purchase of a Minor," below in this supplement in Chapter 12 (Kidnapping and Related Offenses).

As a result of 2013 legislation, S.L. 2013-165, the offense listed as "Selling cigarettes to minors. G.S. 14-313" should read as follows:

> Youth access to tobacco products, tobacco-derived products, vapor products, and cigarette wrapping papers. G.S. 14-313.

As a result of 2016 legislation, S.L. 2016-115, add the following offense to this section:

> Unlawful transfer of custody of minor child. G.S. 14-321.2.

Replace the second to last offense in this list with the following:

> Unlawful payments related to adoption. G.S. 48-10-102.

10

Sexual Assaults

2012 legislation, S.L. 2012-40, amended G.S. 7B-1111(a) to provide that a court may terminate parental rights upon a finding that the parent "has been convicted of a sexually related offense under Chapter 14 of the General Statutes that resulted in the conception of the juvenile." All of the offenses covered in this chapter fall within Chapter 14 of the General Statutes.

2014 legislation, S.L. 2014-100, sec. 17.1(r), amended various sex offender statutes, substituting the words "Department of Public Safety" for the term "Division" in all instances except where the relevant statute refers to the Division of Adult Correction.

2015 legislation substantially reorganized and revised the rape and sex offense statutes. S.L. 2015-181. Specific changes are noted in the sections that follow.

Rape (page 217)

First-Degree Forcible Rape (page 217)

Statute (page 217)

2015 legislation, S.L. 2015-181, secs. 3(a) and (b), recodified and amended the statute. The amended statute provides:

> **§14-27.21. First-degree forcible rape**
> (a) A person is guilty of first degree forcible rape if the person engages in vaginal intercourse with another person by force and against the will of the other person, and does any of the following:
> > (1) Employs or displays a dangerous or deadly weapon or an article which the other person reasonably believes to be a dangerous or deadly weapon.
> > (2) Inflicts serious personal injury upon the victim or another person.
> > (3) The person commits the offense aided and abetted by one or more other persons.
>
> (b) Any person who commits an offense defined in this section is guilty of a Class B1 felony.
>
> (c) Upon conviction, a person convicted under this section has no rights to custody of or rights of inheritance from any child born as a result of the commission of the rape, nor shall the person have any rights related to the child under Chapter 48 or Subchapter 1 of Chapter 7B of the General Statutes.

Punishment (page 218)

As a result of the 2015 legislative change noted above, the statutory citation in this section should be to G.S. 14-27.21(b).

Notes (page 218)

Element (1) (page 218)

As a result of 2015 legislation, S.L. 2015-181, sec. 15, the statutory citation included in the first paragraph of this note should be to G.S. 14-27.36.

There was substantial evidence of vaginal intercourse notwithstanding the child victim's use of ambiguous terms. State v. Combs, 226 N.C. App. 87, 90–91 (2013) (the child used terms such as "manhood" and "middle hole" but went on to explain what these terms meant).

Element (2) (page 218)

As a result of 2015 legislation, S.L. 2015-181, sec. 15, the statutory citation included in this note should be to G.S. 14-27.34.

Element (3) (page 218)

The evidence sufficiently established use of force when, after the victim repeatedly declined the defendant's advances, the defendant pushed her to the ground and got on top of her. State v. Norman, 227 N.C. App. 162, 167–68 (2013) (rape and sexual offense case).

In a second-degree sexual offense case, the court held that the touching was by force and against the victim's will when the defendant surprised a store shopper by putting his hand up her skirt and penetrating her vagina; the court rejected the defendant's argument that because his action surprised the victim, she did not have the opportunity to consent or resist and that therefore he did not act by force and against the victim's will. State v. Henderson, 233 N.C. App. 538, 540–41 (2014).

Evidence (1) that a juvenile threatened the minor victims he had met at a school for special needs with exposing their secrets and their participation with him in sexual activities and (2) of a power differential between the juvenile and the victims was insufficient to establish constructive force; for constructive force to apply, threats resulting in fear, fright, or coercion must be threats of physical harm. *In re* T.W., 221 N.C. App. 193, 199 (2012).

Although constructive force can be inferred from a special relationship, such as between a parent and a child, such an inference is inappropriate where the relationship between a juvenile defendant and the victims was one of "leader to . . . follower[s] among children in school" and did "not involve the same wielding of authority, disparity of power, and degree of fear that occurs between an abusive parent and a child." *Id*. at 200.

Element (4) (page 218)

In a second-degree sexual offense case, the court held that the touching was by force and against the victim's will when the defendant surprised a store shopper by putting his hand up her skirt and penetrating her vagina; the court rejected the defendant's argument that because his action surprised the victim, she did not have the opportunity to consent or resist and that therefore he did not act by force and against the victim's will. *Henderson*, 233 N.C. App. at 540–41.

Element (5)(a) (page 218)

As a result of the 2015 legislation noted above, the statutory citation in the first paragraph of this note should be to G.S. 14-27.21(a)(1).

Element (5)(b) (page 219)

There was sufficient evidence that the victim suffered serious personal injury where she had blood on her lip and bruises on her ribs, arms, and face; the victim was in pain for four or five days after the incident; as a result of feeling unsafe, the victim left her boyfriend, terminated her lease, and moved in with her family; and at the time of trial, roughly a year later, the victim still felt unsafe being alone. State v. Gates, ___ N.C. App. ___, 781 S.E.2d 883, 886–87 (2016).

Jury instructions (new note)

When the evidence of penetration is clear and positive, the trial court does not err by failing to instruct the jury on attempt. State v. Matsoake, ___ N.C. App. ___, 777 S.E.2d 810, 814–15 (2015) (rape case); *Norman*, 227 N.C. App. 162, 168 (same). However, when the evidence of penetration is conflicting, the trial court should instruct on attempt, though it may not be plain error to fail to do so. State v. Carter, 366 N.C. 496, 500–01 (2013) (no plain error; sex offense); State v. Boyett, 229 N.C. App. 576, 578, 741 (2013) (no plain error; rape and incest case).

Defendant under 14 (page 221)

As a result of 2015 legislation, S.L. 2015-181, sec. 15, the statutory citation included in this note should be to G.S. 14-27.35.

Greater and lesser-included offenses (page 221)

For another case holding that assault on a female is not a lesser-included offense of first-degree sexual offense, see *State v. Martin*, 222 N.C. App. 213, 221–22 (2012).

In a 2012 case, the court of appeals held that a defendant cannot be convicted of second-degree sexual offense (mentally disabled victim) and crime against nature (where lack of consent was based on the fact that the victim was mentally disabled, incapacitated, or physically helpless) based on the same conduct (fellatio). State v. Hunt, 221 N.C. App. 489, 495–97 (2012), *aff'd per curiam*, 367 N.C. 700 (2014). The court found that "on the . . . facts of [the] case," crime against nature was a lesser-included offense of second-degree sexual offense and that conviction of both offenses violated double jeopardy. *Id.* However, the North Carolina Supreme Court previously has held that crime against nature is not a lesser-included offense of forcible sexual offense, State v. Etheridge, 319 N.C. 34, 50–51 (1987); State v. Warren, 309 N.C. 224, 230–31 (1983), and that a definitional test—not a factual test—applies when determining whether offenses are lesser-included offenses. State v. Nickerson, 365 N.C. 279, 280 (2011); *Warren*, 309 N.C. at 230–31; *see also* State v. Robinson, 368 N.C 402, 407–08 (2015) (applying a definitional test to the analysis).

As a result of the 2015 legislation noted above, (1) the penultimate sentence of the fifth paragraph in this note should read as follows:

But when a short-form rape indictment is not used and the indictment charges the crime using the language in the rape statute, assault on a female may not be submitted to the jury unless it has been separately charged. *Hedgepeth*, 165 N.C. App. 321 (decided under former G.S. 14-27.2).

As a result of that same legislation, the citations in the last paragraph of this note should read as follows:

G.S. 14-27.23(e); G.S. 14-27.28(d).

Multiple convictions and punishments (page 222)

A defendant may be sentenced for statutory rape and incest arising out of the same transaction. State v. Marlow, 229 N.C. App. 593, 599–600 (2013) (reasoning that the offenses are not the same under the *Blockburger* test).

A defendant may be convicted and sentenced for both statutory rape of a 13, 14, or 15-year-old and second-degree rape of a mentally disabled person when the convictions are based on a single act of sexual intercourse. State v. Banks, 367 N.C. 652, 658–59 (2014).

Convicted defendant has no rights to custody or inheritance (page 223)

As a result of the 2015 legislation noted above, the text of this note should begin as follows: "G.S. 14-27.21(c) provides."

Related Offenses Not in This Chapter (page 223)

Add the following offense to this section:

Committing or attempting to commit sexual penetration on human remains. G.S. 14-401.22(c).

Second-Degree Forcible Rape (page 223)

Statute (page 223)

2015 legislation, S.L. 2015-181, secs. 4(a) and (b), recodified and amended the statute. The new title of the statute is:

§14-27.22. Second-degree forcible rape.

A conforming change was made to subsection (a) so that it now reads:

> (a) A person is guilty of second degree forcible rape if the person engages in vaginal intercourse with another person:

Punishment (page 224)

As a result of the 2015 legislation noted above, the statutory citation in this note should be to G.S. 14-27.22(b).

Elements (page 223)

Remove the "(4)" before the last listed Element. The text listed in Element (4) relates only to Element (3)(b) (with one who is mentally disabled, mentally incapacitated, or physically helpless) and not to Element (3)(a) (by force and against the person's will).

Notes (page 224)

Elements (3)(b)(i), (ii), and (iii) (page 224)

These notes cite G.S. 27.1. That statute was recodified as G.S. 14-27.20 by 2015 legislation. S.L. 2015-181, sec. 2.

Element (3)(b)(i) (page 224)

Reversing a case cited in this note, *State v. Hunt*, 211 N.C. App. 452 (2011), the North Carolina Supreme Court held that expert testimony is not required for the State to establish that the victim had a mental disability for purposes of second-degree sexual offense. State v. Hunt, 365 N.C. 432, 441 (2012).

Convicted defendant has no rights to custody or inheritance (page 225)

As a result of the 2015 legislation noted above, the statutory citation in this note should be to G.S. 14-27.22(c).

First-Degree Statutory Rape (page 225)

Statute (page 225)

2015 legislation, S.L. 2015-181, secs. 3(b) and 6, removed first-degree statutory rape from old G.S. 14-27.2 (recodified by the same legislation as G.S. 14-27.21), recodifying it as follows:

§14-27.24. First degree statutory rape.

> (a) A person is guilty of first degree statutory rape if the person engages in vaginal intercourse with a victim who is a child under the age of 13 years and the defendant is at least 12 years old and is at least four years older than the victim.
> (b) Any person who commits an offense defined in this section is guilty of a Class B1 felony.
> (c) Upon conviction, a person convicted under this section has no rights to custody of or rights of inheritance from any child born as a result of the commission of the rape, nor shall the person have any rights related to the child under Chapter 48 or Subchapter 1 of Chapter 7B of the General Statutes.

No substantive changes were made to the elements of the offense.

Punishment (page 226)

As a result of the 2015 legislation noted above, the statutory citation in this note should now read: G.S. 14-27.24(b).

Notes (page 226)

Element (2) (page 226)

For another case supporting the statement in this note that mistake of age is no defense to this crime, see *State v. Ward*, ___ N.C. App. ___, 792 S.E.2d 579, 585 (2016).

Consent (page 226)

For another case supporting the statement in this note that consent is no defense to this crime, see *State v. Ward*, ___ N.C. App. ___, 792 S.E.2d 579, 585 (2016).

Statutory Rape by an Adult (page 227)

Statute (page 227)

2015 legislation, S.L. 2015-181, secs. 5(a) and (b), recodified and amended the statute. The new title of the statute is:

§14-27.23. Statutory rape of a child by an adult.

A conforming change was made to subsection (a) so that it now reads:

> **(a) A person is guilty of statutory rape of a child by an adult if the person is at least 18 years of age and engages in vaginal intercourse with a victim who is a child under the age of 13 years.**

Due to other recodifications made in that same legislation, conforming changes were made to subsection (e) so that it now reads:

> **(e) The offense under G.S. 14-27.24 is a lesser included offense of the offense in this section.**

Punishment (page 228)

As a result of the 2015 legislation noted above, the statutes referenced in this note should be to the same subsections in new G.S. 14-27.23.

> The trial court has no discretion to sentence the defendant to less than 300 months for this offense. State v. Agustin, 229 N.C. App. 240, 246 (2013).

This note indicates that the statutory provision providing that a defendant may be sentenced to an active term above that normally provided for a Class B1 felony if the judge finds egregious aggravation appears to run afoul of the United States Supreme Court decision in *Blakely v. Washington*, 542 U.S. 296 (2004) (holding that any factor, other than a prior conviction, that increases punishment beyond the prescribed statutory maximum must be submitted to the jury and proved beyond a reasonable doubt). In *State v. Singletary*, ___ N.C. App. ___, 786 S.E.2d 712, 722–24 (2016), the court so held as to the parallel punishment provision for Statutory Sexual Offense by an Adult; that holding almost certainly applies to this offense as well.

Notes (page 228)

Lifetime satellite-based monitoring (page 228)

As a result of the 2015 legislation noted above, the statutory citation in this note should be to G.S. 14-27.23(b).

Convicted defendant has no rights of custody or inheritance (page 228)

As a result of the 2015 legislation noted above, the statutory citation in this note should be to G.S. 14-27.23(d).

Statutory Rape of a Person 15 or Younger by a Defendant Who Is at Least 12 Years Old and at Least Six Years Older Than the Victim (revised title) (page 229)

Statute (page 229)

2015 legislation both amended and recodified the statute. S.L. 2015-62, sec. 1(a); S.L. 2015-181, secs. 7(a) and (b). As amended, the statute now reads as follows:

§ 14-27.25. Statutory rape of person who is 15 years of age or younger.

(a) A defendant is guilty of a Class B1 felony if the defendant engages in vaginal intercourse with another person who is 15 years of age or younger and the defendant is at least 12 years old and at least six years older than the person, except when the defendant is lawfully married to the person.

(b) Unless the conduct is covered under some other provision of law providing greater punishment, a defendant is guilty of a Class C felony if the defendant engages in vaginal intercourse with another person who is 15 years of age or younger and the defendant is at least 12 years old and more than four but less than six years older than the person, except when the defendant is lawfully married to the person.

Elements (page 229)

As a result of the statutory changes noted above, Elements (2) and (3) should be revised to read as follows:

(2) with a child who is 15 years old or younger *and*
(3) the defendant is
    (a) at least 12 years old *and*
    (b) at least six years older than the child.

Punishment (page 229)

As a result of the 2015 legislative change noted above, the statutory citation in this section should be to G.S. 14-27.25(a).

Notes (page 229)

Element (2) (page 229)

As a result of the statutory changes noted above, the crime now applies whenever the victim is 15 years of age or younger.

Exceptions (page 230)

As a result of the 2015 legislation noted above, the statutory citation in this section should be to G.S. 14-27.25(a).

Statutory Rape of a Person 15 or Younger by a Defendant Who Is at Least 12 Years Old and Is More Than Four but Less Than Six Years Older Than the Victim (revised title) (page 231)

Statute (page 231)

2015 legislation both amended and recodified the statute. S.L. 2015-62, sec. 1(a); S.L. 2015-181, secs. 7(a) and (b). The amended statute is reproduced under "Statutory Rape of a Person 15 or Younger by a Defendant Who Is at Least 12 Years Old and Is at Least Six Years Older Than the Victim," above in this supplement.

Elements (page 231)

As a result of the statutory changes noted above, Elements (2) and (3) should be revised to read as follows:

(2) with a child who is 15 years old or younger *and*
(3) the defendant is
    (a) at least 12 years old *and*
    (b) more than four but less than six years older than the child.

Punishment (page 231)

As a result of the 2015 legislation noted above, the statutory citation in this section should be to G.S. 14-27.25(b).

Notes (page 231)

Multiple convictions and punishments (new note)

2015 legislation amended the statute to provide that punishment is as a Class C felony "[u]nless the conduct is covered under some other provision of law providing greater punishment." G.S. 14-27.25(b), as amended by S.L. 2015-62, sec. 1(a); S.L. 2015-181, secs. 7(a) and (b). This means that a defendant cannot be punished for this offense and one that provides for harsher punishment.

Sexual Offenses (page 231)

First-Degree Forcible Sexual Offense (page 231)

Statute (page 231)

2015 legislation, S.L. 2015-181, secs. 8(a) and (b), recodified and amended the statute. The amended statute is as follows:

§14-27.26. First degree forcible sexual offense.

(a) A person is guilty of a first degree forcible sexual offense if the person engages in a sexual act with another person by force and against the will of the other person, and does any of the following:

    (1) Employs or displays a dangerous or deadly weapon or an article which the other person reasonably believes to be a dangerous or deadly weapon.

    (2) Inflicts serious personal injury upon the victim or another person.

    (3) The person commits the offense aided and abetted by one or more other persons.

(b) Any person who commits an offense defined in this section is guilty of a Class B1 felony.

Punishment (page 232)

As a result of the 2015 legislation noted above, the statutory citation in this section should be to G.S. 14-27.26(b).

Notes (page 232)

Element (1) (page 232)

This note cites G.S. 14-27.1. That statute was recodified as G.S. 14-27.20 by 2015 legislation. S.L. 2015-181, sec. 2. This note also cites G.S. 14-27.10. That statute was recodified as G.S. 14-27.36 by the same 2015 legislation. S.L. 2015-181, sec. 15.

The defendant's act of forcing the victim at gunpoint to penetrate her vagina with her own fingers constitutes a sexual act. State v. Green, 229 N.C. App. 121, 128 (2013).

Proof of vaginal penetration cannot support a sexual offense conviction; a sexual act other than vaginal intercourse is required. State v. Spence, 237 N.C. App. 367, 378–79 (2014).

When the sex act is fellatio, proof of penetration is not required. *In re* J.F., 237 N.C. App. 218, 225–26 (2014).

The prosecution need not show that the defendant performed a sexual act on the victim; the State need only prove that the defendant engaged in a sexual act with the victim. *Id.* (victim performed fellatio on the juvenile).

Sexual purpose (new note)

Proof of this crime does not require evidence that the defendant acted with a sexual purpose. *In re* J.F., 237 N.C. App. 218, 224–25 (2014).

Defenses (page 233)

This note cites G.S. 14-27.1. That statute was recodified as G.S. 14-27.20 by 2015 legislation. S.L. 2015-181, sec. 2.

Add the following at the end of this note:

> For the defendant to be entitled to a jury instruction on this affirmative defense, there must be direct testimony that the conduct was for a medically accepted purpose. State v. Stepp, 367 N.C. 772 (2015) (per curiam opinion reversing *State v. Stepp*, 232 N.C. App. 132 (2014), for reasons stated in the dissenting opinion below; the defendant admitted penetrating the victim's genital opening with his finger, but claimed it was for an accepted medical purpose; noting the absence of any direct testimony that this was done for an accepted medical purpose, the dissenting judge found that the defendant was not entitled to a jury instruction on the defense).

Second-Degree Forcible Sexual Offense (page 234)

Statute (page 234)

2015 legislation, S.L. 2015-181, secs. 9(a) and (b), recodified and amended the statute. The new title of the statute is:

§14-27.27. Second degree forcible sexual offense.

A conforming change was made to subsection (a) so that it now reads:

(a) A person is guilty of second degree forcible sexual offense if the person engages in a sexual act with another person:

Elements (page 234)

Remove the "(4)" before the last listed Element. The text presented in Element (4) relates only to Element (3)(b) (with one who is mentally disabled, mentally incapacitated, or physically helpless) and not to Element (3)(a) (by force and against the person's will).

Punishment (page 234)

As a result of the 2015 legislation noted above, the statutory citation in this note should be to G.S. 14-27.27(b).

First-Degree Statutory Sexual Offense (page 235)

Statute (page 235)

2015 legislation, S.L. 2015-181, secs. 8(b) and 11, removed first-degree statutory sexual offense from old G.S. 14-27.4 (recodified by the same legislation as G.S. 14-27.26), recodifying it as follows:

§14-27.29. First degree statutory sexual offense.
(a) A person is guilty of first degree statutory sexual offense if the person engages in a sexual act with a victim who is a child under the age of 13 years and the defendant is at least 12 years old and is at least four years older than the victim.
(b) Any person who commits an offense defined in this section is guilty of a Class B1 felony.

No substantive changes were made to the elements of the offense.

Punishment (page 235)

As a result of the 2015 legislation noted above, the statutory citation in this section should be to G.S. 14-27.29(b).

Statutory Sexual Offense by an Adult (page 236)

Statute (page 236)

2015 legislation, S.L. 2015-181, secs. 10(a) and (b), recodified and amended the statute. The new title of the statute is:

§14-27.28. Statutory sexual offense with a child by an adult.

A conforming change was made to subsection (a) so that it now reads:

> **(a)** A person is guilty of statutory sexual offense with a child by an adult if the person is at least 18 years of age and engages in a sexual act with a victim who is a child under the age of 13 years.

Due to other recodifications made in that same legislation, conforming changes were made to subsection (d) so that it now reads:

> **(d)** The offense under G.S. 14-27.29 is a lesser included offense of the offense in this section.

Punishment (page 237)

As a result of the 2015 legislation noted above, the first two sentences of this section should read as follows:

> Class B1 felony, except that the offense is subject to a mandatory minimum of 300 months of active time. G.S. 14-27.28(b). G.S. 14-27.28(c) provides that a defendant may be sentenced to an active term above that normally provided for a Class B1 felony if the judge finds egregious aggravation.

This note indicates that the statutory provision providing that a defendant may be sentenced to an active term above that normally provided for a Class B1 felony if the judge finds egregious aggravation appears to run afoul of the United States Supreme Court decision in *Blakely v. Washington*, 542 U.S. 296 (2004) (holding that any factor, other than a prior conviction, that increases punishment beyond the prescribed statutory maximum must be submitted to the jury and proved beyond a reasonable doubt). In *State v. Singletary*, ___ N.C. App. ___, 786 S.E.2d 712, 722–24 (2016), the court so held.

Notes (page 237)

Lifetime satellite-based monitoring required (page 238)

As a result of the 2015 legislation noted above, the statutory citation in this note should be to G.S. 14-27.28(b).

Statutory Sexual Offense of a Person 15 or Younger by a Defendant Who Is at Least 12 Years Old and Is at Least Six Years Older Than the Victim (revised title) (page 238)

Statute (page 238)

2015 legislation, S.L. 2015-181, secs. 7(a), 7(b), and 12, removed this offense from G.S. 14-27.7A (which was recodified as G.S. 14-27.25), recodifying it as follows:

> **§14-27.30. Statutory sexual offense with a person who is 15 years of age or younger.**
> (a) A defendant is guilty of a Class B1 felony if the defendant engages in a sexual act with another person who is 15 years of age or younger and the defendant is at least 12 years old and at least six years older than the person, except when the defendant is lawfully married to the person.
> (b) Unless the conduct is covered under some other provision of law providing greater punishment, a defendant is guilty of a Class C felony if the defendant engages in a sexual act with another person who is 15 years of age or younger and the defendant is at least 12 years old and more than four but less than six years older than the person, except when the defendant is lawfully married to the person.

Elements (page 238)

As a result of the statutory changes noted above, Elements (2) and (3) should be revised to read as follows:

(2) with a child who is 15 years old or younger *and*
(3) the defendant is
   (a) at least 12 years old *and*
   (b) at least six years older than the child.

Punishment (page 238)

As a result of the 2015 legislation noted above, the statutory citation in this section should be to G.S. 14-27.30(a).

Notes (page 238)

Element (2) (page 238)

As a result of the statutory changes noted above, the crime now applies whenever the victim is 15 years of age or younger.

Statutory Sexual Offense of a Person 15 or Younger by a Defendant Who Is at Least 12 Years Old and Is More Than Four but Less Than Six Years Older Than the Victim

(revised title) (page 239)

Statute (page 239)

2015 legislation, S.L. 2015-181, secs. 7(a), 7(b), and 12, removed this offense from G.S. 14-27.7A (which was recodified as G.S. 14-27.25), putting it in a new statutory section, G.S. 14-27.30, reproduced under "Statutory Sexual Offense of a Person 15 or Younger by a Defendant Who Is at Least 12 Years Old and Is at Least Six Years Older Than the Victim," above in this supplement.

Elements (page 239)

As a result of the statutory changes noted above, Elements (2) and (3) should be revised to read as follows:

(2) with a child who is 15 years old or younger *and*
(3) the defendant is
   (a) at least 12 years old *and*
   (b) more than four but less than six years older than the child.

Punishment (page 239)

As a result of the 2015 legislation noted above, the statutory citation in this section should be to G.S. 14-27.30(b).

Notes (page 240)

Multiple convictions and punishments (new note)

2015 legislation, S.L. 2015-181, sec. 12, amended the recodified statute to provide that punishment is as a Class C felony "[u]nless the conduct is covered under some other provision of law providing greater punishment." G.S. 14-27.30(b). This means that a defendant cannot be punished for this offense and one that provides for harsher punishment.

Sexual Activity by a Substitute Parent (page 240)

Statute (page 240)

2015 legislation amended and recodified the statute. S.L. 2015-181, secs. 13(a) and (b). The statute now reads:

§14-27.31. Sexual activity by a substitute parent or custodian.

(a) If a defendant who has assumed the position of a parent in the home of a minor victim engages in vaginal intercourse or a sexual act with a victim who is a minor residing in the home, the defendant is guilty of a Class E felony.

> (b) If a person having custody of a victim of any age or a person who is an agent or employee of any person, or institution, whether such institution is private, charitable, or governmental, having custody of a victim of any age engages in vaginal intercourse or a sexual act with such victim, the defendant is guilty of a Class E felony.
>
> (c) Consent is not a defense to a charge under this section.

The statutory amendments did not make any substantive changes to this offense.

Punishment (page 241)

As a result of 2015 legislation noted above, the statutory citation in this note should be to G.S. 14-27.31(a).

Notes (page 241)
Consent (page 241)

As a result of 2015 legislation noted above, the statutory citation in this note should be to G.S. 14-27.31(c).

Sexual Activity by a Custodian (page 242)

Statute (page 242)

2015 legislation amended and recodified the statute. S.L. 2015-181, secs. 13(a) and (b). The amended statute is reproduced under "Sexual Activity by a Substitute Parent," above in this supplement. The statutory amendments did not make any substantive changes to this offense.

Punishment (page 242)

As a result of the 2015 legislation noted above, the statutory citation in this note should be to G.S. 14-27.31(b).

Notes (page 242)
Element (1) (page 242)

As a result of the 2015 legislation noted above, the statutory citation in this note should be to G.S. 14-27.31(b).

Consent (page 243)

As a result of the 2015 legislation noted above, the statutory citation in this note should be to G.S. 14-27.31(c).

Sexual Activity with a Student (page 243)

Sexual Activity with a Student by a Teacher, School Administrator, Student Teacher, Coach, or School Safety Officer (page 243)

Statute (page 243)

2015 legislation amended and recodified the statute. S.L. 2015-181, secs. 14(a) and (b); S.L. 2015-44, sec. 2. The statute now reads as follows:

> §14-27.32. Sexual activity with a student.
>
> (a) If a defendant, who is a teacher, school administrator, student teacher, school safety officer, or coach, at any age, or who is other school personnel, and who is at least

four years older than the victim engages in vaginal intercourse or a sexual act with a victim who is a student, at any time during or after the time the defendant and victim were present together in the same school, but before the victim ceases to be a student, the defendant is guilty of a Class G felony, except when the defendant is lawfully married to the student. The term "same school" means a school at which the student is enrolled and the defendant is employed, assigned, or volunteers.

(b) A defendant who is school personnel, other than a teacher, school administrator, student teacher, school safety officer, or coach, and is less than four years older than the victim and engages in vaginal intercourse or a sexual act with a victim who is a student, is guilty of a Class I felony.

(c) This section shall apply unless the conduct is covered under some other provision of law providing for greater punishment.

(d) Consent is not a defense to a charge under this section.

(e) For purposes of this section, the terms "school", "school personnel", and "student" shall have the same meaning as in G.S. 14-202.4(d). For purposes of this section, the term "school safety officer" shall include a school resource officer or any other person who is regularly present in a school for the purpose of promoting and maintaining safe and orderly schools.

The statutory amendments did not make any substantive changes to this offense.

Punishment (page 243)

As a result of the 2015 legislation noted above, the statutory citation in this section should be to G.S. 14-27.32(a).

Notes (page 243)
Element (1) (page 243)

As a result of the 2015 legislation noted above, the statutory citation in this note should be to G.S. 14-27.32(e).

Element (3) (page 244)

As a result of the 2015 legislation noted above, replace the statutory citations in this note to G.S. 14-27.7(b) with G.S. 14-27.32(e).

Element (4) (page 244)

As a result of the 2015 legislation noted above, the statutory citation in this note should be to G.S. 14-27.32(a).

Exceptions (page 244)

As a result of the 2015 legislation noted above, the statutory citation in this note should be to G.S. 14-27.32(a).

Multiple convictions and punishments (page 244)

As a result of the 2015 legislation noted above, the statutory citation in this note should be to G.S. 14-27.32(c).

Sexual Activity with a Student by School Personnel Other Than a Teacher, School Administrator, Student Teacher, Coach, or School Safety Officer Who Is at Least Four Years Older Than the Student (revised title) (page 244)

Statute (page 244)

2015 legislation amended and recodified the statute. S.L. 2015-181, secs. 14(a) and (b). The new statute is reproduced under "Sexual Activity with a Student by a Teacher, School Administrator, Student Teacher, Coach, or School Safety Officer," above in this supplement. The statutory amendments did not make any substantive changes to this offense.

Punishment (page 245)

As a result of the 2015 legislation noted above, the statutory citation in this note should be to G.S. 14-27.32(a).

Notes (page 245)

Element (1) (page 245)

As a result of the 2015 legislation noted above, replace the citation to G.S. 14-27.7(b) in this note with G.S. 14-27.32(e).

Sexual Activity with a Student by School Personnel Other Than a Teacher, School Administrator, Student Teacher, Coach, or School Safety Officer Who Is Less Than Four Years Older Than the Student (revised title) (page 245)

Statute (page 245)

2015 legislation amended and recodified the statute. S.L. 2015-181, secs. 14(a) and (b); S.L. 2015-44, sec. 2. The new statute is reproduced under "Sexual Activity with a Student by a Teacher, School Administrator, Student Teacher, Coach, or School Safety Officer," above in this supplement.

Punishment (page 246)

As a result of the 2015 legislation noted above, delete the text of this note and replace it with the following:

Class I felony. G.S. 14-27.32(b).

Indecent Liberties (page 246)

Indecent Liberties with a Child (page 246)

Notes (page 246)

Element (2)(a)(i) (page 248)

The defendant's purpose may be inferred from his or her actions. State v. Godley, 234 N.C. App. 562, 569 (2014); State v. Minyard, 231 N.C. App. 605, 621 (2014). For example, there was sufficient evidence of the required purpose when the defendant kissed the victim on the mouth, fondled her under her clothing, touched her breasts and vagina, and engaged in conduct giving rise to first-degree rape charges. Godley, 234 N.C. App. at 569.

There was sufficient proof that the defendant's purpose was to arouse or gratify sexual desire where he repeatedly raped the victim while she was living in his home. State v. Kpaeyeh, ___ N.C. App. ___, 784 S.E.2d 582, 586–87 (2016) (rejecting the defendant's argument that evidence of vaginal penetration is insufficient by itself to prove that a rape was committed for the purpose of arousing or gratifying sexual desire).

Jury instructions (page 249)

Because indecent liberties is a single offense that may be proved by evidence of any one of a number of acts, the trial court did not err by declining to instruct the jury according to a bill of particulars. State v. Stephens, 234 N.C. App. 292, 295–96 (2014) (the trial court properly instructed the jury that it could find the defendant guilty if it found that the defendant willfully took "any immoral, improper, or indecent liberties" with the child; the actual act committed for the purposes of arousing himself or gratifying his sexual desire was immaterial).

In a case involving five counts of indecent liberties, no unanimity issue arose where the trial court framed the jury instructions in terms of the statutory requirements and referenced the indictments, each of which specified a different, non-overlapping time frame; the instructions distinguished the five charges and directed the jurors to find the defendant guilty only if they found that he committed the requisite acts within the designated time period, and each verdict sheet was paired with an indictment. State v. Comeaux, 224 N.C. App. 595, 605 (2012).

The trial judge properly instructed the jury in a case where the indictment tracked the statute and did not allege an evidentiary basis for the charge and the instructions identified the defendant's conduct as placing his penis between the child's feet. State v. Carter, 210 N.C. App. 156, 168–69 (2011) (the instruction was a clarification of the evidence for the jury).

Multiple convictions and punishments (page 249)

Add the following to the second paragraph of this note:

In *State v. Minyard*, 231 N.C. App. 605, 620–21 (2014), the court held that the victim's testimony that the defendant touched the victim's buttocks with his penis "four or five times" supported five indecent liberties convictions. Distinguishing *Laney* and finding the case similar to *James*, the court concluded that the State need not prove that the conduct occurred in discrete, separate settings when it involved acts "more explicit than mere touching." *Id.* at 620.

In *State v. Pierce*, 238 N.C. App. 537, 549–50 (2014), the court, citing *James*, held that the defendant properly was convicted of two counts of indecent liberties when the evidence showed that he had sex with his girlfriend in the presence of the victim, performed oral sex on the victim, and then forced his girlfriend to perform oral sex on the victim while he watched.

Indecent Liberties between Children (page 250)

Notes (page 250)

Element (2) (page 250)

For cases where the evidence was insufficient to establish a juvenile's sexual purpose with respect to the crime of Sexual Battery, see the note on Element (1) to that offense in this supplement.

Taking Indecent Liberties with a Student by a Teacher, School Administrator, Student Teacher, School Safety Officer, or Coach (revised title) (page 251)

Statute (page 251)

2015 legislation, S.L. 2015-44, sec. 3, amended G.S. 14-202.4(b) to read as follows:

> (b) If a defendant, who is school personnel, other than a teacher, school administrator, student teacher, school safety officer, or coach, and who is less than four years older than the victim, takes indecent liberties with a student as provided in subsection (a) of this section, the defendant is guilty of a Class I felony.

That same legislation amended the definition of "school personnel" in G.S. 14-202.4(d)(3) to read as follows:

> (3) "School personnel" means any person included in the definition contained in G.S. 115C-332(a)(2), including those employed by a nonpublic, charter, or regional school, and any person who volunteers at a school or a school sponsored activity.

2015 legislation, S.L. 2015-181, sec. 16, made a conforming change to the last sentence of subsection (d) of the statute. That sentence now reads as follows:

> For purposes of this section, the term indecent liberties does not include vaginal intercourse or a sexual act as defined by G.S. 14-27.20.

Notes (page 252)

    Element (2) (page 252)

This note cites G.S. 14-27.1. That statute was recodified as G.S. 14-27.20 by 2015 legislation. S.L. 2015-181, sec. 2.

    Element (3) (page 252)

    If the victim is enrolled in kindergarten or grade 1 through 12, the victim is a student within the meaning of the statute even if the incident occurs during a school break. State v. Stephens, 234 N.C. App. 292, 296–97 (2014) (incident occurred during summer vacation).

Taking Indecent Liberties with a Student by School Personnel Other Than a Teacher, School Administrator, Student Teacher, School Safety Officer, or Coach Who Is at Least Four Years Older Than the Student (revised title) (page 253)

    Statute (page 253)

As noted above under "Taking Indecent Liberties with a Student by a Teacher, School Administrator, Student Teacher, School Safety Officer, or Coach," 2015 legislation amended the statute.

    Notes (page 253)

        Element (1) (page 253)

As a result of 2015 legislation, S.L. 2015-44, sec. 3, delete the first sentence of this note and replace it with the following:

    "School personnel" means any person included in the definition contained in G.S. 115C-332(a)(2), including those employed by a nonpublic, charter, or regional school, and any person who volunteers at a school or a school-sponsored activity. G.S. 14-202.4(d)(3), as amended by S.L. 2015-44, sec. 3.

Taking Indecent Liberties with a Student by School Personnel Other Than a Teacher, School Administrator, Student Teacher, School Safety Officer, or Coach Who Is Less Than Four Years Older Than the Student (revised title) (page 253)

    Statute (page 253)

As noted above under "Taking Indecent Liberties with a Student by a Teacher, School Administrator, Student Teacher, School Safety Officer, or Coach," 2015 legislation amended the statute.

    Punishment (page 254)

As a result of the 2015 legislation noted above under "Taking Indecent Liberties with a Student by a Teacher, School Administrator, Student Teacher, School Safety Officer, or Coach," delete the text of this section and replace it with the following:

    Class I felony. G.S. 14-202.4(b).

Sexual Battery (page 254)

    Statute (page 254)

2015 legislation recodified the statute as G.S. 14-27.33. Thus, the statute title should now read:

    §14-27.33. Sexual battery.

    Punishment (page 254)

As a result of the 2015 legislation noted above, the statutory citation in this section should be to G.S. 14-27.33(b).

Notes (page 255)

Element (1) (page 255)

The court of appeals has noted that in cases involving adult defendants, "the element of acting for the purpose of sexual arousal, sexual gratification, or sexual abuse may be inferred from the very act itself." *In re* S.A.A. ___N.C. App. ___, ___S.E.2d ___ (Dec. 20, 2016) (quotation omitted). However, that rule does not apply with respect to juveniles. *Id.*; *In re* K.C., 226 N.C. App. 452, 457 (2013). For a juvenile, there must be "evidence of the child's maturity, intent, experience, or other factor indicating his purpose in acting." *S.A.A.* ___ N.C. App. at ___, ___ S.E.2d at ___ (quoting *K.C.*, 226 N.C. App. at 457). For cases where the evidence was held to be insufficient to establish a juvenile's sexual purpose required for this crime, see *K.C.*, 226 N.C. App. at 457–58 (evidence of sexual purpose was insufficient where, among other things, the juvenile and the victim were the same age; there was no evidence that the juvenile exercised control over the situation; and the incident occurred in a public school room during the day), and *S.A.A.*, ___ N.C. App. at ___, ___ S.E.2d at ___ (evidence of sexual purpose was insufficient where, among other things, the juvenile and the girls in question were middle school students; neither the location nor the alleged manner of the touching was secretive in nature; nothing about the juvenile's attitude suggested a sexual motivation; the juvenile made no sexual remarks to the girls; and the juvenile did not attempt to exert any control over the girls). For a case where the evidence was sufficient to establish a juvenile's sexual purpose with respect to the crime of Indecent Liberties between Children, see the note on Element (2) to that crime in the main volume.

Element (2) (page 255)

This note cites G.S. 14-27.1. That statute was recodified as G.S. 14-27.20 by 2015 legislation. S.L. 2015-181, sec. 2.

Sex Offender Crimes (page 258)

Statute (page 258)

2012 legislation, S.L. 2012-153, sec. 3, amended G.S. 14-208.6(4), adding a new subsection, e., as follows:

> e.   A final conviction for a violation of G.S. 14-43.14, only if the court sentencing the individual issues an order pursuant to G.S. 14-43.14(e) requiring the individual to register.

2012 legislation, S.L. 2012-194, sec. 4(a), amended G.S. 14-208.6(5), defining "sexually violent offense," to include the word "former" before G.S. 14-27.6 (attempted rape or sexual offense). 2015 legislation, S.L. 2015-181, sec. 32, made conforming changes to that subsection, so that it now reads as follows:

> (5)   "Sexually violent offense" means a violation of former G.S. 14-27.6 (attempted rape or sexual offense), G.S. 14-27.21 (first-degree forcible rape), G.S. 14-27.22 (second-degree forcible rape), G.S. 14-27.23 (statutory rape of a child by an adult), G.S.14-27.25(a) (statutory rape of a person who is 15 years of age or younger where the defendant is at least six years older), G.S. 14-27.26 (first-degree forcible sexual offense), G.S. 14-27.27 (second-degree forcible sexual offense), G.S. 14-27.28 (statutory sexual offense with a child by an adult), G.S. 14-27.29 (first-degree statutory sexual offense), G.S. 14-27.30(a) (statutory sexual offense with a person who is 15 years of age or younger where the defendant is at least six years older), G.S. 14-27.31 (sexual activity by a substitute parent or custodian), G.S. 14-27.32 (sexual activity with a student), G.S. 14-27.33 (sexual battery), G.S. 14-43.11 (human

trafficking) if (i) the offense is committed against a minor who is less than 18 years of age or (ii) the offense is committed against any person with the intent that they be held in sexual servitude, G.S. 14-43.13 (subjecting or maintaining a person for sexual servitude), G.S. 14-178 (incest between near relatives), G.S. 14-190.6 (employing or permitting minor to assist in offenses against public morality and decency), G.S. 14-190.9(a1) (felonious indecent exposure), G.S. 14-190.16 (first degree sexual exploitation of a minor), G.S. 14-190.17 (second degree sexual exploitation of a minor), G.S. 14-190.17A (third degree sexual exploitation of a minor), G.S. 14-202.1 (taking indecent liberties with children), G.S. 14-202.3 (Solicitation of child by computer or certain other electronic devices to commit an unlawful sex act), G.S. 14-202.4(a) (taking indecent liberties with a student), G.S. 14-205.2(c) or (d) (patronizing a prostitute who is a minor or a mentally disabled person), G.S. 14-205.3(b) (promoting prostitution of a minor or a mentally disabled person), G.S. 14-318.4(a1) (parent or caretaker commit or permit act of prostitution with or by a juvenile), or G.S. 14-318.4(a2) (commission or allowing of sexual act upon a juvenile by parent or guardian). The term also includes the following: a solicitation or conspiracy to commit any of these offenses; aiding and abetting any of these offenses.

2013 legislation, S.L. 2013-205, amended G.S. 14-208.11(a)(1) to read as follows:

(1)   Fails to register as required by this Article, including failure to register with the sheriff in the county designated by the person, pursuant to G.S. 14-208.8, as their expected county of residence.

That same legislation enacted a new subsection, (a2), to G.S. 14-208.11 as follows:

(a2) A person arrested pursuant to subsection (a1) of this section shall be subject to the jurisdiction of the prosecutorial and judicial district that includes the sheriff's office in the county where the person failed to register, pursuant to this Article. If the arrest is made outside of the applicable prosecutorial district, the person shall be transferred to the custody of the sheriff of the county where the person failed to register and all further criminal and judicial proceedings shall be held in that county.

2013 legislation, S.L. 2013-28, amended G.S. 14-208.16(a) to read as follows:

(a) A registrant under this Article shall not knowingly reside within 1,000 feet of the property on which any public or nonpublic school or child care center is located. This subsection applies to any registrant who did not establish his or her residence, in accordance with subsection (d) of this section, prior to August 16, 2006.

2016 legislation, S.L. 2016-102, sec. 1, amended G.S. 14-208.18(a) so that subsection (3) and new subsection (4) read as follows:

(3)   At any place where minors frequently congregate, including, but not limited to, libraries, arcades, amusement parks, recreation parks, and swimming pools, when minors are present.
(4)   On the State Fairgrounds during the period of time each year that the State Fair is conducted, on the Western North Carolina Agricultural Center grounds during the period of time each year that the North Carolina Mountain State Fair is conducted, and on any other fairgrounds during the period of time that an agricultural fair is being conducted.

2015 and 2016 legislation, S.L. 2015-62, sec. 5(a); S.L. 2016-102, sec. 1, amended G.S. 14-208.18(c); it now reads as follows:

(c) The subdivisions of subsection (a) of this section are applicable as follows:
(1)   Subdivisions (1), (3), and (4) of subsection (a) of this section apply to persons required to register under this Article who have committed any of the following offenses:

      a.   Any offense in Article 7A of this Chapter or any federal offense or offense committed in another state, which if committed in this State, is substantially similar to an offense in Article 7A of this Chapter.

      b.   Any offense where the victim of the offense was under the age of 18 years at the time of the offense.

  (2)   Subdivision (2) of subsection (a) of this section applies to persons required to register under this Article if either of the following applies:

      a.   The person has committed any offense in Article 7B of this Chapter or any federal offense or offense committed in another state, which if committed in this State is substantially similar to an offense in Article 7B of this Chapter, and a finding has been made in any criminal or civil proceeding that the person presents, or may present, a danger to minors under the age of 18.

      b.   The person has committed any offense where the victim of the offense was under the age of 18 years at the time of the offense.

Failure to Register, etc. as a Sex Offender (page 268)

Notes (page 269)

Element (1) (page 269)

Registration requirements that became effective on January 1, 1996, and applied to offenders then serving a sentence for a reportable offense applied to the defendant and made him a person required to register where he was convicted in 1994 of indecent liberties, his prison release date for that conviction was September 24, 1995, but he was not actually released until January 24, 1999, because he was serving a consecutive term for crime against nature. State v. Surratt, ___ N.C. App. ___, 773 S.E.2d 327, 331 (2015) (concluding that the defendant's actual release date, January 24, 1999, governs; also concluding that because he was required to register when the 2008 amendments to the registration statutes took effect, the 2008 amendments applied to him as well).

Element (3)(a) (page 269)

2013 legislation, S.L. 2013-205, amended the statute to clarify that failing to register includes failure to register with the sheriff in the county designated by the person as his or her expected county of residence.

Element (3)(b) (page 269)

This prong of the statute applies to a sex offender who has already complied with the initial registration requirements and is later incarcerated and then released. State v. Crockett, 368 N.C. 717, 722 (2016); State v. Barnett, 368 N.C. 710, 714 (2016) (holding that this provision applied where the defendant failed to change his address after being released from a term of incarceration imposed after his initial registration).

The evidence was sufficient to establish this element where (1) after initially registering, the defendant was incarcerated in the county jail and upon his release did not provide notice that he had changed his address from the county jail, *Crockett*, 368 N.C. at 724–25; (2) the defendant moved from North Carolina to South Carolina without providing written notice to the sheriff, *id.* at 725–26; (3) the defendant was not residing at his registered address, State v. McFarland, 234 N.C. App. 274, 280–81 (2014) (the State need not present evidence of the defendant's new address, only that he or she failed to register a change of address); and (4) the defendant may have maintained a permanent residence in one county but he also established a temporary home address at his ex-wife's residence in another county. State v. Pierce, 238 N.C. App. 141, 148–49 (2014).

Element (3)(c) (page 270)

Delete the second sentence of this note and replace it with the following:

To obtain a conviction under this prong of the statute, the State must prove five things: (1) the defendant is required to register, (2) law enforcement mailed a nonforwardable verification form to the defendant's last reported address, (3) the defendant actually received the verification form, (4) law enforcement made a reasonable attempt to verify that the defendant was residing at the registered address, and (5) the defendant willfully failed to return the verification form to the sheriff within three business days. State v. Moore, ___ N.C. App. ___, 770 S.E.2d 131 (2015) (stating these requirements and holding that the State failed to prove that the defendant actually received the verification form, that the sheriff's office made a reasonable attempt to verify that the defendant was still residing at his last reported address, or that the defendant acted willfully); State v. Braswell, 203 N.C. App. 736, 739 (2010) (the State failed to prove that the defendant actually received the verification form).

Element (3)(d) (page 270)

Falsely stating information on any forms submitted pursuant to the sex offender registration program supports a conviction. State v. Pressley, 235 N.C. App. 613, 617 (2014) (in a case where the defendant listed a false address, the court rejected the defendant's argument that the only verification forms that count are the initial verification form and those required to be filed every six months thereafter; the court concluded that the statute criminalizes providing false or misleading information on forms submitted pursuant to the act, regardless of when the forms are submitted). However, the statute only applies to providing false or misleading information on an executed verification form required by the statute; the statute does not apply to oral verifications to a law enforcement officer. State v. Surratt, ___ N.C. App. ___, 773 S.E.2d 327, 333 (2015).

Constitutionality (new note)

Requiring a person adjudicated as an incompetent to notify a sheriff of a change of address is unconstitutional. State v. Young, 140 N.C. App. 1 (2000).

The court of appeals has rejected the argument that the statute's change of address requirement was void for vagueness because it failed to define the term "address." *McFarland*, 234 N.C. App. at 277–79 (the homeless defendant unsuccessfully argued that a person of ordinary intelligence would not know what "address" meant in his case).

Jurisdiction (new note)

2013 legislation, S.L. 2013-205, amended G.S. 14-208.11 to provide that a person arrested for a failure to register violation must be prosecuted in the prosecutorial district that includes the sheriff's office in the county where the defendant failed to register. G.S. 14-208.11(a2). If the arrest is made outside of the applicable prosecutorial district, the defendant must be transferred to the custody of the sheriff of the county where the defendant failed to register. *Id.*

Multiple convictions and punishments (page 271)

Falsely reporting an address on verification forms submitted on two separate occasions supports two convictions. State v. Pressley, 235 N.C. App. 613, 619 (2014) (rejecting the defendant's argument that this constituted a continuing offense and could support only one conviction; submission of each form was a distinct offense).

Knowingly Residing Near a School or Child Care Center (page 272)

Notes (page 272)

Element (5) (page 272)

As a result of 2014 legislation, S.L. 2014-21, add the following sentence at the end of the second paragraph of this note:

> However, a "child care center" does include the permanent locations of organized clubs of Boys and Girls Clubs of America. G.S. 14-208.16(b).

Exceptions (page 272)

As a result of 2013 legislation, S.L. 2013-28, delete the last paragraph of this note and replace it with the following:

> Additionally, this offense does not apply to a person who established his or her residence before August 16, 2006. G.S. 14-208.16(a).

Being Present at a Location Used by Minors (page 274)

Statute (page 274)

As noted in this supplement, 2015 and 2016 legislation, S.L. 2015-62, sec. 5(a), sec. 5(a), S.L. 2016-102, sec.1, amended the statute.

Elements (page 274)

As a result of the 2015 and 2016 legislation noted in this supplement, delete the text of this section and replace it with the following:

> A person guilty of this offense
>
> (1) is required to register as a sex offender
> (2) because of a conviction for any
>   (a) rape, sexual offense, sexual battery, or related offense in G.S. Ch. 14 Art. 7B or substantially similar offense under federal law or the laws of another state *or*
>   (b) offense in which the victim was less than 18 years old *and*
> (3) knowingly
> (4) is present
>   (a) on the premises of any place intended primarily for the use, care, or supervision of minors, including, but not limited to, schools, children's museums, child care centers, nurseries, and playgrounds;
>   (b) within 300 feet of any location intended primarily for the use, care, or supervision of minors when the place is located on premises that are not intended primarily for the use, care, or supervision of minors, including malls, shopping centers, or other property open to the general public and, if the person is required to register because of a rape, sexual offense, sexual battery, or related offense in G.S. Ch. 14 Art. 7B or substantially similar offense under federal law or the laws of another state, a finding has been made in any criminal or civil proceeding that the person presents, or may present, a danger to minors under the age of 18;
>   (c) at any place where minors frequently congregate, including, but not limited to, libraries, arcades, amusement parks, recreation parks, and swimming pools, when minors are present; *or*
>   (d) on the State Fairgrounds when the State Fair is conducted, on the Western North Carolina Agricultural Center grounds when the North Carolina Mountain State Fair is conducted, or on any other fairgrounds when an agricultural fair is being conducted.

Notes (page 274)

Element (2)(b) (new note)

If the prior offense does not include an element as to the victim's age, the State must prove that the victim was younger than the statutory age at the time of the offense. State v. Fryou, ___ N.C. App. ___, 780 S.E.2d 152, 159 (2015).

Element (3) (page 274)

For a case where the evidence was sufficient as to this element, see State v. Fryou, ___ N.C. App. ___, 780 S.E.2d 152, 159–60 (2015) (church widely advertised its preschool and posted a sign at the church entrance indicating that a "nursery" was held on the premises).

Element (4) (page 274)

Although *State v. Fryou*, ___ N.C. App. ___, 780 S.E.2d 152, 160 (2015), held that the State need not prove that minors were actually present at the location at the time of the offense, 2016 legislative changes provide that the ban on being present at any place where minors frequently congregate (Element (4)(c) of this offense) applies only when "minors are present." S.L. 2016-102, sec. 1.

To satisfy Element (4)(b), the State must prove that the location is intended primarily for the use of minors; evidence that minors sometimes use the location is insufficient. State v. Simpson, 235 N.C. App. 398, 403–05 (2014) (the evidence was insufficient where the defendant sat on a park bench in close proximity to the park's batting cage and ball field and the State failed to present evidence that the batting cages and ball fields were intended primarily for use by minors).

Multiple convictions and punishments (new note)

In *State v. Daniels*, 224 N.C. App. 608, 612 (2012), the court held that Elements (4)(a) through (c) constitute three separate and distinct criminal offenses. This holding likely would apply to Element (4)(d) as well.

Constitutionality (new note)

2016 legislation, S.L. 2016-102, sec. 1, amended the statute in response to determinations in a federal district court case that (1) the prior statutory provision banning sex offenders from any place where minors gather for regularly scheduled educational, recreational, or social programs was unconstitutionally vague, Doe v. Cooper, 148 F. Supp. 3d 477, 494 (M.D.N.C. 2015), and (2) the "300 foot rule" ban was unconstitutionally overbroad under the First Amendment. Doe v. Cooper, No. 1:13CV711 (M.D.N.C. Apr. 22, 2016). The General Assembly responded by revising the "any place where minors gather" provision and by adding to the "300 foot rule" a requirement that a finding has been made in any criminal or civil proceeding that the person presents, or may present, a danger to minors under the age of 18. S.L. 2016-102, sec. 1. It also provided that these changes are repealed if the federal district court's determinations are stayed or overturned. *Id.* at sec. 2. The Fourth Circuit affirmed the lower court's rulings in *Doe v. Cooper*, 842 F.3d 833 (4th Cir. 2016).

In *Daniels*, 224 N.C. App. at 621, the court held that prior G.S. 14-208.18(a)(3), which prohibited a sex offender from being "at any place" where minors gather for regularly scheduled programs, was unconstitutionally vague as applied to the defendant. The defendant's two charges arose from his presence at two public parks. The State alleged that on one occasion the defendant was "out kind of close to the parking lot area or that little dirt road area[,]" between the ballpark and the road and that on the second occasion he was at an "adult softball field" adjacent to a "tee ball" field. The court found that on these facts, the portion of G.S. 14-208.18(a)(3) prohibiting presence "at any place" was unconstitutionally vague as applied to the defendant because it fails to give the person of ordinary intelligence a reasonable opportunity to know what is prohibited and it fails to provide explicit standards for those who apply the law. *Id.* at 622. By contrast, the court rejected an as applied vagueness challenge to G.S. 14-208.18(a)(2) in a case involving the defendant's presence at a church that operated a preschool on the premises. State v. Fryou, ___ N.C. App. ___, 780 S.E.2d 152, 161–63 (2015). As noted in this supplement, 2016 legislation amended the prohibitions in G.S. 14-208.18(a)(2) and (3).

Accessing a Social Networking Site (page 274)

Notes (page 275)

Constitutionality (new note)

In *State v. Packingham*, 368 N.C. 380 (2015), *cert granted*, ___ U.S. ___, ___ S. Ct. ___ (Oct. 28, 2016), the court upheld the statute, rejecting the defendant's claim that it was unconstitutional on its face and as applied because it violated free speech rights.

11

Crime against Nature, Incest, Indecent Exposure, and Related Offenses

Crime against Nature (page 281)

Notes (page 281)

Consent (page 282)

Reversing a case cited in this note, *State v. Hunt*, 211 N.C. App. 452 (2011), the North Carolina Supreme Court held that there was sufficient evidence that the victim's conditions rendered her substantially incapable of resisting the defendant's advances and that expert testimony is not required to prove the extent of a victim's mental capacity to consent to sexual acts. State v. Hunt, 365 N.C. 432, 441 (2012).

Penetration required (page 282)

For another case supporting the statement in this note that penetration of or by a sexual organ is required for this offense, see *In re* J.F., 237 N.C. App. 218, 225–27 (2014) (distinguishing *Heil* and finding the evidence insufficient to establish penetration).

Sexual purpose (new note)

Proof of this crime does not require evidence that the defendant acted with a sexual purpose. *In re* J.F., 237 N.C. App. 218, 224–25 (2014).

Greater and lesser-included offenses (page 283)

The court of appeals has held that a defendant cannot be convicted of second-degree sexual offense (mentally disabled victim) and crime against nature (where lack of consent was based on the fact that the victim was mentally disabled, incapacitated, or physically helpless) based on the same conduct (fellatio). State v. Hunt, 221 N.C. App. 489 (2012), *aff'd on other grounds*, 367 N.C. 700 (2014) (per curiam). The court found that on the facts of the case, crime against nature was a lesser-included offense of second-degree sexual offense and that conviction of both violated double jeopardy. *Id.* However, the North Carolina Supreme Court previously has held that crime against nature is not a lesser-included offense of forcible sexual offense, State v. Etheridge, 319 N.C. 34, 50–51 (1987); State v. Warren, 309 N.C. 224, 230–31 (1983), and that a definitional test—not a factual test—applies when determining whether offenses are lesser-included offenses. State v. Nickerson, 365 N.C. 279, 280 (2011); *Warren*, 309 N.C. at 230–31; *see also* State v. Robinson, 368 N.C. 402, 406–08 (2015) (applying a definitional test to the analysis).

Incest Offenses (page 284)

2012 legislation, S.L. 2012-40, amended G.S. 7B-1111(a) to provide that a court may terminate parental rights upon a finding that a parent "has been convicted of a sexually related offense under Chapter 14 of the General Statutes that resulted in the conception of the juvenile." All of the incest offenses covered in this chapter fall within Chapter 14 of the General Statutes.

Incest (page 284)

Notes (page 284)

Jury instructions (new note)

For a discussion of this issue with respect to rape, see this note on "First-Degree Forcible Rape," above in this supplement.

Multiple convictions and punishments (page 285)

A defendant may be sentenced for both statutory rape and incest arising out of the same transaction. State v. Marlow, 229 N.C. App. 593, 599–601 (2013) (reasoning that the offenses are not the same under the *Blockburger* test).

Indecent Exposure (page 289)

Statute (page 289)

2015 legislation, S.L. 2015-250, secs. 2–2.3, amended the statute, adding new subsections as follows:

> (a2) Unless the conduct is prohibited by another law providing greater punishment, any person who shall willfully expose the private parts of his or her person in the presence of anyone other than a consenting adult on the private premises of another or so near thereto as to be seen from such private premises for the purpose of arousing or gratifying sexual desire is guilty of a Class 2 misdemeanor.
> (a4) Unless the conduct is punishable by another law providing greater punishment, any person at least 18 years of age who shall willfully expose the private parts of his or her person in a private residence of which they are not a resident and in the presence of any other person less than 16 years of age who is a resident of that private residence shall be guilty of a Class 2 misdemeanor.
> (a5) Unless the conduct is prohibited by another law providing greater punishment, any person located in a private place who shall willfully expose the private parts of his or her person with the knowing intent to be seen by a person in a public place shall be guilty of a Class 2 misdemeanor.

Misdemeanor Indecent Exposure (page 289)

Notes (page 290)

Element (4) (page 290)

Add the following at the end of the second paragraph of this note:

> The defendant masturbated in a public place when he did so on his own property in front of his garage; the garage was directly off a public road and was in full view from the street and a neighbor's house. State v. Pugh, ___ N.C. App. ___, 780 S.E.2d 226 (2015).

The 2015 legislation noted above created three new Class 2 misdemeanor versions of this offense, all of which apply when the exposure occurs on or near a private place.

Multiple convictions and punishments (page 290)

Add the following at the end of this note:

> ; see also State v. Hayes, ___ N.C. App. ___, 788 S.E.2d 651, 652–53 (2016) (citing the statute and holding that where the defendant simultaneously exposed himself to a minor and an adult, he could not be convicted of both misdemeanor indecent exposure under G.S. 14-190.9(a) (for the exposure to the adult) and felonious indecent exposure under G.S. 14-190.9(a1) (for the exposure to the minor)).

Related Offenses Not in This Chapter (page 291)

> Indecent exposure in a private place. G.S. 14-190.9(a2), (a4), (a5).

Felony Indecent Exposure (page 291)

Notes (page 291)

Multiple convictions and punishments (page 292)

Insert the following at the beginning of this note:

> See this note to "Misdemeanor Indecent Exposure."

Peeping (page 292)

Statute (page 292)

2012 legislation, S.L. 2012-83, sec. 1, amended G.S. 14-202(m)(2) to read:

> (2) Personnel of the Division of Adult Correction of the Department of Public Safety, the Division of Juvenile Justice of the Department of Public Safety, or of a local confinement facility for security purposes or during investigation of alleged misconduct by a person in the custody of the Division or the local confinement facility.

Peeping into a Room Occupied by Another (page 293)

Related Offenses Not in This Chapter (page 294)

As a result of 2014 legislation, S.L. 2014-100, sec. 34.30(e), the following should be added to this section:

> Unlawful distribution of images obtained through the use of an unmanned aircraft device. G.S. 14-401.25.

Peeping while Possessing a Device Capable of Creating a Photographic Image (page 295)

Related Offenses Not in This Chapter (page 296)

As a result of 2014 legislation, S.L. 2014-100, sec. 34.30(e), the following should be added to this section:

> Unlawful distribution of images obtained through the use of an unmanned aircraft device. G.S. 14-401.25.

Disseminating Images Obtained in Violation of the Peeping Statute (page 299)
Related Offenses Not in This Chapter (page 299)

As a result of 2014 legislation, S.L. 2014-100, sec. 34.30(e), the following should be added to this section:

Unlawful distribution of images obtained through the use of an unmanned aircraft device. G.S. 14-401.25.

12
Kidnapping and Related Offenses

First-Degree Kidnapping (page 303)

Notes (page 304)

Element (1)(a) (page 304)

There was sufficient evidence that the defendant confined a child when, while threatening the child and his mother with a gun, the defendant told the mother to put her son in his room and she complied; whenever her son called out, the mother told him to stay in his bedroom. State v. Bell, 221 N.C. App. 535, 547–48 (2012).

Element (1)(b) (page 305)

For a felonious restraint case where the evidence was sufficient to show that the defendant restrained the victim by defrauding her into entering his car and driving to Florida with him, see State v. Lalinde, 213 N.C. App. 308, 315–16 (2013).

Element (3)(b) (page 305)

The plain language of G.S. 14-39(a) does not permit prosecution of a parent for kidnapping, at least when that parent has custodial rights with respect to the children. State v. Pender, ___ N.C. App. ___, 776 S.E.2d 352, 362 (2015). The court of appeals has not decided "whether a parent without custodial rights may be held criminally liable for kidnapping." Id. at n.2.

Element (4)(g) (page 307)

For another case supporting the definition of "terrorizing" described in this note and the point that the relevant fact is not whether the victim was in fact terrorized but rather whether the defendant intended to terrorize the victim, see State v. Pender, ___ N.C. App. ___, 776 S.E.2d 352, 361 (2015).

The evidence was sufficient for the jury to infer an intent to terrorize where (1) the defendant shot victim Nancy's truck parked outside the house in a manner such that everyone inside the house could hear, cut the telephone line to the house at night, shot through the windows multiple times to break into the house, yelled repeatedly on entering the house that he was going to kill Nancy, corralled the occupants of the house into a single room and demanded to know where Nancy was, stated that he was going to kill her, and pointed his shotgun at them; id.; and (2) the defendant threatened to kill the victim and assaulted her, placed her in headlock, and choked her; the victim was in a state of intense fright and apprehension; and witnesses heard the victim yelling for help and saw the defendant punch and choke her, rendering her unconscious, and then drag her across the street. State v. James, ___ N.C. App. ___, 789 S.E.2d 543, 548–49 (2016).

Element (5)(a) (page 308)

Add the following to the bulleted list in this note:

- the defendant dragged the victim to the middle of a gravel driveway and left her there, unconscious and injured; rather than leaving her in the care of nearby witnesses, the defendant ran away after seeing those persons; and the defendant took one of the victim's cell phones, perhaps not realizing that she had a second phone, State v. James, ___ N.C. App. ___, 789 S.E.2d 543, 549–50 (2016);
- the defendant left the traumatized victim in a clearing in the woods near, but not easily visible from, a service road that extended off an interstate exit ramp; the area was very remote and secluded and almost impossible to see from the highway, State v. Gordon, ___ N.C. App. ___, 789 S.E.2d 659, 664 (2016).

Element (5)(b) (page 308)

For a case where the evidence was sufficient to establish this element, see State v. James, ___ N.C. App. ___, 789 S.E.2d 543, 550 (2016) (the victim suffered cuts, bruises, abrasions and scratches requiring emergency room treatment, and serious emotional trauma requiring therapy for many months continuing through the time of trial).

Multiple convictions and punishments(page 309)

For other cases supporting the proposition in this note that a defendant cannot be convicted of both first-degree kidnapping and a sexual assault if the sexual assault is the factor in Element (5) that elevates kidnapping from second-degree to first-degree, see *State v. Barksdale*, 237 N.C. App. 464, 473–74 (2014), and *State v. Holloman*, 231 N.C. App. 426, 432 (2013).

In the first bulletted list under Multiple convictions and punishments, insert the following in the first bulleted paragraph (cases holding that the evidence supported kidnapping and robbery convictions):

State v. Stokes, 367 N.C. 474, 482 (2014) (attempted kidnapping and robbery convictions were proper; after the robbery was completed, the defendant ordered the victim at gunpoint to the back of the store and then into a vehicle outside the store but the victim refused to comply with both commands), *State v. Curtis*, ___ N.C. ___, ___ S.E.2d ___ (Dec. 21, 2016) (per curiam) (after robbing or attempting to rob two victims in a home invasion, the perpetrators moved the victims upstairs, where they restrained them while assaulting a third resident and searching for items that were later stolen), *Bell*, 221 N.C. App. at 546–47.

In the first bulleted list under Multiple convictions and punishments, insert the following in the second bulleted paragraph (cases holding that the evidence was sufficient to sustain kidnapping and sexual assault convictions):

State v. King, ___ N.C. App. ___, ___ S.E.2d. ___ (Sept. 6, 2016) (the defendant forced the victim into his car after sexually assaulting her), *State v. Knight*, ___ N.C. App. ___, 785 S.E.2d 324, 339, *review allowed*, ___ N.C. ___, 787 S.E.2d 17 (2016) (commission of the rape did not require the defendant to seize and restrain the victim and to carry her from her living room couch to her bedroom), *Bell*, 221 N.C. App. at 547.

In the first bulleted list under Multiple convictions and punishments, insert the following in the fourth bulleted paragraph (cases holding that the evidence was sufficient to sustain kidnapping and assault convictions):

State v. James, ___ N.C. App. ___, 789 S.E.2d 543, 548 (2016) (two separate, distinct restraints sufficient to support convictions for both kidnapping and assault by strangulation).

In the second bulleted list under Multiple convictions and punishments, insert the following in the second bulleted paragraph (cases holding that the evidence was insufficient to sustain kidnapping and sexual assault convictions):

State v. Parker, 237 N.C. App. 546, 549–50 (2014) (restraint supporting the kidnapping charge was inherent in the charged rapes and sexual assault), *State v. Martin*, 222 N.C. App. 213, 219–21 (2012).

In the second bulleted list under Multiple convictions and punishments, insert the following as a new bulleted paragraph:

- The defendant's restraint of the victim was inherent in an assault by strangulation of the victim, and thus the kidnapping conviction was improper. *Martin*, 222 N.C. App. at 221.

Abduction of a Child (page 315)

Related Offenses Not in This Chapter (page 316)

As a result of 2016 legislation, S.L. 2016-115, add the following offense to this section:

Unlawful transfer of custody of minor child. G.S. 14-321.2.

Human Trafficking, Involuntary Servitude, and Sexual Servitude (page 316)

Statute (page 316)

2013 legislation, S.L. 2013-368, sec. 1, amended subsection (a) of G.S. 14-43.11, the human trafficking statute, to read as follows:

(a) A person commits the offense of human trafficking when that person (i) knowingly or in reckless disregard of the consequences of the action recruits, entices, harbors, transports, provides, or obtains by any means another person with the intent that the other person be held in involuntary servitude or sexual servitude or (ii) willfully or in reckless disregard of the consequences of the action causes a minor to be held in involuntary servitude or sexual servitude.

That same law also enacted a new subsection, (c1), to G.S. 14-43.11 as follows:

(c1) Mistake of age is not a defense to prosecution under this section. Consent of a minor is not a defense to prosecution under this section.

S.L. 2013-368, sec. 2, amended subsection (a) of G.S. 14-43.12, the involuntary servitude statute, to read as follows:

(a) A person commits the offense of involuntary servitude when that person knowingly and willfully or in reckless disregard of the consequences of the action holds another in involuntary servitude.

That same law also enacted a new subsection, (c1), to G.S. 14-43.12 as follows:

(c1) Mistake of age is not a defense to prosecution under this section. Consent of a minor is not a defense to prosecution under this section.

S.L. 2013-368, sec. 3, amended subsection (a) of G.S. 14-43.13, the sexual servitude statute, to read as follows:

(a) A person commits the offense of sexual servitude when that person knowingly or in reckless disregard of the consequences of the action subjects or maintains another in sexual servitude.

That same law also increased the punishment for this offense to a Class D felony and enacted a new subsection, (b1), to G.S. 14-43.13 as follows:

(b1) Mistake of age is not a defense to prosecution under this section. Consent of a minor is not a defense to prosecution under this section.

Human Trafficking (page 318)

Elements (page 318)

As a result of 2013 legislation, S.L. 2013-368, sec. 1, the Elements of this offense should read as follows:

A person guilty of this offense

    (1) (a) knowingly or in reckless disregard of the consequences

           (b) recruits, entices, harbors, transports, provides, or obtains

           (c) another person

           (d) with the intent that the other person be held in involuntary or sexual servitude *or*

    (2) (a) willfully or in reckless disregard of the consequences

           (b) causes a minor to be held in involuntary or sexual servitude.

Notes (page 318)

Element (4) (page 318)

Retitle this note to read:

Elements (1)(d) and (2)(b)

Mistake of age and consent (new note)
Neither mistake of age nor consent by a minor is a defense to prosecution. G.S. 14-43.11(c1) (enacted by S.L. 2013-368).

Greater and lesser-included offenses (new note)
"Sale, Surrender, or Purchase of a Minor" (new crime), discussed below in this supplement, is a lesser-included offense of this crime. G.S. 14-43.14(d).

Sex offender registration (new note)
2013 legislation, S.L. 2013-33, provides that human trafficking is a sexually violent offense under G.S. 14-208.6(5) requiring sex offender registration if the offense is committed against

- a minor who is less than 18 years of age or
- any person with the intent that they be held in sexual servitude.

Involuntary Servitude (page 318)

Elements (page 318)

As a result of 2013 legislation, S.L. 2013-368, sec. 2, Element (1) of this offense should read as follows:

A person guilty of this offense

    (1) (a) knowingly and willfully *or*

           (b) in reckless disregard of the consequences

Notes (page 319)

Mistake of age and consent (new note)
Neither mistake of age nor consent by a minor is a defense to prosecution. G.S. 14-43.12(c1) (enacted by S.L. 2013-368).

Sexual Servitude (page 319)

Elements (page 319)

As a result of 2013 legislation, S.L. 2013-368, sec. 3, Element (1) of this offense should read as follows:

A person guilty of this offense

(1) (a) knowingly *or*
    (b) in reckless disregard of the consequences

Punishment (page 319)

As a result of 2013 legislation, S.L. 2013-368, sec. 3, delete the first sentence of this note and replace it with the following:

Class D felony if the victim is an adult.

Notes (page 319)

Mistake of age and consent (new note)

Neither mistake of age nor consent by a minor is a defense to prosecution. G.S. 14-43.13(b1) (enacted by S.L. 2013-368).

Sale, Surrender, or Purchase of a Minor (new crime)

This offense was enacted by 2012 legislation. S.L. 2012-153, sec. 1.

Statute

§ 14-43.14. Unlawful sale, surrender, or purchase of a minor.

(a) A person commits the offense of unlawful sale, surrender, or purchase of a minor when that person, acting with willful or reckless disregard for the life or safety of a minor, participates in any of the following: the acceptance, solicitation, offer, payment, or transfer of any compensation, in money, property, or other thing of value, at any time, by any person in connection with the unlawful acquisition or transfer of the physical custody of a minor, except as ordered by the court. This section does not apply to actions that are ordered by a court, authorized by statute, or otherwise lawful.

(b) A person who violates this section is guilty of a Class F felony and shall pay a minimum fine of five thousand dollars ($5,000). For each subsequent violation, a person is guilty of a Class F felony and shall pay a minimum fine of ten thousand dollars ($10,000).

(c) A minor whose parent, guardian, or custodian has sold or attempted to sell a minor in violation of this Article is an abused juvenile as defined by G.S. 7B-101(1). The court may place the minor in the custody of the Department of Social Services or with such other person as is in the best interest of the minor.

(d) A violation of this section is a lesser included offense of G.S. 14-43.11.

(e) When a person is convicted of a violation of this section, the sentencing court shall consider whether the person is a danger to the community and whether requiring the person to register as a sex offender pursuant to Article 27A of this Chapter would further the purposes of that Article as stated in G.S. 14-208.5. If the sentencing court rules that the person is a danger to the community and that the person shall register, then an order shall be entered requiring the person to register.

Elements

A person guilty of this offense

(1) (a) willfully *or*
    (b) with reckless disregard for the life or safety of a minor
(2) participates in any acceptance, solicitation, offer, payment, or transfer of any compensation, in money, property, or other thing of value by any person

(3) in connection with the unlawful acquisition or transfer of the physical custody of a minor.

Punishment

Class F felony. G.S. 14-43.14(b). For a first offense, the defendant must pay a minimum fine of $5,000; for subsequent violations, the defendant must pay a minimum fine of $10,000. *Id.*

Notes

Element (1)(a). See Willfully" in Chapter 1 (States of Mind) of the main volume.

Exceptions. The statute does not apply to actions that are ordered by a court, are authorized by statute, or are otherwise lawful. G.S. 14-43.14(a). A parent may not be prosecuted for this offense when the parent abandons an infant less than seven days of age by voluntarily delivering the infant in compliance with the provisions of G.S. 7B-500(b) or (d) and does not express an intention to return for the infant. G.S. 14-322.3 (as amended by S.L. 2012-153, sec. 4).

Minor declared abused. A minor whose parent, guardian, or custodian has sold or attempted to sell the minor in violation of the statute is an abused juvenile and may be placed in appropriate custody. G.S. 14-43.14(c).

Greater and lesser-included offenses. This offense is a lesser-included offense of human trafficking. G.S. 14-43.14(d).

Sex offender registration. The sentencing judge must require registration if he or she finds that a person convicted of this crime is a danger to the community and that requiring the person to register as a sex offender would further the purpose of the sex offender statute. G.S. 14-43.14(e).

Related Offenses Not in This Chapter

See "Child Abuse" offenses and "Contributing to a Juvenile's Being Delinquent, Undisciplined, Abused, or Neglected" in Chapter 9 (Abuse and Neglect) of the main volume.

See "Failure to Report the Disappearance of a Child" (new crime) in Chapter 9 of this supplement.

Unlawful payments related to adoption. G.S. 48-10-102.

13

Larceny, Possession of Stolen Goods, Embezzlement, and Related Offenses

Larceny (page 323)

Misdemeanor Larceny (page 323)

Statute (page 323)

2012 legislation, S.L. 2012-154, enacted G.S. 14-72(b)(6), proscribing the crime of "Habitual Misdemeanor Larceny" (new crime), discussed below in this supplement.

> (6) Committed after the defendant has been convicted in this State or in another jurisdiction for any offense of larceny under this section, or any offense deemed or punishable as larceny under this section, or of any substantially similar offense in any other jurisdiction, regardless of whether the prior convictions were misdemeanors, felonies, or a combination thereof, at least four times. A conviction shall not be included in the four prior convictions required under this subdivision unless the defendant was represented by counsel or waived counsel at first appearance or otherwise prior to trial or plea. If a person is convicted of more than one offense of misdemeanor larceny in a single session of district court, or in a single week of superior court or of a court in another jurisdiction, only one of the convictions may be used as a prior conviction under this subdivision; except that convictions based upon offenses which occurred in separate counties shall each count as a separate prior conviction under this subdivision.

Elements (page 324)

The first line of this section should read:

A person guilty of this offense

Notes (page 324)

Element (1) (page 324)

A taking occurred in a robbery case when (1) the defendant grabbed the victim's cell phone and threw it away; the brevity of the taking is irrelevant, State v. Mason, 222 N.C. App. 223, 228 (2012), and (2) the defendant forced the victim at gunpoint to take the defendant as a passenger in the victim's car; the fact that the victim was physically present in the car did not negate the inference that the defendant had sole control of the car. State v. Watkins, 218 N.C. App. 94, 103–04 (2012).

Element (3) (page 325)

No larceny occurred where the defendant withdrew money from his account after learning that it had been erroneously deposited in his name. State v. Jones, ___ N.C. App. ___, 781 S.E.2d 333, 337, *review allowed*, ___ N.C. ___, 784 S.E.2d 466 (2016) (although a larceny may occur when possession is obtained by trick or artifice, the defendant engaged in no such activity; because the money was erroneously deposited into the defendant's account it was in his possession when taken).

Greater and lesser-included offenses (page 326)

Include the following after the citation to *State v. Watson* in the first paragraph of this note:

State v. Hole, ___ N.C. App. ___, 770 S.E.2d 760, 763 (2015) (same but concluding that no plain error occurred when the trial court failed to instruct on the lesser-included offense).

Related Offenses Not in This Chapter (page 329)

Add the following offense to this section:

Taking, etc., of certain wild plants from land of another. G.S. 14-129.

As a result of 2014 legislation, S.L. 2014-120, sec. 52(a), the following new offense should be added to this section:

Felony taking of Venus flytrap. G.S. 14-129.3.

As a result of 2012 legislation, S.L. 2012-127, the following offense should be added to this section:

Theft of waste kitchen grease. G.S. 14-79.2.

Habitual Misdemeanor Larceny (new crime)

Statute

2012 legislation, S.L. 2012-154, enacted G.S. 14-72(b)(6), reproduced above under "Misdemeanor Larceny."

Elements

A person guilty of this offense

(1) commits a larceny *and*
(2) has four prior larceny convictions.

Punishment

Class H felony. G.S. 14-72(a).

Notes

Element (1). See "Misdemeanor Larceny" in the main volume.

Element (2). The prior offense can be

- a North Carolina conviction under G.S. 14-72 or
- a substantially similar offense in any other jurisdiction.

G.S. 14-72(b)(6). The priors can be misdemeanors, felonies, or a combination of the two. *Id.* A prior conviction cannot be counted unless the defendant was represented by or waived counsel. *Id.* If a person is convicted of more than one offense of misdemeanor larceny in a single session of district court or in a single week of superior court or a court in another jurisdiction, only one of the convictions may be used as a prior conviction, except that convictions based on offenses that occurred in separate counties each count as a separate prior conviction. *Id.*

Related Offenses Not in This Chapter

See the offenses listed under "Misdemeanor Larceny" in the main volume.

Felony Larceny (page 330)

Notes (page 330)

Element (8)(a) (page 331)

For another case holding that fair market value is the relevant measure, see *State v. Redman*, 224 N.C. App. 363, 366 (2012). A witness need not be an expert to give an opinion as to value; one who has knowledge of value gained from experience, information, and observation may give his or her opinion of the value of the stolen item. *Id.* Where a vehicle owner testified to a vehicle's value, there was sufficient evidence of this element. *Id.* at 367. For a case where the State presented sufficient evidence that the fair market value of the stolen boat batteries was more than $1,000, see *State v. Fish*, 229 N.C. App. 584, 587–89 (2013).

Element (8)(b) (page 331)

A larceny was from the person when the defendant (1) stole the victim's purse from the child's seat of her grocery cart; at the time, the victim was looking at a store product and was within hand's reach of her cart and realized that the larceny was occurring as it happened, State v. Sheppard, 228 N.C. App. 266, 269–70 (2013), and (2) stole the victim's laptop from an apartment; the victim had taken a momentary break from doing her homework on the laptop and was about three feet away from it. State v. Hull, 236 N.C. App. 415, 418–19 (2014).

Multiple convictions and punishments (page 332)

A defendant may not be sentenced for both larceny from the person and larceny of goods worth more than $1,000 based on a single larceny. *Sheppard*, 228 N.C. App. at 270–71 (the crimes are not separate offenses but, rather, alternative ways to establish a felony larceny; while it is proper to indict on alternative theories of felony larceny and allow the jury to determine guilt as to each theory, where there is only one larceny, judgment may only be entered for one larceny).

Larceny of a Chose in Action (page 333)

Notes (page 333)

Element (2) (page 333)

A blank check is not a chose in action. State v. Grier, 224 N.C. App. 150, 155 (2012).

Relation to other offenses (new note)

Forgery and larceny of a chose in action are not mutually exclusive offenses. *Grier*, 224 N.C. App. at 153.

Unauthorized Use of a Motor-Propelled Conveyance (page 334)

Notes (page 334)

Element (5) generally (new note)

For a case where the evidence was insufficient on the issue of lack of consent, see *In re A.N.C.*, 225 N.C. App. 315, 325 (2013).

Greater and lesser-included offenses (page 335)

Delete the first paragraph of this note and replace it with the following:

North Carolina courts have held that unauthorized use of a motor-propelled conveyance is not a lesser-included offense of possession of stolen goods, *see* State v. Nickerson, 365 N.C. 279,

281–83 (2011) (applying the definitional test and concluding that unauthorized use of a motor-propelled conveyance contains at least one element not present in possession of stolen goods), nor is it a lesser-included offense of possession of a stolen vehicle. State v. Robinson, 368 N.C. 402, 406–08 (2015) (applying a definitional analysis).

Include the following at the beginning of the second paragraph of this note:

Notwithstanding *Nickerson* and *Robinson*, the court of appeals has held that

Include the following after the citation to *State v. Watson* in the second paragraph of this note:

State v. Hole, ___ N.C. App. ___, 770 S.E.2d 760, 763 (2015) (same but concluding that no plain error occurred when the trial court failed to instruct on the lesser-included offense).

Possession of Stolen Goods (page 335)

Misdemeanor Possession of Stolen Goods (page 335)

Notes (page 336)

Element (1) (page 336)

The evidence was insufficient to establish that the defendant constructively possessed jewelry when it showed only that the defendant was a high-ranking member of a gang to which the others involved in a robbery and subsequent transfer of stolen goods belonged; the defendant accompanied a person in possession of stolen property to an enterprise at which a legitimate transaction occurred; the defendant made ambiguous references to "more scrap gold" and "rings" unaccompanied by any indication that these items were stolen. State v. Privette, 218 N.C. App. 459, 472–73 (2012).

Element (3) (page 336)

For a case where the evidence was sufficient to establish that the defendant knew or had reasonable grounds to believe that the items were stolen, see *State v. Jester*, ___ N.C. App. ___, 790 S.E.2d 368, 378 (2016) (although valued at more than $1,000, the defendant sold the property for $114, told a detective that he obtained the property from a "white man" but could not give the man's name, did not state that he had purchased the items, and did not produce a receipt for them).

Greater and lesser-included offenses (page 337)

Delete the citation to *Oliver* in this note.

Related Offenses Not in This Chapter (page 338)

The following offense, enacted by 2012 legislation, S.L. 2012-46, should be added to this section:

Secondary metals recycler purchase violations. G.S. 66-419; -424.

Vehicle and Vehicle Part Offenses (page 345)

The following offense, enacted by 2012 legislation, S.L. 2012-46, should be added as a related offense to the vehicle and vehicle part offenses covered here:

> Secondary metals recycler purchase of catalytic converters in certain circumstances. G.S. 66-419.

Possession of a Stolen Vehicle (page 345)

Notes (page 345)

Greater and lesser-included offenses (new note)

Unauthorized use is not a lesser-included offense of possession of a stolen vehicle. State v. Robinson, 368 N.C. 402, 406–08 (2015).

Altering, Destroying, etc. any Stolen Motor Vehicle or Part (page 347)

Statute (page 347)

2013 legislation, S.L. 2013-323, amended subsection (a) of G.S. 14-72.7 to read as follows:

> (a) A person is guilty of a Class G felony if that person engages in any of the following activities, without regard to the value of the property in question:
> (1) Altering, destroying, disassembling, dismantling, reassembling, or storing any motor vehicle or motor vehicle part the person knows or has reasonable grounds to believe has been illegally obtained by theft, fraud, or other illegal means.
> (2) Permitting a place to be used for any activity prohibited by this section, where the person either owns or has legal possession of the place, and knows or has reasonable grounds to believe that the place is being used for any activity prohibited by this section.
> (3) Purchasing, disposing of, selling, transferring, receiving, or possessing a motor vehicle or motor vehicle part either knowing or having reasonable grounds to believe that the vehicle identification number of the motor vehicle, or vehicle part identification number of the vehicle part, has been altered, counterfeited, defaced, destroyed, disguised, falsified, forged, obliterated, or removed.
> (4) Purchasing, disposing of, selling, transferring, receiving, or possessing a motor vehicle or motor vehicle part to or from a person engaged in any activity prohibited by this section, knowing or having reasonable grounds to believe that the person is engaging in that activity.

Elements (page 348)

As a result of 2013 legislation, S.L. 2013-323, the Elements for this offense should read as follows:

> A person guilty of this offense
> (1) (a) alters,
>   (b) destroys,
>   (c) disassembles,
>   (d) dismantles,
>   (e) reassembles, *or*
>   (f) stores

(2) any
   (a) motor vehicle *or*
   (b) motor vehicle part
(3) knowing or having reasonable grounds to believe that it was illegally obtained.

Punishment (page 348)

As a result of 2013 legislation, S.L. 2013-323, delete the text in this section and replace it with the following:

Class G felony. G.S. 14-72.7(a).

Notes (page 348)

Element (1) (page 348)

As a result of 2013 legislation, S.L. 2013-323, delete this note.

Element (3) (page 348)

This note should be titled Element (2).

Element (4) (page 348)

As a result of 2013 legislation, S.L. 2013-323, delete this note.

Related Offenses Not in This Chapter (page 349)

The following offenses should be added to this section:

Purchase of vehicles for purposes of scrap or parts only. G.S. 20-62.1.
Secondary metals recycler purchase of catalytic converters in certain circumstances.
   G.S. 66-419.

Permitting a Place to Be Used to Violate the Chop Shop Laws (page 349)

Elements (page 349)

As a result of 2013 legislation, S.L. 2013-323, the Elements for this offense should read as follows:

A person guilty of this offense
   (1) permits
   (2) a place that the person owns or has legal possession of
   (3) to be used for any activity prohibited by G.S. 14-72.7 *and*
   (4) knows or has reasonable grounds to believe that the place is being used for the prohibited activity.

Punishment (page 349)

As a result of 2013 legislation, S.L. 2013-323, delete the text in this section and replace it with the following:

Class G felony. G.S. 14-72.7(a).

Notes (page 349)

Element (1) (page 349)

As a result of 2013 legislation, S.L. 2013-323, delete this note.

Related Offenses Not in This Chapter (page 349)

The following offenses should be added to this section:

Purchase of vehicles for purposes of scrap or parts only. G.S. 20-62.1.
Secondary metals recycler purchase of catalytic converters in certain circumstances.
   G.S. 66-419.

Purchasing, Selling, etc. of a Motor Vehicle or Part with an Altered Identification Number (page 349)

Elements (page 349)

As a result of 2013 legislation, S.L. 2013-323, the Elements for this offense should read as follows:

A person guilty of this offense

(1) (a) purchases,
    (b) disposes of,
    (c) sells,
    (d) transfers,
    (e) receives, *or*
    (f) possesses

(2) (a) a motor vehicle *or*
    (b) a motor vehicle part

(3) knowing or having reasonable grounds to believe that the vehicle identification number has been altered, counterfeited, defaced, destroyed, disguised, falsified, forged, obliterated, or removed.

Punishment (page 350)

As a result of 2013 legislation, S.L. 2013-323, delete the text in this section and replace it with the following:

Class G felony. G.S. 14-72.7(a).

Notes (page 350)

As a result of 2013 legislation, S.L. 2013-323, causing a renumbering and revision of the Elements of this offense, delete the text in this section and replace it with the following:

Element (1)(c). For an explanation of the term "sells" in the context of drug offenses, see the note on Element (2)(a) to "Sale or Delivery of a Controlled Substance" in Chapter 27 (Drug Offenses) of the main volume.

Element (1)(e). For a discussion of the term "receives," see the note on Element (1) to "Misdemeanor Receiving of Stolen Goods" in the main volume.

Element (1)(f). For a discussion of the term "possesses," see the note on Element (1) to "Misdemeanor Possession of Stolen Goods" in the main volume.

Element (2). For a definition of the term "motor vehicle" as used in the context of motor vehicle offenses, see the note on Element (2) to "Driving While License Revoked" in Chapter 28 (Motor Vehicle Offenses) of the main volume.

Element (3). For definitions of the terms "vehicle identification number" and "vehicle part identification number," see G.S. 14-72.7(f)(2) and (3).

Exceptions. See this note to "Altering, Destroying, etc. Any Stolen Motor Vehicle or Part" in the main volume.

Seizure and forfeiture. See this note to "Altering, Destroying, etc. Any Stolen Motor Vehicle or Part" in the main volume.

Related Offenses Not in This Chapter (page 350)

The following offenses should be added to this section:

Purchase of vehicles for purposes of scrap or parts only. G.S. 20-62.1.
Secondary metals recycler purchase of catalytic converters in certain circumstances.
    G.S. 66-419.

Purchasing, Disposing of, etc. a Motor Vehicle or Part in Connection with a Chop Shop Violation (page 350)

Elements (page 350)

As a result of 2013 legislation, S.L. 2013-323, the Elements for this offense should read as follows:

A person guilty of this offense

    (1) (a) purchases,
          (b) disposes of,
          (c) sells,
          (d) transfers,
          (e) receives, *or*
          (f) possesses
    (2) (a) a motor vehicle *or*
          (b) motor vehicle part
    (3) to or from a person
    (4) engaged in any activity prohibited by G.S. 14-72.7
    (5) knowing or having reasonable grounds to believe that the person is engaging in that activity.

Punishment (page 351)

As a result of 2013 legislation, S.L. 2013-323, delete the text in this section and replace it with the following:

Class G felony. G.S. 14-72.7(a).

Notes (page 351)

As a result of 2013 legislation, S.L. 2013-323, causing a renumbering and revision of the Elements of this offense, delete the text in this section and replace it with the following:

Element (1)(c). For an explanation of the term "sells" in the context of drug offenses, see the note on Element (2)(a) to "Sale or Delivery of a Controlled Substance" in Chapter 27 (Drug Offenses) of the main volume.

Element (1)(e). For a discussion of the term "receives," see the note on Element (1) to "Misdemeanor Receiving of Stolen Goods" in the main volume.

Element (1)(f). For a discussion of the term "possesses," see the note on Element (1) to "Misdemeanor Possession of Stolen Goods" in the main volume.

Element (2). For a definition of the term "motor vehicle" as used in the context of motor vehicle offenses, see the note on Element (2) to "Driving While License Revoked" in Chapter 28 (Motor Vehicle Offenses) of the main volume.

Exceptions. See this note to "Altering, Destroying, etc. Any Stolen Motor Vehicle or Part" in the main volume.

Seizure and forfeiture. See this note to "Altering, Destroying, etc. Any Stolen Motor Vehicle or Part" in the main volume.

Related Offenses Not in This Chapter (page 351)

The following offenses should be added to this section:

Purchase of vehicles for purposes of scrap or parts only. G.S. 20-62.1.
Secondary metals recycler purchase of catalytic converters in certain circumstances.
    G.S. 66-419.

Larceny of a Motor Vehicle Part (page 351)

Related Offenses Not in This Chapter (page 352)

The following offense, enacted by 2012 legislation, S.L. 2012-46, should be added to this section:

> Secondary metals recycler purchase of catalytic converters in certain circumstances. G.S. 66-419.

Financial Transaction Card Theft (page 359)

Taking or Withholding a Card (page 360)

Notes (page 360)

Element (5) (page 360)

For a case where the evidence was sufficient to establish this element, see *State v. Sellers*, ___ N.C. App. ___, 789 S.E.2d 459, 464 (2016) (someone other than the victim used the card at two stores on the day it was stolen; surveillance video showed the defendant at one of the stores when the card was swiped, and an employee testified that the defendant tried to use a card issued in another person's name).

Embezzlement Offenses (page 364)

Embezzlement by Employee (page 364)

Related Offenses Not in This Chapter (page 366)

Delete the text of this section and replace it with the following:

> See the offenses listed under "Embezzlement," below, and under "Embezzlement" in the main volume.

Embezzlement (page 366)

Notes (page 367)

Element (1) (page 367)

The State can establish the requisite intent by direct or circumstantial evidence. State v. Parker, 233 N.C. App. 577, 580 (2014) (evidence was sufficient where the defendant used school system funds for improper purchases).

Element (2) (page 367)

For another case supporting the proposition in this note that the person entrusted with the property need not convert it to his or her own use, see *Parker*, 233 N.C. App. at 580.

Element (4) (page 367)

For a case holding that there was sufficient evidence that the defendant was an agent of the company and not an independent contractor, see *State v. Smalley*, 220 N.C. App. 142, 144–45 (2012) (the defendant was alleged to have improperly written company checks to herself).

There was sufficient evidence that the defendant had constructive possession of the corporation's money when she was given complete access to the corporation's accounts and could write checks on behalf of the corporation and delegate where the corporation's money went. *Id.*

There was sufficient evidence of embezzlement where the defendant, a bookkeeper controller for the victim company, was instructed to close the company's credit cards but failed to do so, instead incurring personal charges on the cards and paying the card bills from company funds. State v. Renkosiak, 226 N.C. App. 377, 378–79 (2013).

Related Offenses Not in This Chapter (page 369)

As a result of 2012 legislation, S.L. 2012-56, the following offense should be added to this section:

Embezzlement from a bank. G.S. 53C-8-11.

14
Robbery, Extortion, and Blackmail

Common Law Robbery (page 379)

Notes (page 379)

Element (3) (page 380)

In a multi-count robbery case, there was sufficient evidence that victim Adrienne relinquished her property because of violence or intimidation; although Adrienne herself did not testify, evidence showed that she was a resident of premises where the robbery occurred, another victim heard her screaming during the intrusion, her face was injured, two witnesses testified that she had been beaten, and her personal belongings were taken. State v. Jones, ___ N.C. App. ___, 772 S.E.2d 470, 477 (2015).

Multiple convictions and punishments (page 381)

Where the defendant attempted to rob two victims inside a residence, two charges were proper; the fact that only one residence was involved was irrelevant where the defendant demanded that each victim turn over his personal property. State v. Jastrow, 237 N.C. App. 325, 329–30 (2014).

Armed Robbery (page 381)

Notes (page 382)

Element (3) (page 382)

For a case where the evidence was sufficient to show that either the defendant or his accomplice used a firearm to induce the victim to part with her purse, see *State v. James*, 226 N.C. App. 120, 125 (2013).

For a case where there was sufficient evidence that a lawn chair was a dangerous weapon, see *State v. Mills*, 221 N.C. App. 409, 413 (2012).

An unopened knife wielded by the defendant can be a dangerous weapon. State v. Whisenant, ___ N.C. App. ___, 791 S.E.2d 122, 125 (2016) (in a case where the defendant yelled, "I will kill you," while brandishing the knife, the court held: "the unopened knife was a dangerous weapon when Defendant threatened to use it to cause great bodily harm or death").

Element (4) (page 383)

The evidence was sufficient to establish that an unopened knife endangered or threatened the victim's life where, while the victim attempted to disarm the defendant, the defendant threatened, "I will kill you," and the victim felt afraid. State v. Whisenant, ___ N.C. App. ___, 791 S.E.2d 122, 125 (2016).

Timing of elements (page 384)

There was sufficient evidence that a theft and use of force were part of a continuous transaction where the defendant went to the victim's home with the intent to rob him, shot and killed the victim, and left with money and drugs. State v. Rogers, 227 N.C. App. 617, 622–23 (2013).

Jury instructions (new note)

Where the evidence showed that the defendant displayed and threatened to use a weapon by pointing it at the victim, the trial court was not required to give the mere possession instruction in footnote 6 to element seven of N.C.P.I.—Crim. 217.20. State v. Bell, 227 N.C. App. 339, 345 (2013).

Attempt (page 384)

For cases where the evidence was sufficient to prove an attempted armed robbery, see *State v. Calderon*, ___ N.C. App. ___, 774 S.E.2d 398, 408 (2015) (the defendant did not consummate the offense because the victim was passed out or asleep and therefore could not be induced to give up his money due to the threat that the accomplices' weapons presented and because no one saw the defendant take anything from the victim's pockets), and *State v. Evans*, 228 N.C. App. 454, 461–62 (2013) (the defendant planned a robbery with an accomplice, waited in a vehicle until the accomplice went into the residence and sent a message with the location of each individual inside, entered the apartment and went directly to the victim's bedroom, and proceeded to wield his firearm in a threatening manner toward the victim; the evidence was sufficient even though the defendant did not make a specific demand for money).

Even though assault with a deadly weapon is a lesser-included offense of armed robbery, a defendant may be convicted for that assault and armed robbery when each conviction arises from discrete conduct. State v. Ortiz, 238 N.C. App. 508, 515 (2014).

Greater and lesser-included offenses (page 385)

Extortion is not a lesser-included offense of armed robbery. State v. Wright, ___ N.C. App. ___, 770 S.E.2d 757, 759 (2015) (applying a definitional rather than a factual test).

"Presumption" of the use of a dangerous weapon (page 385)

The trial court did not err by failing to instruct the jury on common law robbery and by denying the defendant's motion to dismiss armed robbery charges where there was no evidence that the gun was inoperable or unloaded and thus no evidence to rebut the presumption that the firearm was functioning properly. State v. Williamson, 220 N.C. App. 512, 515–16 (2012).

Although a defendant's testimony that a gun was unloaded extinguished the presumption that a dangerous weapon was used, a permissive inference remained and supported denial of a motion to dismiss. *Bell*, 227 N.C. App. at 342–44 (in addition to the victim's testimony that the defendant entered her business, pointed a gun at her, and demanded money, evidence showed that upon leaving, the defendant saw the police and ran into the woods, where he left his hoodie and gun and jumped off of an embankment).

Although the fact that a BB pistol and a pellet gun were found outside the residence where the robbery occurred extinguished the presumption that a dangerous weapon was used, in light of the victim's testimony that the defendant used handguns, a permissive inference remained and supported denial of a motion to dismiss. State v. Holt, ___ N.C. App. ___, 773 S.E.2d 542, 547 (2015) (noting that no evidence conclusively connected BB pistol or pellet gun to the robbery).

Extortion (page 386)

Notes (page 386)

Element (2) (page 386)

The statute requires proof that the defendant intentionally utilized unjust or unlawful means in attempting to obtain the property or other acquittance, advantage, or immunity; it does not require proof that the defendant sought to achieve an end to which he or she had no entitlement. State v. Privette, 218 N.C. App. 459, 477 (2012).

Jury instructions (new note)

The trial judge properly instructed the jury on extortion using the pattern jury instruction. *Id.*

Greater and lesser-included offenses (new note)

Extortion is not a lesser-included offense of armed robbery. State v. Wright, ___ N.C. App. ___, 770 S.E.2d 757, 759 (2015) (applying a definitional rather than a factual test).

Defenses (new note)

North Carolina does not recognize a "claim of right" defense to extortion. *Id.*; *Privette*, 218 N.C. App. at 477.

15
Burglary, Breaking or Entering, and Related Offenses

First-Degree Burglary (page 391)

Notes (page 392)

Element (2) (page 393)

An entering did not occur when (1) the defendant used a shotgun to break a window and the end of the shotgun entered the premises, State v. Watkins, 218 N.C. App. 94, 100–01 (2012), or (2) the defendants used landscaping bricks and a fire pit bowl to break a home's window but there was no evidence that they entered the premises. State v. Lucas, 234 N.C. App. 247, 251–54 (2014) (following *Watkins* and distinguishing *State v. Salters*, 137 N.C. App. 553 (2000) (evidence of a splintered door frame and broken lock along with evidence that a suitcase missing from inside was seen in the defendant's possession was sufficient to establish an entering)).

Element (7) (page 394)

There was sufficient evidence that a burglary occurred at nighttime when the defendant left his girlfriend's apartment after 10 p.m. and did not return until 6 a.m. the next day; the burglary occurred during that time period; after taking judicial notice of the time of civil twilight (5:47 a.m.) and the driving distance between the victim's residence and the apartment, the court concluded that it would have been impossible for the defendant to commit the crime after 5:47 a.m. and be back at the apartment by 6 a.m. State v. Brown, 221 N.C. App. 383, 387–88 (2012).

Element (8) (page 395)

For another case supporting the statement in the first paragraph of this note that the defendant must intend to commit the required crime inside the dwelling, see *State v. Allah*, 231 N.C. App. 88, 93–95 (2013) (insufficient evidence that the defendant intended to commit a felonious restraint inside the building; that offense requires that the defendant transport the victim by motor vehicle or other conveyance, and his car was left running outside).

Evidence that items were missing after a breaking or entering can be sufficient to prove the defendant's intent to commit a larceny inside the premises. State v. Northington, 230 N.C. App. 575, 579 (2013).

The evidence was sufficient to establish the requisite intent when (1) the defendants were walking from house to house in the neighborhood to determine whether the houses were occupied and were trying to open doors of parked cars, State v. Lucas, 234 N.C. App. 247, 254–55 (2014), and (2) the defendant unlawfully broke and entered a church late at night; he did not have permission to be there and could not remember what he did there; and the defendant's wallet was found near where missing items had been stored. *State v. Campbell*, 368 N.C. 83 (2015).

The sixth paragraph of this note states that the fact that an intruder broke and entered a dwelling at nighttime is sufficient, in the absence of contrary evidence, to support a finding that the intruder intended to steal. This inference is sometimes called the *McBryde* inference, after the seminal case *State v. McBryde*, 97 N.C. 393 (1887). For another case applying the *McBryde* inference, see *State v. Mims*, ___ N.C. App. ___, 774 S.E.2d 349, 353 (2015). Additionally, in *Mims* the court applied the *McBryde* inference to an attempted breaking or entering that occurred during daylight hours.

Doctrine of recent possession (page 396)

When the victim's laptop and other items were found in the defendant's possession hours after the burglary, the doctrine of recent possession provided sufficient evidence that the defendant was the perpetrator. *Brown*, 221 N.C. App. at 388.

Felony Breaking or Entering of a Building (page 398)

Statute (page 398)

2013 legislation, S.L. 2013-95, added subsection (a1) to G.S. 14-54 as follows:

> (a1) Any person who breaks or enters any building with intent to terrorize or injure an occupant of the building is guilty of a Class H felony.

Elements (page 398)

As a result of the 2013 legislation, S.L. 2013-95, Element (5) should be revised as follows:

(5) with the intent to
   (a) commit any felony or larceny therein *or*
   (b) terrorize or injure an occupant of the building.

Notes (page 399)

Element (5) (page 400)

The 2013 statute does not define the term "terrorize." That term is, however, used in the context of kidnapping, where it has been defined by case law. See the note on Element (4)(g) to "First-Degree Kidnapping" in Chapter 12 (Kidnapping and Related Offenses) of the main volume.

Greater and lesser-included offenses (page 400)

For another case supporting the statement in this note that first-degree trespass is a lesser-included offense of this one, see *State v. Lucas*, 234 N.C. App. 247, 256 (2014).

Breaking or Entering a Vehicle (page 402)

Statute (page 402)

2015 legislation, S.L. 2015-286, sec. 3.3(a), amended the statute, putting the existing text in subsection (a) and creating a new subsection (b) as follows:

> (b) It shall not be a violation of this section for any person to break or enter any railroad car, motor vehicle, trailer, aircraft, boat, or other watercraft of any kind to provide assistance to a person inside the railroad car, motor vehicle, trailer, aircraft, boat, or watercraft of any kind if one or more of the following circumstances exist:
>
> (1) The person acts in good faith to access the person inside the railroad car, motor vehicle, trailer, aircraft, boat, or watercraft of any kind in order to provide first aid or emergency health care treatment or because the person inside is, or is in imminent danger of becoming unconscious, ill, or injured.
>
> (2) It is reasonably apparent that the circumstances require prompt decisions and actions in medical, other health care, or other assistance for the person inside the railroad car, motor vehicle, trailer, aircraft, boat, or watercraft of any kind.
>
> (3) The necessity of immediate health care treatment or removal of the person from the railroad car, motor vehicle, trailer, aircraft, boat, or other watercraft of any kind is so reasonably apparent that any delay in the rendering of treatment or removal would seriously worsen the physical condition or endanger the life of the person.

Notes (page 403)

Element (5) (page 403)

For a case where the State failed to present evidence that the boats in question contained items of value, see *State v. Fish*, 229 N.C. App. 584, 590 (2013) (rejecting the State's argument that boat batteries constituted items of value, reasoning that they were part of the boats themselves).

Element (6) (page 403)

For another case supporting the statement in this note that the intended felony or larceny may be a theft of the motor vehicle that is the subject of the breaking or entering, see *State v. Mitchell*, 234 N.C. App. 423, 428 (2014) (citing *Clark*).

Jury instructions (new note)

When an indictment alleges that the defendant broke *and* entered a vehicle, the trial court does not err by instructing the jury that the defendant can be found guilty if he or she broke *or* entered the vehicle. *Id.* at 428–29 (citing similar case law regarding breaking or entering a building).

Good Samaritan exception (new note)

The offense does not occur if a person breaks or enters to assist someone inside if the requirements of G.S. 14-56(b) are satisfied.

16

Fraud, Forgery, False Pretenses, and Related Offenses

Worthless Checks (page 411)

Worthless Checks—Making or Uttering (page 411)

Statute (page 411)

2013 legislation, S.L. 2013-244, sec. 4, amended the title of G.S. 14-107 and subsections (a) and (b) to read as follows:

> **§ 14-107. Worthless checks; multiple presentation of checks.**
>
> (a) It is unlawful for any person, firm or corporation, to draw, make, utter or issue and deliver to another, any check or draft on any bank or depository, for the payment of money or its equivalent, knowing at the time of the making, drawing, uttering, issuing and delivering the check or draft, that the maker or drawer of it:
>
> > (1)   Has not sufficient funds on deposit in or credit with the bank or depository with which to pay the check or draft upon presentation, or
> >
> > (2)   Has previously presented the check or draft for the payment of money or its equivalent.
>
> (b) It is unlawful for any person, firm or corporation to solicit or to aid and abet any other person, firm or corporation to draw, make, utter or issue and deliver to any person, firm or corporation, any check or draft on any bank or depository for the payment of money or its equivalent, being informed, knowing or having reasonable grounds for believing at the time of the soliciting or the aiding and abetting that the maker or the drawer of the check or draft:
>
> > (1)   Has not sufficient funds on deposit in, or credit with, the bank or depository with which to pay the check or draft upon presentation, or
> >
> > (2)   Has previously presented the check or draft for the payment of money or its equivalent.

Another piece of 2013 legislation, S.L. 2013-360, sec. 18B.14(b), amended subsection (d)(1) so that the first sentence now provides:

> > (1)   Except as provided in subdivision (3) or (4) of this subsection, the person is guilty of a Class 3 misdemeanor.

Elements (page 412)

As a result of 2013 legislation, S.L. 2013-244, sec. 4, Element (4) should be revised as follows:

> (4) knowing that
> > (a) there are insufficient funds or credit available for the payment *or*
> >
> > (b) the maker or drawer has previously presented the check or draft for the payment.

Punishment (page 412)

As a result of 2013 legislation, S.L. 2013-360, sec 18B.14(b), the first three words of this section should read:

Class 3 misdemeanor

Notes (page 412)

Elements (3) and (4) (page 413)

In the note on Element (3), delete the second sentence of the second paragraph. Add the following text at the end of the first paragraph of the note on Element (4):

A postdated check implies no more than that on its date the drawer will have or expects to have funds or credit in the bank to insure its payment at that time. State v. Crawford, 198 N.C. 522 (1930); State v. Byrd, 204 N.C. 162 (1933).

Obtaining Property for a Worthless Check (page 416)

Statute (page 416)

2013 legislation, S.L. 2013-360, sec. 18B.14(a), amended the statute to lower the punishment for this offense to a Class 3 misdemeanor.

Punishment (page 416)

As a result of 2013 legislation, S.L. 2013-360, sec. 18B.14(a), delete the text of this section and replace it with the following:

Class 3 misdemeanor. G.S. 14-106.

Obtaining Property by False Pretenses (page 417)

Notes (page 417)

Element (1) (page 417)

The evidence was sufficient to establish this element where the defendant (1) uttered a forged check, State v. Conley, 220 N.C. App. 50, 60–61 (2012); (2) approached two elderly women, falsely told them that their roofs needed repair, took payment for the work and then performed shoddy work or failed to complete the job, State v. Barker, ___ N.C. App. ___, 770 S.E.2d 142, 148 (2015); (3) submitted false invoices for moving expenses from companies that did not exist in North Carolina, State v. Holanek, ___ N.C. App. ___, 776 S.E.2d 225, 234 (2015).

Element (2) (page 418)

For a case where the evidence showed that the defendant falsely represented to a pawn shop that items sold to the shop were not stolen, see *State v. Greenlee*, 227 N.C. App. 133, 137–38 (2013).

The State failed to offer sufficient evidence to establish that the defendant made a false representation with the intent to deceive when he told the victims that he intended to invest money that they loaned him in legitimate institutions and would repay it with interest at a specified time; the evidence showed only that the defendant, "after seriously overestimating his investing skills, made a promise that he was unable to keep." State v. Braswell, 225 N.C. App. 734, 742 (2013).

Element (3) (page 418)

The State failed to offer sufficient evidence to establish that the defendant made a false representation with the intent to deceive when he told the victims that he intended to invest the money they loaned him in legitimate institutions and would repay it with interest at a specified time; the evidence showed only that the defendant, "after seriously overestimating his investing skills, made a promise that he was unable to keep." *Braswell*, 225 N.C. App. at 742.

For a case where the evidence was sufficient to prove an intent to deceive, see *State v. Pendergraft*, 238 N.C. App. 516, 527 (2014) (rejecting the defendant's argument that his honest but mistaken belief that he could obtain title to a property by adverse possession precluded a finding that he had the required intent to deceive).

Element (4) (page 418)

In a case where the defendant obtained money by selling to company BIMCO electrical wire falsely represented not to have been stolen, there was sufficient evidence that his false representation in fact deceived BIMCO; the court rejected the defendant's argument that BIMCO was indifferent to legal ownership and employed a "nod and wink system" in which no actual deception occurred, noting evidence that the defendant represented himself as the lawful owner of the material and that BIMCO paid him for it. State v. Hallum, ___ N.C. App. ___, 783 S.E.2d 294, 299 (2016).

Attempt (page 420)

This offense was committed even though the defendant returned the victim's payment; the defendant's actions were sufficient to constitute an attempt. State v. Seelig, 226 N.C. App. 147, 162 (2013).

Related Offenses Not in This Chapter (page 420)

The following offenses should be added to this section:

> Hiring with intent to defraud. G.S. 14-168.
> Unemployment insurance fraud. G.S. 96-18.

As a result of 2012 legislation, S.L. 2012-185, the offense listed in this section as "Improper receipt of decedent's retirement allowance. G.S. 135-18.11, 128-38.5, 135-75.2, and 120-4.34" should read:

> Improper receipt of decedent's retirement allowance or monthly benefit under the Disability Income Plan. G.S. 135-18.11, 128-38.5, 135-75.2, and 120-4.34.

Exploitation of a Disabled or Elder Adult (page 421)

Exploitation of a Disabled or Older Adult through a Position of Trust or Business Relationship (revised title) (page 421)

Statute (page 421)

2013 legislation, S.L. 2013-337, replaced the term "elder adult" with "older adult" throughout G.S. 14-112.2. It also amended subsection (a)(2) to read as follows:

> (2) Older adult.—A person 65 years of age or older.

That same legislation also amended subsection (c) to read as follows:

> (c) It is unlawful for a person to knowingly, by deception or intimidation, obtain or use, endeavor to obtain or use, or conspire with another to obtain or use an older adult's or disabled adult's funds, assets, or property with the intent to temporarily or permanently deprive the older adult or disabled adult of the use, benefit, or possession of the funds, assets, or property, or benefit someone other than the older adult or disabled adult. This subsection shall not apply to a person acting within the scope of that person's lawful authority as the agent for the older adult or disabled adult.

Another 2013 law, S.L. 2013-203, amended the statute, adding a new subsection, (f), as follows:

> (f) If a person is charged with a violation of this section that involves funds, assets, or property valued at more than five thousand dollars ($5,000), the district attorney may file a petition in the pending criminal proceeding before the court with jurisdiction over the pending charges to freeze the funds, assets, or property of the defendant in an amount up to one hundred fifty percent (150%) of the alleged value of funds, assets, or property in the defendant's pending criminal proceeding for purposes of restitution to the victim. The standard of proof required to freeze the defendant's funds, assets, or property shall be by clear and convincing evidence. The procedure for petitioning the court under this subsection shall be governed by G.S. 14-112.3.

Elements (page 422)

As a result of 2013 legislation noted above, replace the term "elder adult" with "older adult" throughout this section.

Notes (page 423)

Element (2) (page 423)

As a result of 2013 legislation, S.L. 2013-337, delete the second paragraph of this note and replace it with the following:

> An "older adult" is a person 65 years old or older. G.S. 14-112.2(a)(2). Prior to 2013 legislative changes, the statute applied to an "elder adult." Interpreting the latter provision, one case held that there was sufficient evidence that the victim was an elder adult when the victim was at least 99 years old and received help to pay his bills, cash his checks, and perform personal hygiene tasks, among other things. State v. Forte, 206 N.C. App. 699, 704–05 (2010).

Asset freeze (new note)

> If the offense involves funds, assets, or property valued at more than $5,000, new G.S. 14-112.2(f) allows the district attorney to file a petition to freeze the defendant's funds, assets, or property for purposes of restitution. New G.S. 14-112.3 sets out the relevant procedure.

Exploitation of a Disabled or Older Adult Lacking Capacity (revised title) (page 423)

Elements (page 423)

As a result of 2013 legislation, S.L. 2013-337, the Elements of this offense are revised to read:

> A person guilty of this offense
>
> (1) knowingly *and*
> (2) by deception or intimidation
> (3) obtains, uses, endeavors to obtain or use, or conspires with another to obtain or use an older or disabled adult's funds, assets, or property
> (4) with the intent to
>   (a) temporarily or permanently deprive the older or disabled adult of the use, benefit, or possession of the funds, assets, or property *or*
>   (b) benefit someone other than the older or disabled adult.

Notes (page 423)

Element (1) (new note)

See "Knowingly" in Chapter 1 (States of Mind) of the main volume.

Element (2) (page 423)

Delete the text of this note and replace it with the following:

> For definitions of "older adult" and "disabled adult," see the note on Element (2) to "Exploitation of a Disabled or Older Adult through a Position of Trust or Business Relationship" (revised title), above in this supplement and in the main volume.

Asset freeze (new note)

See this note to "Exploitation of a Disabled or Older Adult through a Position of Trust or Business Relationship" (revised title), above in this supplement.

Identity Theft and Frauds (page 424)

Identity Theft (page 426)

Notes (page 427)

Element (2)(b) (page 427)

The evidence was sufficient to establish that the defendant "used" or "possessed" another person's Social Security number to avoid legal consequences when, after being detained and questioned for shoplifting, the defendant falsely gave the officer his name as Roy Lamar Ward and provided the officer with the name of an employer, date of birth, and possible address; the officer then obtained Ward's Social Security number, wrote it on the citation, and issued the citation to the defendant, but the defendant neither signed the citation nor confirmed the listed Social Security number. State v. Sexton, 223 N.C. App. 341, 345 (2012).

Element (2)(c) (page 427)

See discussion of *Sexton*, 223 N.C. App. 341, immediately above.

Element (4) (new note)

Where the evidence showed that the defendant had used other individuals' credit card numbers, it was sufficient to show that he possessed the victims' credit cards with the intent to fraudulently represent that he was those individuals for the purpose of making financial transactions in their names. State v. Jones, 367 N.C. 299, 305 (2014). The fact that the defendant used false names not matching those on the victims' credit cards did not negate the defendant's intent to fraudulently represent that he was the cardholder. *Id.* at 306.

Crimes Involving Security Interests (page 430)

Fraudulent Filings (page 431)

Statute (page 431)

2012 legislation, S.L. 2012-150, sec. 6, amended the statute, making the crime a Class I felony.

Punishment (page 432)

As a result of the 2012 legislation noted above, delete the text of this section and replace it with the following:

Class I felony. G.S. 14-401.19.

Related Offenses Not in This Chapter (page 432)

The following offense should be added to this section:

Simulation of court process in connection with collection of claim, demand or account. G.S. 14-118.1.

False Liens (new crime)

This offense was enacted in 2012, S.L. 2012-150. It was amended in 2013, S.L. 2013-170; S.L. 2013-410, sec. 27.8, and in 2015, S.L. 2015-87. The statute now reads as follows:

Statute

§ 14-118.6. Filing false lien or encumbrance.

(a) It shall be unlawful for any person to present for filing or recording in a public record or a private record generally available to the public a false lien or encumbrance against the real or personal property of a public officer, a public employee, or an immediate family member of that public officer or public employee on account of the performance of the public officer or public employee's official duties, knowing or having reason to know that the lien or encumbrance is false or contains a materially false, fictitious, or fraudulent statement or representation. For purposes of this subsection, the term "immediate family member" means a spouse or a child. Any person who violates this subsection shall be guilty of a Class I felony.

(b) When presented to the register of deeds for recording, if a register of deeds has a reasonable suspicion that the lien or encumbrance is false, as described in subsection (a) of this section, the register of deeds may refuse to record the lien or encumbrance. Neither the register of deeds nor any other entity shall be liable for recording or the refusal to record a lien or encumbrance as described in subsection (a) of this section. If the recording of the lien or encumbrance is denied, the register of deeds shall allow the recording of a Notice of Denied Lien or Encumbrance Filing on a form adopted by the Secretary of State, for which no filing fee shall be collected. The Notice of Denied Lien or Encumbrance Filing shall not itself constitute a lien or encumbrance. When recording is denied, any interested person may initiate a special proceeding in the county where the recording was denied within ten (10) business days of the filing of the Notice of Denied Lien or Encumbrance Filing asking the superior court of the respective county to find that the proposed recording has a statutory or contractual basis and to order that the document be recorded. If, after hearing, upon a minimum of five (5) days' notice as provided in Rule 5 of the Rules of Civil Procedure and opportunity to be heard to all interested persons and all persons claiming an ownership interest in the property, the court finds that there is a statutory or contractual basis for the proposed recording, the court shall order the document recorded. A lien or encumbrance recorded upon order of the court under this subsection shall have a priority interest as of the time of the filing of the Notice of Denied Lien or Encumbrance Filing. If the court finds that there is no statutory or contractual basis for the proposed recording, the court shall enter an order finding that the proposed recording is null and void and that it shall not be filed, indexed, or recorded and a certified copy of that order shall be recorded by the register of deeds that originally denied the recording. The review by the judge under this subsection shall not be deemed a finding as to any underlying claim of the parties involved. If a special proceeding is not initiated under this subsection within ten (10) business days of the filing of the Notice of Denied Lien or Encumbrance Filing, the lien or encumbrance is deemed null and void as a matter of law.

(b1) When a lien or encumbrance is presented to a clerk of superior court for filing and the clerk of court has a reasonable suspicion that the lien or encumbrance is false as described in subsection (a) of this section, the clerk of court may refuse to file the lien or encumbrance. Neither the clerk of court nor the clerk's staff shall be liable for filing or the refusal to file a lien or encumbrance under this subsection. The clerk of superior court shall not file, index, or docket the document against the property of a public officer or public employee until that document is approved for filing by the clerk of superior court by any judge of the judicial district having subject matter jurisdiction. If the judge determines that the filing is not false, the clerk shall index the claim of lien. A lien or encumbrance filed upon order of the court under this subsection shall have a priority interest as of the date and time of indexing by the clerk of superior court. If the court finds that there is no statutory or contractual basis for the proposed filing, the court shall enter an order that the proposed filing is null and void as a matter of law, and that it shall not be filed or indexed.

The clerk of superior court shall serve the order and return the original denied filing to the person or entity that presented it. The person or entity shall have 30 days from the entry of the order to appeal the order. If the order is not appealed within the applicable time period, the clerk may destroy the filing.

(c) Upon being presented with an order duly issued by a court of competent jurisdiction of this State declaring that a lien or encumbrance already recorded or filed is false, as described in subsection (a) of this section, and therefore null and void as a matter of law, the register of deeds or clerk of court that received the recording or filing, in addition to recording or filing the court's order finding the lien or encumbrance to be false, shall conspicuously mark on the first page of the original record previously filed the following statement: "THE CLAIM ASSERTED IN THIS DOCUMENT IS FALSE AND IS NOT PROVIDED FOR BY THE GENERAL LAWS OF THIS STATE."

(d) In addition to any criminal penalties provided for in this section, a violation of this section shall constitute a violation of G.S. 75-1.1.

(e) Subsections (b), (b1), and (c) of this section shall not apply to filings under Article 9 of Chapter 25 of the General Statutes or under Chapter 44A of the General Statutes.

Elements

A person guilty of this offense

(1) presents for filing in a public record or a private record generally available to the public
(2) a false lien or encumbrance
(3) against the real or personal property of
  (a) a public officer or public employee *or*
  (b) an immediate family member of the public officer or public employee
(4) on account of the performance of the public officer or public employee's official duties
(5) knowing or having reason to know that the lien or encumbrance is false or contains a materially false, fictitious, or fraudulent statement or representation.

Punishment

Class I felony. G.S. 14-118.6(a).

Notes

Element (3) generally. For the definition of the term "real property," see the note on Element (3) to "Injury to Real Property" in Chapter 18 (Trespass, Property Damage, and Littering) of the main volume. For the definition of the term "personal property," see the note on Element (3) to "Injury to Personal Property," also in Chapter 18 of the main volume.

Element (3)(b). The term "immediate family member" means a spouse or child. G.S. 14-118.6(a).

Related Offenses Not in This Chapter

No docketing of lien unless authorized by statute. G.S. 44A-12.1.

Residential Mortgage Fraud (page 433)

Statute (page 433)

2012 legislation, S.L. 2012-150, sec. 5, amended G.S. 14-118.12, adding a new subsection, (a)(5), as follows:

(5) Knowingly files in a public record or a private record generally available to the public a document falsely claiming that a mortgage loan has been satisfied, discharged, released, revoked, or terminated or is invalid.

Elements (page 434)

As a result of the 2012 legislation noted above, a new Element, (3)(d), should be added to this offense as follows:

> (d) knowingly files in a public or private record generally available to the public a document falsely claiming that a mortgage loan has been satisfied, discharged, released, revoked, or terminated or is invalid.

Related Offenses Not in This Chapter (page 435)

The following offenses should be added to this section:

> Simulation of court process in connection with collection of claim, demand or account. G.S. 14-118.1.
> Bank fraud. G.S. 53C-8-11.

Forgery and Related Offenses (page 435)

Forgery and Counterfeiting of Instruments (page 437)

Notes (page 438)

Relation to other offenses (new note)
Forgery and larceny of a chose in action are not mutually exclusive offenses. State v. Grier, 224 N.C. App. 150, 153 (2012).

Uttering Forged Instruments or Instruments with False Endorsements (page 439)

Notes (page 440)

Element (3) (page 440)
For a case where there was sufficient evidence that a check was falsely made, see *State v. Conley*, 220 N.C. App. 50, 60–61 (2012).

Electronic Food and Nutrition Benefits Fraud (page 456)

Fraudulently Obtaining or Transferring Electronic Food and Nutrition Benefits (page 456)

Notes (page 456)

Element (3) (new note)
The trial court did not err by denying the defendant's motion to dismiss where the evidence showed that the defendant knowingly submitted a fraudulent wage verification form to obtain food benefits to which he was not entitled. State v. Davis, 230 N.C. App. 50, 53–54 (2013).

Computer Fraud (page 461)

Accessing a Government Computer to Defraud or Obtain Property (page 465)
Notes (page 465)

Element (1) (page 465)
For a case where the court found this Element satisfied, see *State v. Barr*, 218 N.C. App. 329, 336–40 (2012).

Element (4)(b) (new note)
The evidence was sufficient to sustain a conviction under G.S. 14-454.1(a)(2) where the State alleged that the defendant, who worked for a private license plate agency, submitted false information into the State Title and Registration System (STARS) so that a car dealer whose dealer number was invalid could transfer title and the defendant admitted that she personally accessed STARS to make three transfers for the dealer, that she told a co-worker to run a fourth transaction in a similar fashion, and that she received payment for doing so. *Barr*, 218 N.C. App. at 334–35.

Willful Failure to File a State Tax Return, Supply State Tax Information, or Pay State Tax (page 467)
Related Offenses Not in This Chapter (page 468)
As a result of 2013 legislation, S.L. 2013-301, the following offense should be added to this list:

Possession, transfer, or use of automated sales suppression device. G.S. 14-118.7.

17
Arson and Burning Offenses

Arson Offenses (page 471)

First-Degree Arson (page 471)
Notes (page 471)

Element (1) (page 471)

Delete the second sentence of this note and replace it with the following:

> As used for arson, these terms mean that the act was done "voluntarily and without excuse or justification and without any bona fide claim of right." State v. White, 288 N.C. 44, 50 (1975); State v. Eubanks, 83 N.C. App. 338, 339 (1986). An intent or animus against either the property itself or its owner is not required. *White*, 288 N.C. at 50; *Eubanks*, 83 N.C. App. at 339.

Add the following at the end of this note:

> The evidence was sufficient to establish malice where, among other things, the defendant was enraged at the property owner for evicting him. State v. Burton, 224 N.C. App. 120, 126 (2012).

Setting Fire Offenses (page 483)

Setting Fire to Woods and Fields (page 483)
Statute (page 483)

2015 legislation, S.L. 2015-263, sec. 36(a), amended the statute, replacing "Department of Environmental Quality" with "Department of Agriculture and Consumer Services."

Elements (page 483)

As a result of the 2015 legislative change noted above, Element (4) should now read as follows:

> (4) in any county that is under the protection of the Department of Agriculture and Consumer Services in its work of forest fire control.

18

Trespass, Property Damage, and Littering

Trespass Offenses (page 489)

First-Degree Trespass (page 489)

Statute (page 489)

2012 legislation, S.L. 2012-168, sec. 1, amended G.S. 14-159.12, modifying subsection (b) and adding new subsections (c) through (e).

2014 legislation, S.L. 2014-103, sec. 10(a), added a new subsection, (c)(1)d.

2016 legislation, S.L. 2016-26, sec. 1, added a new subsection (f) and further amended subsection (b).

The revised statute reads:

> (b) Except as otherwise provided in subsection (c), (d), or (f) of this section, first degree trespass is a Class 2 misdemeanor.
> (c) Except as otherwise provided in subsection (d) of this section, a violation of subsection (a) of this section is a Class A1 misdemeanor if all of the following circumstances exist:
>   (1) The offense is committed on the premises of any of the following:
>   a. A facility that is owned or operated by an electric power supplier as defined in G.S. 62-133.8(a)(3) and that is either an electric generation facility, a transmission substation, a transmission switching station, a transmission switching structure, or a control center used to manage transmission operations or electrical power generating at multiple plant locations.
>   b. Any facility used or available for use in the collection, treatment, testing, storing, pumping, or distribution of water for a public water system.
>   c. Any facility, including any liquefied natural gas storage facility or propane air facility, that is owned or operated by a natural gas local distribution company, natural gas pipeline carrier operating under a certificate of public convenience and necessity from the Utilities Commission, municipal corporation operating a municipally owned gas distribution system, or regional natural gas district organized and operated pursuant to Article 28 of Chapter 160A of the General Statutes used for transmission, distribution, measurement, testing, regulating, compression, control, or storage of natural gas.

        d.   Any facility used or operated for agricultural activities, as that term is defined in G.S. 106-581.1.

    (2)   The person actually entered a building, or it was necessary for the person to climb over, go under, or otherwise surmount a fence or other barrier to reach the facility.

(d) If, in addition to the circumstances set out in subsection (c) of this section, the violation also includes any of the following elements, then the offense is a Class H felony:

    (1)   The offense is committed with the intent to disrupt the normal operation of any of the facilities described in subdivision (1) of subsection (c) of this section.

    (2)   The offense involves an act that places either the offender or others on the premises at risk of serious bodily injury.

(e) As used in subsections (c) and (d) of this section, the term "facility" shall mean a building or other infrastructure.

(f) A violation of subsection (a) of this section is a Class I felony and shall include a fine of not less than one thousand dollars ($1,000) for each violation, if any of the following circumstances exist:

    (1) The offense occurs on real property where the person has reentered after having previously been removed pursuant to the execution of a valid order or writ for possession.

    (2) The offense occurs under color of title where the person has knowingly created or provided materially false evidence of an ownership or possessory interest.

Punishment (page 489)

As per the legislative changes noted above, in certain circumstances the offense is elevated to a Class A1 misdemeanor or a Class H or I felony. G.S. 14-159.12(c), (d), or (f). Whenever the elevated version of this offense is charged, the relevant facts must be alleged in the charging instrument and proved to the jury beyond a reasonable doubt.

Notes (page 489)

Greater and lesser-included offenses (page 490)

For another case supporting the statement in this note that first-degree trespass is a lesser-included offense of felony breaking or entering, see *State v. Lucas*, 230 N.C. App. 50, 53–54 (2014).

Related Offenses Not in This Chapter (page 490)

As a result of 2014 legislation, S.L. 2014-120, sec. 52(a); 2014-100, sec. 34.30(b) and (e), the following new offenses should be added to this section:

Felony taking of Venus flytrap. G.S. 14-129.3.
Unlawful distribution of images taken through use of unmanned aircraft system. G.S. 14-401.25.

As a result of 2012 legislation, S.L. 2012-168, sec. 1, the following new offense should be added to this section:

Trespass on utility facility. G.S. 14-159.12(c) and (d).

After the offense "Trespassing for purposes of hunting, etc., without written consent a misdemeanor (including trespass to remove pine needles or straw). G.S. 14-159.6," add the following:

(2012 legislation, S.L. 2012-52, amended the statute to provide for a broader version of this offense applying in Granville County only.)

Domestic Criminal Trespass (page 492)

Related Offenses Not in This Chapter (page 493)

The citation to the last item in this list should read as follows:

> G.S. 14-269.8; 50B-3.1(j).

Injury to Property Offenses (page 495)

Injury to Real Property (page 495)

Notes (page 495)

Element (3) (page 495)

An air conditioning unit attached to the exterior of a mobile home was real property where it was affixed in a manner such that it "became an irremovable part of" the home and attached to the home for the use and enjoyment of the home's renter. State v. Hardy, ___ N.C. App. ___, 774 S.E.2d 410, 418 (2015).

Related Offenses Not in This Chapter (page 495)

As a result of 2014 legislation, S.L. 2014-120, sec. 52(a), the following new offense should be added to this section:

> Felony taking of Venus flytrap. G.S. 14-129.3.

The following offense, enacted by 2012 legislation, S.L. 2012-46, sec. 31, should be added to this section:

> Cutting, mutilating, defacing, or injuring property to obtain nonferrous metals. G.S. 14-159.4.

The following offense, enacted by 2015 legislation, S.L. 2015-72, should be added to this section:

> Graffiti vandalism. G.S. 14-127.1.

Defacing a Public Building, Statue, or Monument (page 496)

Statute (page 496)

2014 legislation, S.L. 2014-100, sec. 17.1(w), amended G.S. 14-132(c)(3) to now read as follows:

> (3) Designated by the Director of the State Bureau of Investigation in accordance with G.S. 143B-987.

2015 legislation, S.L. 2015-72, sec. 2, amended G.S. 14-132(d) to now read as follows:

> (d) Unless the conduct is covered under some other provision of law providing greater punishment, any person who violates any provision of this section is guilty of a Class 2 misdemeanor.

Notes (page 497)

Multiple convictions and punishments (new note)

The "[u]nless the conduct is covered" language added to the punishment provision in 2015 means that a defendant may not be punished for this offense and one that carries a more severe punishment.

Related Offenses Not in This Chapter (page 497)

The following offenses, enacted by 2012 legislation, S.L. 2012-46, sec. 31, should be added to this section:

Interfering with gas, water, or electric meters. G.S. 14-151.
Cutting, mutilating, defacing, or injuring property to obtain nonferrous metals. G.S. 14-159.4.

The following offense, enacted by 2015 legislation, S.L. 2015-72, should be added to this section:

Graffiti vandalism. G.S. 14-127.1.

Injury to Personal Property (page 497)
Related Offenses Not in This Chapter (page 498)

The following offenses, enacted by 2012 legislation, S.L. 2012-127 and S.L. 2012-46, sec. 31, respectively, should be added to this section:

Damaging or contaminating waste kitchen grease or container. G.S. 14-79.2.
Cutting, mutilating, defacing, or injuring property to obtain nonferrous metals. G.S. 14-159.4.

19

Disorderly Conduct, Riot, and Gang Offenses

Drunk and Disruptive (page 507)

Statute (page 507)

2015 legislation, S.L. 2015-247, sec. 3(c), amended subsection (b) of the statute to read as follows:

> (b) Any person who violates this section shall be guilty of a Class 3 misdemeanor.

Notes (page 508)
Guilty pleas (page 508)

As a result of the 2015 legislation noted above, delete this note.

Disorderly Conduct (page 508)

Statute (page 508)

2012 legislation, S.L. 2012-12, sec. 2(b), amended G.S. 14-288.4(a)(4)c. to read:

> c.   If an emergency is occurring or is imminent within the institution, an order given by any law-enforcement officer acting within the scope of the officer's authority.

2013 legislation, S.L. 2013-6, sec. 1, amended G.S. 14-288.4(a)(8) to read:

> (8)   Engages in conduct with the intent to impede, disrupt, disturb, or interfere with the orderly administration of any funeral, memorial service, or family processional to the funeral or memorial service, including a military funeral, service, or family processional, or with the normal activities and functions occurring in the facilities or buildings where a funeral or memorial service, including a military funeral or memorial service, is taking place. Any of the following conduct that occurs within two hours preceding, during, or within two hours after a funeral or memorial service shall constitute disorderly conduct under this subdivision:
> > a.   Displaying, within 500 feet of the ceremonial site, location being used for the funeral or memorial, or the family's processional route to the funeral or memorial service, any visual image that conveys fighting

       words or actual or imminent threats of harm directed to any person or property associated with the funeral, memorial service, or processional route.

    b.   Uttering, within 500 feet of the ceremonial site, location being used for the funeral or memorial service, or the family's processional route to the funeral or memorial service, loud, threatening, or abusive language or singing, chanting, whistling, or yelling with or without noise amplification in a manner that would tend to impede, disrupt, disturb, or interfere with a funeral, memorial service, or processional route.

    c.   Attempting to block or blocking pedestrian or vehicular access to the ceremonial site or location being used for a funeral or memorial.

That same legislation also amended G.S. 14-288.4(c), the punishment provision of the statute, to make a first offense a Class 1 misdemeanor, a second offense a Class I felony, and a third or subsequent offense a Class H felony.

Disorderly Conduct by Fighting (page 510)

Related Offenses Not in This Chapter (page 510)

The following offenses were enacted by 2012 legislation, S.L. 2012-12, sec. 1(d), and should be added to this section:

    Violating Governor's order during a state of emergency. G.S. 166A-19.30(d); G.S. 14-288.20A(2).

    Violating county or municipality's ordinance during a state of emergency. G.S. 166A-19.31(h); G.S. 14-288.20A(1).

    Willfully refusing to leave a public building as directed under a Governor's order. G.S. 14-288.20A(3).

The following offenses were repealed by 2012 legislation, S.L. 2012-12, sec. (e), and should be removed from this section:

    Violation of state of emergency ordinance. G.S. 14-288.12 through -288.15.

    Governor's power to order evacuation of public building. G.S. 14-288.19.

The following offense was repealed by 2015 legislation, S.L. 2015-286, sec. 1.1, and should be removed from this section:

    Using profane or indecent language on public highways. G.S. 14-197.

Disorderly Conduct by Disrupting Students (page 513)

Notes (page 513)

Element (1) (new note)

The evidence was sufficient to show that a juvenile acted intentionally where he was described as "very defiant" and he could have avoided the physical contact at issue. *In re* M.J.G., 234 N.C. App. 350, 357–58 (2014).

Element (3) (page 513)

The evidence showed that the juvenile's conduct substantially interfered with the operation of the school where the juvenile's conduct required intervention by several teachers, the assistant principal, and the school resource officer, and a group of special needs students missed their buses because of the disturbance. *Id.* at 360–61.

Disorderly Conduct by Disrupting a Funeral (page 515)

Punishment (page 515)

2013 legislation, S.L. 2013-6, changed the punishments for this offense. As a result, delete the text in this section and replace it with the following:

> Class 1 misdemeanor for a first offense, Class I felony for a second offense, and Class H felony for a third or subsequent offense. G.S. 14-288.4(c). If an elevated version of this offense is charged, the fact elevating punishment must be alleged in a charging instrument and proved at trial, unless the defendant pleads guilty or no contest to the issue. *See* G.S. 15A-928 (alleging and proving prior convictions).

Notes (page 515)

Element (3) (page 515)

As a result of 2013 legislation, S.L. 2013-6, delete the text of this note and replace it with the following:

> The statute expressly includes military funerals and services. G.S. 14-288.4(a)(8). It also provides that any of the following conduct occurring within the time period beginning two hours before the service and ending two hours after the service constitutes disorderly conduct:
>
> - displaying, within 500 feet of the ceremonial site or processional route, any visual image that conveys fighting words or actual or imminent threats of harm directed to any person or property associated with the event or processional route;
> - uttering, within 500 feet of the ceremonial site or processional route, loud, threatening, or abusive language or singing, chanting, whistling, or yelling with or without noise amplification in a manner that would tend to impede, disrupt, disturb, or interfere with a funeral, memorial service, or processional route; or
> - attempting to block or blocking pedestrian or vehicular access to the ceremonial site or location being used for a funeral or memorial.
>
> *Id.*

Disorderly Conduct in a Public Building (page 516)

Statute (page 516)

2014 legislation, S.L. 2014-100, sec. 17.1(w), amended G.S. 14-132(c)(3) to now read:

> (3)   Designated by the Director of the State Bureau of Investigation in accordance with G.S. 143B-987.

Notes (page 517)

Constitutionality (new note)

In *State v. Dale*, ___ N.C. App. ___, 783 S.E.2d 222, 229–30 (2016), the court rejected the defendant's void for vagueness and as applied constitutional challenges to a conviction for this offense.

Failure to Disperse on Command (page 526)

Related Offenses Not in This Chapter (page 527)

The following offenses were enacted by 2012 legislation, S.L. 2012-12, sec. 1(d), and should be added to this section:

> Violating Governor's order during a state of emergency. G.S. 166A-19.30(d); G.S. 14-288.20A(2).
>
> Violating county or municipality's ordinance during a state of emergency. G.S. 166A-19.31(h); G.S. 14-288.20A(1).
>
> Willfully refusing to leave a public building as directed under a Governor's order. G.S. 14-288.20A(3).

The following offense was repealed by 2012 legislation, S.L. 2012-12, sec. 2(c), and should be removed from this section:

> Transporting dangerous weapon or substance during emergency; possessing off premises. G.S. 14-288.7.

Gang-Related Crimes (page 527)

Street Gang Activity (page 528)

Notes (page 528)

Element (3) (page 528)

As a result of 2013 legislation, S.L. 2013-165, the last offense in the bulleted list should read:

- G.S. 14-313 (Youth access to tobacco products, tobacco-derived products, vapor products, and cigarette wrapping papers).

The following offense was repealed by 2015 legislation, S.L. 2015-286, sec. 1.1, and should be removed from the bulleted list in this note:

- G.S. 14-197 (Using profane or indecent language on public highways; counties exempt);

Real property declared a public nuisance (page 529)

Delete this note and replace it with the following:

> **Street gangs and real property used by them a public nuisance.** 2012 legislation, S.L. 2012-28, enacted the N.C. Street Gang Abatement Act, declaring street gangs and real property used by street gangs public nuisances and providing for specified remedies. G.S. 14-50.31 through -50.33.

20

Bombing, Terrorism, and Related Offenses

Terrorism (new crime)

This offense was enacted by 2012 legislation, S.L. 2012-38, and applies to offenses committed on or after December 1, 2012. *Id.*

Statute

§ 14-10.1. Terrorism.

(a) As used in this section, the term "act of violence" means a violation of G.S. 14-17; a felony punishable pursuant to G.S. 14-18; any felony offense in this Chapter that includes an assault, or use of violence or force against a person; any felony offense that includes either the threat or use of any explosive or incendiary device; or any offense that includes the threat or use of a nuclear, biological, or chemical weapon of mass destruction.

(b) A person is guilty of the separate offense of terrorism if the person commits an act of violence with the intent to do either of the following:

    (1)   Intimidate the civilian population at large, or an identifiable group of the civilian population.

    (2)   Influence, through intimidation, the conduct or activities of the government of the United States, a state, or any unit of local government.

(c) A violation of this section is a felony that is one class higher than the offense which is the underlying act of violence, except that a violation is a Class B1 felony if the underlying act of violence is a Class A or Class B1 felony offense. A violation of this section is a separate offense from the underlying offense and shall not merge with other offenses.

(d) All real and personal property of every kind used or intended for use in the course of, derived from, or realized through an offense punishable pursuant to this Article shall be subject to lawful seizure and forfeiture to the State as set forth in G.S. 14-2.3 and G.S. 14-7.20. However, the forfeiture of any real or personal property shall be subordinate to any security interest in the property taken by a lender in good faith as collateral for the extension of credit and recorded as provided by law, and no real or personal property shall be forfeited under this section against an owner who made a bona fide purchase of the property, or a person with rightful possession of the property, without knowledge of a violation of this Article.

Elements

A person guilty of this offense

    (1)   commits an act of violence

    (2)   with the intent to

(a) intimidate the civilian population, or an identifiable group of the civilian population, *or*

(b) influence, through intimidation, a government's conduct or activities.

Punishment

This offense is punished as a felony that is one class higher than the offense that constitutes the underlying act of violence, except that a violation is a Class B1 felony if the underlying act of violence is a Class A or B1 felony. G.S. 14-10.1(c).

Notes

Element (1). G.S. 14-10.1(a) defines the term "act of violence" to include

- murder under G.S. 14-17;
- manslaughter under G.S. 14-18;
- any Chapter 14 felony that includes an assault or use of violence or force against a person;
- any felony that includes either the threat or use of any explosive or incendiary device; and
- any offense that includes the threat or use of a nuclear, biological, or chemical weapon of mass destruction.

The statute does not define the phrase "explosive or incendiary device." That term is defined in two other statutory provisions, but it is not clear which of these definitions is meant to apply to this offense. Specifically, G.S. 14-50.1 defines an "explosive or incendiary device or material" as including "nitroglycerine, dynamite, gunpowder, other high explosive, incendiary bomb or grenade, other destructive incendiary device, or any other destructive incendiary or explosive device, compound, or formulation; any instrument or substance capable of being used for destructive explosive or incendiary purposes against persons or property, when the circumstances indicate some probability that such instrument or substance will be so used; or any explosive or incendiary part or ingredient in any instrument or substance included above, when the circumstances indicate some probability that such part or ingredient will be so used." G.S. 14-72(b)(3) defines an "explosive or incendiary device or substance" as "any explosive or incendiary grenade or bomb; any dynamite, blasting powder, nitroglycerin, TNT, or other high explosive; or any device, ingredient for such device, or type or quantity of substance primarily useful for large-scale destruction of property by explosive or incendiary action or lethal injury to persons by explosive or incendiary action." That section further provides that the definition does not include "fireworks; or any form, type, or quantity of gasoline, butane gas, natural gas, or any other substance having explosive or incendiary properties but serving a legitimate non-destructive or nonlethal use in the form, type, or quantity stolen." G.S. 14-72(b)(3).

Presumably the phrase "any offense that includes the threat or use of a nuclear, biological, or chemical weapon of mass destruction" refers to the nuclear, biological, or chemical weapon of mass destruction offenses in G.S. 14-288.21 through -288.24.

Element (2)(b). The governments covered include the federal government, any state government, and any unit of local government. G.S. 14-10.1(b)(2).

Multiple convictions and punishments. A defendant may be convicted and punished for both this offense and the underlying offense that constitutes the act of violence. G.S. 14-10.1(c).

Seizure and forfeiture of property. All real and personal property used or intended for use in the course of, derived from, or realized through this offense is subject to seizure and forfeiture pursuant to G.S. 14-2.3 and 14-7.20. G.S. 14-10.1(d). However, the forfeiture is subordinate to any security interest in the property taken by a lender in good faith as collateral for the extension of credit and recorded as provided by law. *Id.* Also, no property may be forfeited against an owner who made a bona fide purchase of it, or a person with rightful possession of the property, without knowledge of the criminal violation. *Id.*

Related Offenses Not in This Chapter

"Riot" (Chapter 19)
"Gang-Related Crimes" (Chapter 19)

Malicious Damage by Use of Explosives or Incendiaries (page 537)

Malicious Damage to Occupied Property by Use of an Explosive or Incendiary (page 537)

Related Offenses Not in This Chapter (page 538)

The following offense was repealed by 2012 legislation, S.L. 2012-12, sec. 2(c), and should be removed from this section:

Transporting dangerous weapon or substance during emergency; possessing off premises. G.S. 14-288.7.

As a result of 2014 legislation, S.L. 2014-100, sec. 34.30(b) through (d), add the following to this section:

Interference with manned aircraft by unmanned aircraft systems. G.S. 14-280.3.
Unlawful possession and use of unmanned aircraft systems. G.S. 14-401.24.

Perpetrating a Hoax by Use of a False Bomb or Other Device (page 543)

Perpetrating a Hoax in or at a Public Building (page 543)

Notes (page 543)

Element (1) (new note)

For a case where there was sufficient evidence that the defendant intended to perpetrate a hoax with a false bomb, see *State v. Golden*, 224 N.C. App. 136, 147 (2012).

Element (2) (new note)

For a case in which there was sufficient evidence that the defendant placed or concealed a false bomb in his vehicle, see *Golden*, 224 N.C. App. at 146.

21
Perjury, Bribery, Obstruction, Resisting, and Related Crimes

Obstruction of Justice (page 557)

Notes (page 557)

Element (2) (page 557)

Add the following at the end of the bulleted list in this note:

- making false statements to law enforcement officers about a crime under investigation. State v. Cousin, 233 N.C. App. 523, 530–31 (2014) (the defendant gave eight different written statements to authorities providing a wide array of scenarios surrounding the victim's death and identifying four different individuals as being the perpetrator; he also admitted that he had been untruthful to investigators).

Multiple convictions and punishments (new note)

No double jeopardy violation occurred when the trial court sentenced the defendant for felony obstruction of justice and accessory after the fact to murder arising out of the same conduct. *Cousin*, 233 N.C. App. at 535–37 (reasoning that each offense contains an element not in the other).

Interfering with Witnesses (page 558)

Intimidating a Witness (page 559)

Notes (page 559)

Element (1) (page 559)

For a case where there was sufficient evidence that a rape defendant threatened the victim, see *State v. Barnett*, ___ N.C. App. ___, 784 S.E.2d 188, 192–93, *review allowed*, ___ N.C. ___, 784 S.E.2d 474 (2016) (among other things, on the day of the incident the defendant threatened to kill the victim if she called the police and subsequently sent her a letter stating, "What did I tell you, [sic] would happen, if you took charges; [sic] out on me? You remember what I told you. And I'ma [sic] stand by my word. Because you knew not to press charges or go to the hospital. You knew better then [sic] that.").

Element (2) (page 559)

In *State v. Shannon*, 230 N.C. App. 583, 586 (2013), the court of appeals held that the statute applied to a person who is a prospective witness but who has not been formally summoned. *See also* State v. Jones, 237 N.C. App. 526, 533–35 (2014) (trial court did not err by instructing the jury that "it is immaterial that the victim was regularly summoned or legally bound to attend").

The State need not prove the specific court proceeding that the defendant intended to deter the witness from attending. State v. Barnett, ___ N.C. App. ___, 784 S.E.2d 188, 193, *review allowed*, ___ N.C. ___, 784 S.E.2d 474 (2016) (the State need only prove that the witness had been summoned or was acting as a witness in a state court proceeding).

Because the statute covers attempts to intimidate a witness, a defendant may be convicted of this offense even if the victim did not receive the defendant's threatening letters. *Id.* at 194.

Perjury Offenses (page 562)

Perjury (page 562)
Related Offenses Not in This Chapter (page 563)

As a result of 2012 legislation, S.L. 2012-56, sec. 4, the following offenses should be added to this section:

False or fraudulent report by bank examiner. G.S. 53C-8-7.
False reports and statements regarding a bank. G.S. 53C-8-11(a)(5).

As a result of 2014 legislation, S.L. 2014-100, sec. 17.1(p), delete the offense listed as False swearing in fire investigation by Attorney General. G.S. 58-79-10 and replace it with the following:

False swearing in fire investigation by Director of the State Bureau of Investigation.
G.S. 58-79-10.

Bribery Offenses (page 564)

Taking or Agreeing to Take a Bribe (page 564)
Related Offenses Not in This Chapter (page 566)

As a result of 2012 legislation, S.L. 2012-56, sec. 4, the following offense should be added to this section:

Keeping or accepting a bribe by bank examiner. G.S. 53C-8-7.

Resisting, Delaying, or Obstructing an Officer (page 567)

Notes (page 567)

Element (1) (page 567)

For cases where there was sufficient evidence of willfulness, see *State v. Smith*, 225 N.C. App. 471, 478 (2013), and *State v. Cornell*, 222 N.C. App. 184, 189 (2012).

Element (2) (page 567)

Add the following at the end of the second full paragraph on page 568:

The evidence was also sufficient to sustain a conviction when (6) during a 10- to 15-second incident the defendant stepped between an officer and gang members and refused the officer's instructions to step away, *Cornell*, 222 N.C. App. at 189, and (7) the defendant refused to provide the officer with his identification so that the officer could issue the defendant a citation for a seatbelt violation. State v. Friend, 237 N.C. App. 490, 493–94 (2014).

Add the following at the end of the last paragraph of this note:

In *State v. Friend*, 237 N.C. App. 490, 493–94 (2014), the North Carolina Court of Appeals stated that "failure to provide information about one's identity during a lawful stop can constitute resistance, delay, or obstruction within the meaning of [the statute]." Note that *Friend* requires that the defendant's failure to identify actually delay the officer in completing a lawful task, there issuing a seatbelt citation to the defendant-passenger. *Id.* Note also that the *Friend* court qualified its ruling, stating: "There are, of course, circumstances where one would be excused from providing his or her identity to an officer," such as when doing so would violate the Fifth Amendment's protection against compelled self-incrimination. *Id.*

Element (5) (page 569)

Because the officer did not read or produce a copy of the search warrant as required by G.S. 15A-252 before seeking to search the defendant, the officer was not engaged in lawful conduct and the evidence was insufficient to support a conviction based on the defendant's refusal to allow the officer to search him pursuant to the warrant. State v. Carter, 237 N.C. App. 274, 279–80 (2014).

Defenses (new note)

For a case where the court rejected the defendant's argument that his conduct was justified on grounds that he acted out of concern for a minor in his care, see *Cornell*, 222 N.C. App. at 189.

Related Offenses Not in This Chapter (page 570)

The following offenses were enacted by 2012 legislation, S.L. 2012-12, sec. 1(d), and should be added to this section:

Violating Governor's order during a state of emergency. G.S. 166A-19.30(d);
G.S. 14-288.20A(2).
Violating county or municipality's ordinance during a state of emergency. G.S. 166A-19.31(h);
G.S. 14-288.20A(1).
Willfully refusing to leave a public building as directed under a Governor's order.
G.S. 14-288.20A(3).

The following offenses were repealed by 2012 legislation, S.L. 2012-12, sec. 2(e), and should be removed from this section:

Violation of state of emergency ordinance. G.S. 14-288.12 through -288.14.
Violating a provision of a proclamation of the Governor in an emergency. G.S. 14-288.15.
Failure to evacuate on Governor's command. G.S. 14-288.19.

False Report to Law Enforcement Agencies or Officers (page 571)

Statute (page 571)

2013 legislation, S.L. 2013-52, sec. 6, amended the statute to read as follows:

§ 14-225. False reports to law enforcement agencies or officers.

(a) Except as provided in subsection (b) of this section, any person who shall willfully make or cause to be made to a law enforcement agency or officer any false, deliberately misleading or unfounded report, for the purpose of interfering with the operation of a law enforcement agency, or to hinder or obstruct any law enforcement officer in the performance of his duty, shall be guilty of a Class 2 misdemeanor.

(b) A violation of subsection (a) of this section is punishable as a Class H felony if the false, deliberately misleading, or unfounded report relates to a law enforcement investigation involving the disappearance of a child as that term is defined in G.S. 14-318.5 or child victim of a Class A, B1, B2, or C felony offense. For purposes of this subsection, a child is any person who is less than 16 years of age.

Elements (page 571)

As a result of 2013 legislation, S.L. 2013-52, sec. 6, Element (4) should read as follows:

(4) a false or deliberately misleading or unfounded report

Punishment (page 571)

As a result of 2013 legislation, S.L. 2013-52, sec. 6, this section should read as follows:

Class 2 misdemeanor. G.S. 14-225(a). Class H felony if the report relates to a law enforcement investigation involving

- the disappearance of a child (as defined by G.S. 14-318.5) or
- a child victim of a Class A through C felony.

G.S. 14-225(b). A child is a person less than 16 years of age. *Id.* Any fact elevating punishment must be alleged in the charging instrument and proved to a jury, unless the defendant pleads guilty or no contest to the issue.

Concealing a Death (page 573)

Statute (page 573)

As a result of 2013 legislation, S.L. 2013-52, sec. 5, G.S. 14-401.22 has been revised to read:

(a) Except as provided in subsection (a1) of this section, any person who, with the intent to conceal the death of a person, fails to notify a law enforcement authority of the death or secretly buries or otherwise secretly disposes of a dead human body is guilty of a Class I felony.

(a1) Any person who, with the intent to conceal the death of a child, fails to notify a law enforcement authority of the death or secretly buries or otherwise secretly disposes of a dead child's body is guilty of a Class H felony. For purposes of this subsection, a child is any person who is less than 16 years of age.

To save space, subsections (b) through (f) are not reproduced here.

Punishment (page 573)

As a result of 2013 legislation, S.L. 2013-52, sec. 5, this section should be revised to read as follows:

Class I felony. G.S. 14-401.22(a). If the body is of a child less than 16 years old, the offense is a Class H felony. G.S. 14-401.22(a1). If the defendant knew or had reason to know that the person did not die of natural causes, the offense is a Class D felony. G.S. 14-401.22(e). All facts elevating punishment must be alleged in the charging instrument and proved to the jury, unless the defendant pleads guilty or no contest to the issue.

Related Offenses Not in This Chapter (page 573)

Add the following offense to this section:

Disturbing, vandalizing, or desecrating human remains; committing sexual penetration on human remains. G.S. 14-401.22(c).

Prison and Other Escapes (page 574)

Prison Breach and Escape from County or Municipal Confinement Facilities or Officers (page 574)

Statute (page 574)

2013 legislation, S.L. 2013-389, sec. 3, amended subsection (1) to read as follows:

> (1)   He has been charged with or convicted of a felony and has been committed to the facility pending trial or transfer to the State prison system; or

Punishment (page 574)

As a result of the 2013 legislation noted above, the second sentence of this note should read as follows:

Class H felony if the defendant

- has been charged with or convicted of a felony and has been committed to the facility pending trial or transfer to the state prison system or
- is serving a sentence imposed on conviction of a felony.

S.L. 2013-389.

Related Offenses Not in This Chapter (page 574)

As a result of 2015 legislation, S.L. 2015-47, delete the seventh offense listed in this section and replace it with the following:

Furnishing poison, controlled substances, deadly weapons, cartridges, ammunition, or alcoholic beverages to inmates; furnishing tobacco or mobile phones to inmates; furnishing mobile phones to delinquent juveniles. G.S. 14-258.1.

22
Weapons Offenses

Possession of a Firearm by a Felon (page 581)

Notes (page 582)

Element (2)(c) (page 582)

There was insufficient evidence of constructive possession where (1) the defendant did not have exclusive control of the apartment in which guns were found and the State failed to present evidence of other incriminating circumstances, State v. Perry, 222 N.C. App. 813, 819 (2012); (2) the defendant did not have exclusive control of the car that he owned but in which he was a passenger when the rifle was found; the rifle was registered to the defendant's girlfriend, who was driving; the defendant and his girlfriend had equal access to the location where the weapon was found; and there was no physical evidence, such as fingerprints, tying the defendant to the rifle. State v. Bailey, ___ N.C. App. ___, 757 S.E.2d 491, 494 (2014).

The fact that a person is aware of a weapon does not, by itself, establish constructive possession. *Id.* at 494.

There was sufficient evidence that the defendant constructively possessed (1) drugs and a rifle found in a bedroom that was not under his exclusive control; among other things, photographs, a Father's Day card, a cable bill, a cable installation receipt, and a pay stub found in the bedroom linked him to the contraband and placed him in the room within two days of when the contraband was found, State v. Bradshaw, 366 N.C. 90, 96–97 (2012); (2) a firearm when the defendant was driving a rental vehicle, had a female passenger, and the gun was found in a purse in the car's glove container; the court reasoned that the defendant was driving the car, and his interactions with the police showed that he was aware of the vehicle's contents, State v. Mitchell, 224 N.C. App. 171, 178 (2012); and (3) a gun where an anonymous 911 caller reported seeing a man wearing a plaid shirt holding a gun near a black car beside a field; someone saw the man drop the gun; an officer saw the defendant standing near a black car wearing a plaid shirt; the defendant later returned to the scene claiming ownership of the car; and officers found a firearm in a vacant lot approximately 10 feet from the car. State v. McKiver, ___ N.C. App. ___, 786 S.E.2d 85, 89, *temporary stay allowed*, ___ N.C. ___, 787 S.E.2d 15 (2016) (noting that additional incriminating circumstances existed, beyond the defendant's mere presence at the scene and proximity to the firearm, to infer that he constructively possessed the firearm), *temporary stay allowed*, ___ N.C. ___, 787 S.E.2d 15 (2016).

Exceptions (page 584)

Add the following at the end of the first paragraph to this note:

> *See* Booth v. North Carolina, 227 N.C. App. 484 (2013) (offense does not apply to a person who has received a Pardon of Forgiveness for his or her prior felony).

Constitutionality (page 584)

This note cites *Baysden v. North Carolina*, 217 N.C. App. 20 (2011), as holding that the statute was unconstitutional as applied to the plaintiff. With one justice taking no part in consideration of the case, an equally divided North Carolina Supreme Court left undisturbed that opinion, which stands without precedential value. Baysden v. State, 366 N.C. 370 (2013). Because of that decision and one additional case, delete all text in this paragraph from the words "Post-*Britt* North Carolina Court of Appeals cases" onward and replace it with the following:

> Post-*Britt* North Carolina Court of Appeals cases include *State v. Whitaker*, 201 N.C. App. 190, 202–07 (2009) (distinguishing *Britt* and rejecting an as applied challenge to the statute), *aff'd*, 364 N.C. 404 (2010); *State v. Price*, 233 N.C. App. 386, 397–98 (2014) (following *Whitaker*); and *State v. Bonetsky*, ___ N.C. App. ___, 784 S.E.2d 637, 639–44 (2016) (rejecting the defendant's as applied challenge).

Add the following to this note:

> In *Johnston v. State*, 367 N.C. 164 (2013), the court per curiam affirmed the decision below, *Johnston v. State*, 224 N.C. App. 282 (2012), which reversed the trial court's ruling that G.S. 14-415.1 violated the plaintiff's substantive due process right under the U.S. and N.C. constitutions and remanded to the trial court for additional proceedings; the court of appeals also reversed the trial court's ruling that the statute was facially invalid on procedural due process grounds, under both the U.S. and N.C. constitutions.

Defenses (page 586)

Add the following after the second sentence of this note:

> State v. Monroe, 367 N.C. 771 (2015) (per curiam); State v. Edwards, ___ N.C. App. ___, 768 S.E.2d 619, 621 (2015);

Related Offenses Not in This Chapter (page 586)

As a result of 2015 legislation, S.L. 2015-47, delete the fourth item listed in this section and replace it with the following:

> Furnishing poison, controlled substances, deadly weapons, cartridges, ammunition or alcoholic beverages to inmates; furnishing tobacco products or mobile phones to inmates; furnishing mobile phones to delinquent juveniles. G.S. 14-258.1.

The following offense was repealed by 2012 legislation, S.L. 2012-12, sec. 2(c), and should be removed from this section:

> Transporting dangerous weapon or substance during emergency. G.S. 14-288.7.

As a result of 2014 legislation, S.L. 2014-100, sec. 34.30(d), add the following to this section:

> Unlawful possession and use of unmanned aircraft systems with weapon attached. G.S. 14-401.24.

The citation for the listed offense, "Purchase or possession of firearms by person subject to domestic violation order prohibited," should read:

> G.S. 14-269.8; 50B-3.1(j).

Carrying a Concealed Weapon (page 587)

Statute (page 587)

2015 legislation, S.L. 2015-264, sec. 3, amended subsection (a), replacing the word "shurikin" with "shuriken." That same legislation also amended subsections (a), (a1), and (b1), making them gender-neutral.

2013 legislation, S.L. 2013-369, sec.1, enacted subsection (a2) of G.S. 14-269 as follows:

> **(a2)** This prohibition does not apply to a person who has a concealed handgun permit issued in accordance with Article 54B of this Chapter, has a concealed handgun permit considered valid under G.S. 14-415.24, or is exempt from obtaining a permit pursuant to G.S. 14-415.25, provided the weapon is a handgun, is in a closed compartment or container within the person's locked vehicle, and the vehicle is in a parking area that is owned or leased by State government. A person may unlock the vehicle to enter or exit the vehicle, provided the handgun remains in the closed compartment at all times and the vehicle is locked immediately following the entrance or exit.

2015 legislation, S.L. 2015-215, sec. 2.5, enacted a new subsection (b)(3a) as follows:

> **(3a)** A member of the North Carolina National Guard who has been designated in writing by the Adjutant General, State of North Carolina, who has a concealed handgun permit issued in accordance with Article 54B of this Chapter or considered valid under G.S. 14-415.24, and is acting in the discharge of his or her official duties, provided that the member does not carry a concealed weapon while consuming alcohol or an unlawful controlled substance or while alcohol or an unlawful controlled substance remains in the member's body.

2015 legislation, S.L. 2015-195, sec. 1(a), amended subsection (b)(4a) to now read as follows:

> **(4a)** Any person who is a district attorney, an assistant district attorney, or an investigator employed by the office of a district attorney and who has a concealed handgun permit issued in accordance with Article 54B of this Chapter or considered valid under G.S. 14-415.24; provided that the person shall not carry a concealed weapon at any time while in a courtroom or while consuming alcohol or an unlawful controlled substance or while alcohol or an unlawful controlled substance remains in the person's body. The district attorney, assistant district attorney, or investigator shall secure the weapon in a locked compartment when the weapon is not on the person of the district attorney, assistant district attorney, or investigator. Notwithstanding the provisions of this subsection, a district attorney may carry a concealed weapon while in a courtroom;

2013 legislation, S.L. 2013-369, sec. 25, amended subsection (b)(4b) to read as follows:

> **(4b)** Any person who is a qualified retired law enforcement officer as defined in G.S. 14-415.10 and meets any one of the following conditions:
> a. Is the holder of a concealed handgun permit in accordance with Article 54B of this Chapter.
> b. Is exempt from obtaining a permit pursuant to G.S. 14-415.25.
> c. Is certified by the North Carolina Criminal Justice Education and Training Standards Commission pursuant to G.S. 14-415.26;

Section 21 of that same law enacted subsections (b)(4d) and (4e) as follows:

> **(4d)** Any person who is a North Carolina district court judge, North Carolina superior court judge, or a North Carolina magistrate and who has a concealed handgun permit issued in accordance with Article 54B of this Chapter or considered valid under G.S. 14-415.24; provided that the person shall not carry a concealed weapon at any time while consuming alcohol or an unlawful controlled substance or while alcohol or an unlawful controlled substance

remains in the person's body. The judge or magistrate shall secure the weapon in a locked compartment when the weapon is not on the person of the judge or magistrate;

(4e) Any person who is serving as a clerk of court or as a register of deeds and who has a concealed handgun permit issued in accordance with Article 54B of this Chapter or considered valid under G.S. 14-415.24; provided that the person shall not carry a concealed weapon at any time while consuming alcohol or an unlawful controlled substance or while alcohol or an unlawful controlled substance remains in the person's body. The clerk of court or register of deeds shall secure the weapon in a locked compartment when the weapon is not on the person of the clerk of court or register of deeds. This subdivision does not apply to assistants, deputies, or other employees of the clerk of court or register of deeds;

2015 legislation, S.L. 2015-5, enacted subsection (b)(7) as follows:

(7) State correctional officers, when off-duty, provided that an officer does not carry a concealed weapon while consuming alcohol or an unlawful controlled substance or while alcohol or an unlawful controlled substance remains in the officer's body. If the concealed weapon is a handgun, the correctional officer must meet the firearms training standards of the Division of Adult Correction of the Department of Public Safety.

An additional piece of 2015 legislation, S.L. 2015-195, sec. 1(a), enacted new subsections (b)(7) and (8). As noted, other 2015 legislation also enacted a subsection (b)(7). Presumably this overlap will be reconciled by the codifier. The new subsections read as follows:

(7) A person employed by the Department of Public Safety who has been designated in writing by the Secretary of the Department, who has a concealed handgun permit issued in accordance with Article 54B of this Chapter or considered valid under G.S. 14-415.24, and has in the person's possession written proof of the designation by the Secretary of the Department, provided that the person shall not carry a concealed weapon at any time while consuming alcohol or an unlawful controlled substance or while alcohol or an unlawful controlled substance remains in the person's body.

(8) Any person who is an administrative law judge described in Article 60 of Chapter 7A of the General Statutes and who has a concealed handgun permit issued in accordance with Article 54B of this Chapter or considered valid under G.S. 14-415.24, provided that the person shall not carry a concealed weapon at any time while consuming alcohol or an unlawful controlled substance or while alcohol or an unlawful controlled substance remains in the person's body.

2014 legislation, S.L. 2014-119, sec. 12(a), amended subsection (c) of the statute to read:

(c) Any person violating the provisions of subsection (a) of this section shall be guilty of a Class 2 misdemeanor. Any person violating the provisions of subsection (a1) of this section shall be guilty of a Class 2 misdemeanor for the first offense and a Class H felony for a second or subsequent offense. A violation of subsection (a1) of this section punishable under G.S. 14-415.21(a) is not punishable under this section.

Carrying a Concealed Pistol or Gun (page 589)

Punishment (page 589)

As a result of 2014 legislation, S.L. 2014-119, sec. 12(a), punishment for a second or subsequent offense has been elevated to a Class H felony.

Elements (page 589)

The North Carolina Court of Appeals has held that the exception in G.S. 14-269(a1)(2) (having a permit) is a defense, not an element of this offense. State v. Mather, 221 N.C. App. 593, 602 (2012). This exception is listed as Element (5)(b). If this holding applies to the other (a1) exceptions, Element (5) in its entirety would be deleted and Elements (5)(a) through (c) would constitute defenses as well.

Notes (page 589)

Element (3) (page 589)

There was sufficient evidence that a weapon was concealed about the defendant's person where officers found one razor blade under a table in a room adjoining the defendant's cell and where the defendant had been seated earlier in the day; they found another on a ledge below the window in the defendant's cell, moments after he held such a blade in his hand while threatening an officer. State v. Hill, 227 N.C. App. 371, 380–82 (2013).

Element (5) generally (page 589)

The exception in G.S. 14-269(a1)(2) (having a permit) is a defense, not an essential element of this offense. *Mather*, 221 N.C. App. at 602. This holding is likely to apply to the (a1)(1) and (a1)(3) exceptions as well.

Element 5(b) (page 590)

This note mentions and cites G.S. 14-415.27 as exempting district attorneys and related individuals from the limitations in G.S. 14-415.11(c), provided the exemption is consistent with federal law. 2013 legislation, S.L. 2013-269, sec. 22, expanded the scope of G.S. 14-415.27 to also include judges, magistrates, clerks of court, and registers of deeds. 2015 legislation further expanded the scope of that provision. S.L. 2015-195, sec. 1(c).

As a result of 2013 and 2015 legislation, S.L. 2013-369, sec. 16; S.L. 2015-195, sec. 9, add the following to the end of the second paragraph of this note:

Additionally, a person who has a valid permit but carries a concealed handgun in violation of G.S. 14-415.11(c2) is guilty of a Class 1 misdemeanor. G.S. 14-415.21(a1).

Constitutionality (page 591)

G.S. 14-415.12 (criteria to qualify for a concealed handgun permit) was not unconstitutional as applied to the petitioner because the petitioner's right to carry a concealed handgun did not fall within the scope of the Second Amendment. Kelly v. Riley, 223 N.C. App. 261, 268 (2012).

Defenses (page 591)

The exception in G.S. 14-269(a1)(2) (having a permit) is a defense, not an element of this offense. *Mather*, 221 N.C. App. at 602. The State has no initial burden of producing evidence to show that the defendant's carrying a concealed weapon does not fall within the (a1) exception. *Id.* However, once the defendant puts forth evidence showing that his or her conduct falls within an exception, the burden of persuasion to show that the defendant's action was outside the exception falls on the prosecution. *Id.* These rules are likely to apply to the (a1)(1) and (a1)(3) exceptions as well.

Exceptions (page 591)

With respect to the fifth bullet in this list, 2015 legislation, S.L. 2015-195, sec. 1(a), amended the exception in G.S. 14-269(b)(4a) to provide, in relevant part: "Notwithstanding the provisions of this subsection, a district attorney may carry a concealed weapon while in a courtroom."

As a result of 2013 legislation, S.L. 2013-269, sec. 25, the sixth bullet in this note should be modified to read:

- qualified retired law enforcement officers, as defined in G.S. 14-415.10, who have concealed handgun permits in accordance with G.S. Chapter 14, Article 54B, are exempt from obtaining permits under G.S. 14-415.25, or are certified by the North Carolina Criminal Justice Education and Training Standards Commission under G.S. 14-415.26;

2013 legislation, S.L. 2013-269, secs. 1 and 21, enacted new exceptions to this crime. First, new G.S. 14-269(a2) provides that this offense does not apply to a person who has or is exempted from obtaining a concealed handgun permit when the weapon is a handgun, it is in a closed compartment or container in the person's locked vehicle, and the vehicle is in a parking area that is owned or leased by state government. Second, new G.S. 14-269(b)(4d) and (4e) provide exceptions for certain judges, magistrates, clerks, or registers of deeds in certain circumstances.

2015 legislation added additional exceptions. S.L. 2015-215, sec. 2.5, added an exception in new G.S. 14-269(b)(3a) pertaining to members of the North Carolina National Guard. S.L. 2015-5 added an exception in new G.S. 14-269(b)(7) pertaining to off-duty state correctional officers. S.L. 2015-195, sec. 1(a), added exceptions for certain persons employed by the Department of Public Safety and certain administrative law judges.

Multiple convictions and punishments (new note)

2014 legislation, S.L. 2014-119, sec. 12(a), amended G.S. 14-269(c) to provide that a violation of G.S. 14-269(a1) that is punishable under G.S. 14-415.21(a) (person with valid permit who is found to be carrying concealed handgun without the permit or who fails to disclose to any officer that the person holds a valid permit and is carrying a concealed handgun) is not punishable under G.S. 14-269.

Carrying a Concealed Weapon Other Than a Pistol or Gun (page 592)

Elements (page 592)

As a result of 2015 legislation, S.L. 2015-264, sec. 3, Element (4)(h) should now read as follows:

(h) shuriken

Possession of Weapons on School Grounds (page 594)

Statute (page 594)

2013 legislation, S.L. 2013-360, sec. 8.45(a), added a new subsection, (3a), to G.S. 14-269.2(a) as follows:

(3a) Volunteer school safety resource officer.—A person who volunteers as a school safety resource officer as provided by G.S. 162-26 or G.S. 160A-288.4.

As a result of recent legislation, S.L. 2013-360, sec. 8.45(b); S.L. 2014-119, sec. 9(a), G.S. 14-269.2(g) now reads as follows:

(g) This section shall not apply to any of the following:
(1)   A weapon used solely for educational or school-sanctioned ceremonial purposes, or used in a school-approved program conducted under the supervision of an adult whose supervision has been approved by the school authority.
(1a)   A person exempted by the provisions of G.S. 14-269(b).

(2) Firefighters, emergency service personnel, North Carolina Forest Service personnel, detention officers employed by and authorized by the sheriff to carry firearms, and any private police employed by a school, when acting in the discharge of their official duties.

(3) Home schools as defined in G.S. 115C-563(a).

(4) Weapons used for hunting purposes on the Howell Woods Nature Center property in Johnston County owned by Johnston Community College when used with the written permission of Johnston Community College or for hunting purposes on other educational property when used with the written permission of the governing body of the school that controls the educational property.

(5) A person registered under Chapter 74C of the General Statutes as an armed armored car service guard or an armed courier service guard when acting in the discharge of the guard's duties and with the permission of the college or university.

(6) A person registered under Chapter 74C of the General Statutes as an armed security guard while on the premises of a hospital or health care facility located on educational property when acting in the discharge of the guard's duties with the permission of the college or university.

(7) A volunteer school safety resource officer providing security at a school pursuant to an agreement as provided in G.S. 115C-47(61) and either G.S. 162-26 or G.S. 160A-288.4, provided that the volunteer school safety resource officer is acting in the discharge of the person's official duties and is on the educational property of the school that the officer was assigned to by the head of the appropriate local law enforcement agency.

2013 legislation, S.L. 2013-369, sec. 2, added new subsections, (i), (j), and (k), to the statute. 2015 legislation, S.L. 2015-195, sec. 2, amended subsection (k). The subsections now read as follows:

(i) The provisions of this section shall not apply to an employee of an institution of higher education as defined in G.S. 116-143.1 or a nonpublic post-secondary educational institution who resides on the campus of the institution at which the person is employed when all of the following criteria are met:

(1) The employee's residence is a detached, single-family dwelling in which only the employee and the employee's immediate family reside.

(2) The institution is either:
   a. An institution of higher education as defined by G.S. 116-143.1.
   b. A nonpublic post-secondary educational institution that has not specifically prohibited the possession of a handgun pursuant to this subsection.

(3) The weapon is a handgun.

(4) The handgun is possessed in one of the following manners as appropriate:
   a. If the employee has a concealed handgun permit that is valid under Article 54B of this Chapter, or who is exempt from obtaining a permit pursuant to that Article, the handgun may be on the premises of the employee's residence or in a closed compartment or container within the employee's locked vehicle that is located in a parking area of the educational property of the institution at which the person is employed and resides. Except for direct transfer between the residence and the vehicle, the handgun must remain at all times either on the premises of the employee's residence or in the closed compartment of the employee's locked vehicle. The employee may unlock the vehicle to enter or exit, but must lock the vehicle immediately following the entrance or exit if the handgun is in the vehicle.
   b. If the employee is not authorized to carry a concealed handgun pursuant to Article 54B of this Chapter, the handgun may be on the premises of the employee's residence, and may only be in the employee's vehicle

when the vehicle is occupied by the employee and the employee is immediately leaving the campus or is driving directly to their residence from off campus. The employee may possess the handgun on the employee's person outside the premises of the employee's residence when making a direct transfer of the handgun from the residence to the employee's vehicle when the employee is immediately leaving the campus or from the employee's vehicle to the residence when the employee is arriving at the residence from off campus.

(j) The provisions of this section shall not apply to an employee of a public or non-public school who resides on the campus of the school at which the person is employed when all of the following criteria are met:

(1) The employee's residence is a detached, single-family dwelling in which only the employee and the employee's immediate family reside.

(2) The school is either:

    a. A public school which provides residential housing for enrolled students.

    b. A nonpublic school which provides residential housing for enrolled students and has not specifically prohibited the possession of a handgun pursuant to this subsection.

(3) The weapon is a handgun.

(4) The handgun is possessed in one of the following manners as appropriate:

    a. If the employee has a concealed handgun permit that is valid under Article 54B of this Chapter, or who is exempt from obtaining a permit pursuant to that Article, the handgun may be on the premises of the employee's residence or in a closed compartment or container within the employee's locked vehicle that is located in a parking area of the educational property of the school at which the person is employed and resides. Except for direct transfer between the residence and the vehicle, the handgun must remain at all times either on the premises of the employee's residence or in the closed compartment of the employee's locked vehicle. The employee may unlock the vehicle to enter or exit, but must lock the vehicle immediately following the entrance or exit if the handgun is in the vehicle.

    b. If the employee is not authorized to carry a concealed handgun pursuant to Article 54B of this Chapter, the handgun may be on the premises of the employee's residence, and may only be in the employee's vehicle when the vehicle is occupied by the employee and the employee is immediately leaving the campus or is driving directly to their residence from off campus. The employee may possess the handgun on the employee's person outside the premises of the employee's residence when making a direct transfer of the handgun from the residence to the employee's vehicle when the employee is immediately leaving the campus or from the employee's vehicle to the residence when the employee is arriving at the residence from off campus.

(k) The provisions of this section shall not apply to a person who has a concealed handgun permit that is valid under Article 54B of this Chapter, or who is exempt from obtaining a permit pursuant to that Article, if any of the following conditions are met:

(1) The person has a handgun in a closed compartment or container within the person's locked vehicle or in a locked container securely affixed to the person's vehicle and only unlocks the vehicle to enter or exit the vehicle while the firearm remains in the closed compartment at all times and immediately locks the vehicle following the entrance or exit.

(2) The person has a handgun concealed on the person and the person remains in the locked vehicle and only unlocks the vehicle to allow the entrance or exit of another person.

(3) The person is within a locked vehicle and removes the handgun from concealment only for the amount of time reasonably necessary to do either of the following:

a. Move the handgun from concealment on the person to a closed compartment or container within the vehicle.

b. Move the handgun from within a closed compartment or container within the vehicle to concealment on the person.

2015 legislation, S.L. 2015-195, sec. 3, added a new subsection (l) as follows:

(l) It is an affirmative defense to a prosecution under subsection (b) or (f) of this section that the person was authorized to have a concealed handgun in a locked vehicle pursuant to subsection (k) of this section and removed the handgun from the vehicle only in response to a threatening situation in which deadly force was justified pursuant to G.S. 14-51.3.

Possession of Firearms on School Grounds (page 596)

Notes (page 596)

Element (1) (page 596)

Although the court of appeals held that the State must prove that the defendant both knowingly possessed or carried a prohibited weapon and knowingly entered educational property with that weapon, State v. Huckelba, ___ N.C. App. ___, 771 S.E.2d 809, 820 (2015), that decision was reversed by the supreme court on grounds that even if the trial court erred in its jury instructions, the error did not rise to the level of plain error. State v. Huckelba, 368 N.C. 569 (2015).

No criminal intent required (page 597)

Delete this note. Although *Haskins* held that no criminal intent was required, the statute subsequently was amended to add the element that the defendant acts knowingly.

Exceptions (page 597)

Recent legislation added several new exceptions to this offense:

- S.L. 2014-119, sec. 9(a), amended subsection G.S. 14-269.2(g)(2), creating an exception for detention officers employed by and authorized by the sheriff to carry firearms.
- S.L. 2013-360, sec. 8.45(b), added a new subsection G.S. 14-269.2(g)(7), creating an exception for certain volunteer school safety resource officers when acting in the discharge of their official duties on educational property.
- S.L. 2013-369, sec. 2, added new subsections G.S. 14-269.2(i) and (j), providing that the offense does not apply to certain school employees who reside at educational institutions and schools.
- S.L. 2013-369, sec. 2, also added new subsection G.S. 14-269.2(k), subsequently amended by S.L. 2015-195, sec. 2, providing that the offense does not apply to individuals who either have a valid concealed handgun permit or are exempt from obtaining a permit and have a handgun in a locked vehicle under circumstances specified in the statute.

Affirmative defense (new note)

It is an affirmative defense to a prosecution under subsection G.S. 14-269.2(b) or (f) that the person was authorized to have a concealed handgun in a locked vehicle pursuant to G.S. 14-269.2(k) and removed the handgun from the vehicle only in response to a threatening situation in which deadly force was justified pursuant to G.S. 14-51.3. G.S. 14-269.2(l).

Storing a Firearm in a Manner Accessible to a Minor (page 601)

Notes (page 602)

Element (5) (new note)

For a case where there was sufficient circumstantial evidence that the defendant stored or left a gun in a condition and manner accessible to a minor, see *State v. Lewis*, 222 N.C. App. 747, 750–51 (2012).

Carrying a Gun into an Assembly or Establishment Where Alcoholic Beverages Are Sold and Consumed (page 602)

Statute (page 602)

2013 legislation, S.L. 2013-369, sec. 3, amended subsection (b) of G.S. 14-269.3 to read as follows:

(b) This section shall not apply to any of the following:
  (1) A person exempted from the provisions of G.S. 14-269.
  (2) The owner or lessee of the premises or business establishment.
  (3) A person participating in the event, if the person is carrying a gun, rifle, or pistol with the permission of the owner, lessee, or person or organization sponsoring the event.
  (4) A person registered or hired as a security guard by the owner, lessee, or person or organization sponsoring the event.
  (5) A person carrying a handgun if the person has a valid concealed handgun permit issued in accordance with Article 54B of this Chapter, has a concealed handgun permit considered valid under G.S. 14-415.24, or is exempt from obtaining a permit pursuant to G.S. 14-415.25. This subdivision shall not be construed to permit a person to carry a handgun on any premises where the person in legal possession or control of the premises has posted a conspicuous notice prohibiting the carrying of a concealed handgun on the premises in accordance with G.S. 14-415.11(c).

Notes (page 603)
Exceptions (page 603)

As a result of 2013 legislation, S.L. 2013-369, sec. 3, add the following text at the end of this section:

- a person carrying a handgun who has a valid concealed handgun permit, who has a permit considered valid under G.S. 14-415.24, or who is exempt from obtaining a permit.

G.S. 14-269.3(b)(5). However, this last exception does not apply if the person in legal possession or control of the premises has posted a conspicuous notice prohibiting the carrying of a concealed handgun on the premises in accordance with G.S. 14-415.11(c). *Id.*

Weapons at Parades, etc. (page 604)

Statute (page 604)

2013 legislation, S.L. 2013-369, sec. 15, amended G.S. 14-277.2, adding a new subsection, (d), as follows:

> (d) The provisions of this section shall not apply to concealed carry of a handgun at a parade or funeral procession by a person with a valid permit issued in accordance with Article 54B of this Chapter, with a permit considered valid under G.S. 14-415.24, or who is exempt from obtaining a permit pursuant to G.S. 14-415.25. This subsection shall not be construed to permit a person to carry a concealed handgun on any premises where the person in legal possession or control of the premises has posted a conspicuous notice prohibiting the carrying of a concealed handgun on the premises in accordance with G.S. 14-415.11(c).

Notes (page 604)

Exceptions (page 604)

Pursuant to 2013 legislation, S.L. 2013-369, sec. 15, this offense does not apply to the concealed carry of a handgun at a parade or funeral procession by a person with a valid permit, with a permit considered valid under G.S. 14-415.24, or with an exemption from getting a permit under G.S. 14-415.25. G.S. 14-277.2(d) (enacted by S.L. 2013-369, sec. 15). However, this exception does not allow a person to carry a concealed handgun on premises where the person in legal possession or control has posted a conspicuous notice prohibiting the carrying of a concealed handgun in accordance with G.S. 14-415.11(c). *Id.*

Going Armed to the Terror of the People

This is not a new crime. It was deleted from the 7th edition of North Carolina Crimes but appears here again in response to requests for its inclusion.

Statute

This is a common law offense. State v. Dawson, 272 N.C. 535, 541–42 (1968); State v. Huntly, 25 N.C. 418, 418 (1843); State v. Staten, 32 N.C. App. 495, 496–97 (1977) (citing *Dawson*).

Elements

A person guilty of this offense

    (1) arms himself or herself with an unusual and dangerous weapon

    (2) for the purpose of terrifying others *and*

    (3) goes about on public highways

    (4) in a manner to cause terror to the people.

Punishment

Class 1 misdemeanor. G.S. 14-3(a); *Dawson*, 272 N.C. at 549 (offense is a misdemeanor).

Notes

Generally. For the elements of this offense, see *Dawson*, 272 N.C. at 549, and *Staten*, 32 N.C. App. at 497.

For a case where the evidence was sufficient to establish this offense, see, for example, *State v. Dawson*, 272 N.C. 531, 549 (1968) (armed with a carbine and four pistols, the defendant and three others drove on the public highways at night, firing bullets into a store and two homes).

Element (1). In *Huntly*, the court held that any gun is an unusual and dangerous weapon for purposes of this offense. State v. Huntly, 25 N.C. 418, 422 (1843). In that case it was argued that a gun cannot constitute an unusual weapon, "for there is scarcely a man in the community who does not own and occasionally use a gun of some sort." *Id.* The court rejected that argument, concluding: "A gun is an 'unusual weapon,' wherewith to be armed and clad. No man amongst us carries it about with him, as one of his every day accoutrements—as a part of his dress—and never we trust will the day come when any deadly weapon will be worn or wielded in our peace loving and law-abiding State, as an appendage of manly equipment." *Id.*; *see also* State v. Toler, ___ N.C. App. ___, 716 S.E.2d 875, *6 (2011) (unpublished) (gun was an unusual and dangerous weapon).

In *State v. Lanier*, 71 N.C. 288, 289 (1874), the defendant was charged with going armed to the terror of the people after riding a horse, at a canter, through a courthouse after court had adjourned. Witnesses saw no arms of any kind. The North Carolina Supreme Court "attach[ed] no importance to the fact that the defendant had no arms," stating, "we think it may be conceded that the driving or riding without arms through a court house or a crowded street at such a rate or in such a manner as to endanger the safety of the inhabitants amounts to a breach of the peace and is an indictable offence at common law." *Id.* at 290 (but going on to conclude that the trial court erred by instructing the jury that if they believed either one of the two witnesses, they must find the defendant guilty; the court determined that the circumstances of the defendant's act were relevant and created a jury issue, stating: "We conceive that the riding through a court house or a street at 12 o'clock at night, when no one is present, is a very different thing from riding through at 12 o'clock in the day, when the court house or street is full of people. The same act may be criminal or innocent, according to the surrounding circumstances.").

Element (2). The crime requires that the defendant act for the purpose of terrifying others. *See, e.g., Toler*, ___ N.C. App. ___, 716 S.E.2d 875, at *6 (the evidence was sufficient to establish that the defendant acted with the required purpose when he shot his gun on a public highway while driving closely behind another vehicle with his high beams on).

Element (3). It appears that the offense would not occur if the defendant remained on private property.

Element (4). In an unpublished case involving a charge of going armed to the terror of the people, the North Carolina Court of Appeals found this element satisfied where the defendant shot his gun while driving closely behind another vehicle on a public highway with his high beams on. State v. Toler, ___ N.C. App. ___, 716 S.E.2d 875, *6 (2011) (unpublished) (rejecting the defendant's argument that his actions were not "to the terror of the people" where the only people involved were those in the victim's car).

The offense of affray involves fighting in public to the terror of the people. For purposes of that offense, cases hold that if members of the public experience fear, the "to the terror of the people" element is satisfied. *In re* May, 357 N.C. 423, 428 (2003).

Relation to open carry. Because of the elements noted above, this offense would not apply to mere open carry. State v. Huntly, 25 N.C. 418, 422–23 (1843) ("[I]t is to be remembered that the carrying of a gun per se constitutes no offence. For any lawful purpose—either of business or amusement—the citizen is at perfect liberty to carry his gun. It is the wicked purpose—and the mischievous result—which essentially constitute the crime. He shall not carry about this or any other weapon of death to terrify and alarm, and in such manner as naturally will terrify and alarm, a peaceful people.").

23
Prostitution

2013 legislation, S.L. 2013-368, rewrote the state's prostitution offenses. As a result, delete the text of this chapter and replace it with the content that follows.

2015 legislation, S.L. 2015-181, secs. 17 and 18, made conforming changes to G.S. 14-203(5) and G.S. 14-205.2, which are reflected in the statutory text reproduced below.

Prostitution (new crime)

Statute

§ 14-203. Definition of terms.

The following definitions apply in this Article:

(1) Advance prostitution.—The term includes all of the following:

   a. Soliciting for a prostitute by performing any of the following acts when acting as other than a prostitute or a patron of a prostitute:

      1. Soliciting another for the purpose of prostitution.
      2. Arranging or offering to arrange a meeting of persons for the purpose of prostitution.
      3. Directing another to a place knowing the direction is for the purpose of prostitution.
      4. Using the Internet, including any social media Web site, to solicit another for the purpose of prostitution.

   b. Keeping a place of prostitution by controlling or exercising control over the use of any place that could offer seclusion or shelter for the practice of prostitution and performing any of the following acts when acting as other than a prostitute or a patron of a prostitute:

      1. Knowingly granting or permitting the use of the place for the purpose of prostitution.
      2. Granting or permitting the use of the place under circumstances from which the person should reasonably know that the place is used or is to be used for purposes of prostitution.
      3. Permitting the continued use of the place after becoming aware of facts or circumstances from which the person should know that the place is being used for the purpose of prostitution.

(2) Minor.—Any person who is less than 18 years of age.

(3) Profit from prostitution.—When acting as other than a prostitute, to receive anything of value for personally rendered prostitution services or to receive anything of value from a prostitute, if the thing received is not for lawful consideration and the person knows it was earned in whole or in part from the practice of prostitution.

(4)   Prostitute.—A person who engages in prostitution.

(5)   Prostitution.—The performance of, offer of, or agreement to perform vaginal intercourse, any sexual act as defined in G.S. 14-27.20, or any sexual contact as defined in G.S. 14-27.20, for the purpose of sexual arousal or gratification for any money or other consideration.

§ 14-204. Prostitution.

(a) Offense.—Any person who willfully engages in prostitution is guilty of a Class 1 misdemeanor.

(b) First Offender; Conditional Discharge.

(1)   Whenever any person who has not previously been convicted of or placed on probation for a violation of this section pleads guilty to or is found guilty of a violation of this section, the court, without entering a judgment and with the consent of such person, shall place the person on probation pursuant to this subsection.

(2)   When a person is placed on probation, the court shall enter an order specifying a period of probation of 12 months and shall defer further proceedings in the case until the conclusion of the period of probation or until the filing of a petition alleging violation of a term or condition of probation.

(3)   The conditions of probation shall be that the person (i) not violate any criminal statute of any jurisdiction, (ii) refrain from possessing a firearm or other dangerous weapon, (iii) submit to periodic drug testing at a time and in a manner as ordered by the court, but no less than three times during the period of the probation, with the cost of the testing to be paid by the probationer, (iv) obtain a vocational assessment administered by a program approved by the court, and (v) attend no fewer than 10 counseling sessions administered by a program approved by the court.

(4)   The court may, in addition to other conditions, require that the person do any of the following:

    a.   Make a report to and appear in person before or participate with the court or such courts, person, or social service agency as directed by the court in the order of probation.

    b.   Pay a fine and costs.

    c.   Attend or reside in a facility established for the instruction or residence of defendants on probation.

    d.   Support the person's dependents.

    e.   Refrain from having in the person's body the presence of any illicit drug prohibited by the North Carolina Controlled Substances Act, unless prescribed by a physician, and submit samples of the person's blood or urine or both for tests to determine the presence of any illicit drug.

(5)   Upon violation of a term or condition of probation, the court may enter a judgment on its original finding of guilt and proceed as otherwise provided.

(6)   Upon fulfillment of the terms and conditions of probation, the court shall discharge the person and dismiss the proceedings against the person. Upon the discharge of the person and dismissal of the proceedings against the person under this subsection, the person is eligible to apply for expunction of records pursuant to G.S. 15A-145.6.

(7)   Discharge and dismissal under this subsection shall not be deemed a conviction for purposes of structured sentencing or for purposes of disqualifications or disabilities imposed by law upon conviction of a crime.

(8)   There may be only one discharge and dismissal under this section.

(c) Immunity From Prosecution for Minors.—Notwithstanding any other provision of this section, if it is determined, after a reasonable detention for investigative purposes, that a person suspected of or charged with a violation of this section is a minor, that person shall be immune from prosecution under this section and instead shall be taken into temporary protective custody as an undisciplined juvenile pursuant to Article 19 of Chapter 7B of the General Statutes. Pursuant to the provisions of G.S. 7B-301, a law enforcement officer who takes a minor into custody under this section shall immediately report an allegation of a violation of G.S. 14-43.11 and G.S. 14-43.13 to the director of the department of social services in the county where the minor resides or is found, as appropriate, which shall commence an initial investigation into child abuse or child neglect within 24 hours pursuant to G.S. 7B-301 and G.S. 7B-302.

Elements

A person guilty of this offense

(1) willfully

(2) engages in prostitution.

Punishment

Class 1 misdemeanor. G.S. 14-204(a). For conditional discharge, see G.S. 14-204(b). For special probation conditions, see G.S. 14-205.4.

Notes

Element (1). See "Willfully" in Chapter 1 (States of Mind) of the main volume.

Element (2). "Prostitution" is the performance of, offer of, or agreement to perform vaginal intercourse, a sexual act, or sexual contact for the purpose of sexual arousal or gratification and for money or other consideration. G.S. 14-203(5).

"Sexual act" includes cunnilingus, fellatio, analingus, anal intercourse, and the penetration by any object into the genital or anal opening of another person's body, except when for accepted medical purposes. G.S. 14-203(5); 14-27.1(4) (this statute was recodified as G.S. 14-27.20 by 2015 legislation, S.L. 2015-181, sec. 2).

"Sexual contact" includes touching the sexual organ, anus, breast, groin, or buttocks of another; touching another with one's own sexual organ, anus, breast, groin, or buttocks; and ejaculating, emitting, or placing semen, urine, or feces on another. G.S. 14-203(5); 14-27.1(5) (this statute was recodified as G.S. 14-27.20 by 2015 legislation, S.L. 2015-181, sec. 2). "Touching" means physical contact, including through clothing. G.S. 14-27.1(6) (this statute was recodified as G.S. 14-27.20 by 2015 legislation, S.L. 2015-181, sec. 2).

Evidence issues. G.S. 14-206 provides that "testimony of a prior conviction, or testimony concerning the reputation of any place, structure, or building, and of the person or persons who reside in or frequent the same, and of the defendant" is admissible to prove this offense.

Immunity for minors. The law provides for immunity from prosecution for persons less than 18 years of age. G.S. 14-204(c); 14-203(2) (defining a "minor").

Related Offenses Not in This Chapter

"Crime against Nature" (Chapter 11)

"Fornication and Adultery" (Chapter 11)

Opposite sexes occupying same bedroom at hotel for immoral purposes; falsely registering as husband and wife. G.S. 14-186.

Keeping bawdy house. G.S. 14-188.

Solicitation of Prostitution

2015 legislation, S.L. 2015-183, amended the statute to now read as follows:

Statute

> **§ 14-205.1. Solicitation of prostitution.**
>
> (a) Except as otherwise provided in this section, any person who solicits another for the purpose of prostitution is guilty of a Class 1 misdemeanor for a first offense and a Class H felony for a second or subsequent offense. Any person 18 years of age or older who willfully solicits a minor for the purpose of prostitution is guilty of a Class G felony. Any person who willfully solicits a person who is severely or profoundly mentally disabled for the purpose of prostitution is guilty of a Class E felony. Punishment under this section may include participation in a program devised for the education and prevention of sexual exploitation (i.e. "John School"), where available. A person who violates this subsection shall not be eligible for a disposition of prayer for judgment continued under any circumstances.
>
> (b) Immunity From Prosecution for Minors.—Notwithstanding any other provision of this section, if it is determined, after a reasonable detention for investigative purposes, that a person suspected of or charged with a violation of this section is a minor who is soliciting as a prostitute, that person shall be immune from prosecution under this section and instead shall be taken into temporary protective custody as an undisciplined juvenile pursuant to Article 19 of Chapter 7B of the General Statutes. Pursuant to the provisions of G.S. 7B-301, a law enforcement officer who takes a minor into custody under this section shall immediately report an allegation of a violation of G.S. 14-43.11 and G.S. 14-43.13 to the director of the department of social services in the county where the minor resides or is found, as appropriate, which shall commence an initial investigation into child abuse or child neglect within 24 hours pursuant to G.S. 7B-301 and G.S. 7B-302.

Elements

A person guilty of this offense

(1) solicits another

(2) for prostitution.

Punishment

Class 1 misdemeanor for a first offense; Class H felony for a second or subsequent offense. G.S. 14-205.1. The statute provides for two enhanced versions of this offense. First, a person 18 years or older who willfully solicits a minor under 18 years old is guilty of a Class G felony. *Id.*; G.S. 14-203(2). Second, a person who willfully solicits a severely or profoundly mentally disabled person is guilty of a Class E felony. G.S. 14-205.1. The term "severely or profoundly mentally disabled" is not defined. The additional facts enhancing punishment must be alleged in the charging instrument and found by a jury, unless the defendant pleads guilty or no contest to the issue. For all versions of the offense, punishment may include participation in a "John School." *Id.* A prayer for judgment continued (PJC) is not allowed. *Id.* For special probation conditions, see G.S. 14-205.4.

Notes

Element (2). See "Prostitution," above in this supplement.

Evidence issues. See this note to "Prostitution," above in this supplement.

Immunity from prosecution (new note)
The statute provides for immunity from prosecution for minors who solicit as prostitutes. G.S. 14-205.1(b).

Related Offenses Not in This Chapter

See the offenses listed under "Prostitution," above in this supplement.

Patronizing a Prostitute

Statute

§ 14-205.2. Patronizing a prostitute.

(a) Any person who willfully performs any of the following acts with a person not his or her spouse commits the offense of patronizing a prostitute:

    (1)   Engages in vaginal intercourse, any sexual act as defined in G.S. 14-27.20, or any sexual contact as defined in G.S. 14-27.20, for the purpose of sexual arousal or gratification with a prostitute.

    (2)   Enters or remains in a place of prostitution with intent to engage in vaginal intercourse, any sexual act as defined in G.S. 14-27.20, or any sexual contact as defined in G.S. 14-27.20, for the purpose of sexual arousal or gratification.

(b) Except as provided in subsections (c) and (d) of this section, a first violation of this section is a Class A1 misdemeanor. Unless a higher penalty applies, a second or subsequent violation of this section is a Class G felony.

(c) A violation of this section is a Class F felony if the defendant is 18 years of age or older and the prostitute is a minor.

(d) A violation of this section is a Class D felony if the prostitute is a severely or profoundly mentally disabled person.

Elements

A person guilty of this offense

(1) willfully

(2) (a) (i)   engages in vaginal intercourse, a sexual act, or a sexual contact

          (ii) for the purpose of sexual arousal or gratification

          (iii) with a prostitute *or*

     (b) (i)   enters or remains

          (ii) in a place of prostitution

          (iii) with intent to engage in vaginal intercourse, a sexual act, or a sexual contact

          (iv) for the purpose of sexual arousal or gratification *and*

(3) the acts are done with a person who is not the defendant's spouse.

Punishment

A first offense is a Class A1 misdemeanor; a second or subsequent offense is a Class G felony. G.S. 14-205.2(b). There are two enhanced versions of this offense. First, a violation is a Class F felony if the defendant is 18 years old or older and the prostitute is less than 18 years old. G.S. 14-205.2(c); 14-203(2). Second, a violation is a Class D felony if the prostitute is severely or profoundly mentally disabled. G.S. 14-205.2(d). The additional facts enhancing punishment must be alleged in the charging instrument and found by a jury, unless the defendant pleads guilty or no contest to the issue. The term "severely or profoundly mentally disabled" is not defined. Both elevated versions of this offense qualify as sexually violent offenses for the purposes of the sex offender registration statutes. G.S. 14-190.13(5). For special probation conditions, see G.S. 14-205.4.

Notes

Element (1). See "Willfully" in Chapter 1 (States of Mind) of the main volume.

Element (2). The terms "sexual act" and "sexual contact" are defined in the note on Element (2) to "Prostitution," above in this supplement. A prostitute is "a person who engages in prostitution." G.S. 14-203(4).

Element (3). It is not clear if this provision is an element of the offense or a defense.

Evidence issues. See this note to "Prostitution," above in this supplement.

Related Offenses Not in This Chapter

See the offenses listed under "Prostitution," above in this supplement.

Promoting Prostitution

Statute

§ 14-205.3. Promoting prostitution.

(a) Any person who willfully performs any of the following acts commits promoting prostitution:

    (1)   Advances prostitution as defined in G.S. 14-203.

    (2)   Profits from prostitution by doing any of the following:

        a.   Compelling a person to become a prostitute.

        b.   Receiving a portion of the earnings from a prostitute for arranging or offering to arrange a situation in which the person may practice prostitution.

        c.   Any means other than those described in sub-subdivisions a. and b. of this subdivision, including from a person who patronizes a prostitute. This sub-subdivision does not apply to a person engaged in prostitution who is a minor. A person cannot be convicted of promoting prostitution under this sub-subdivision if the practice of prostitution underlying the offense consists exclusively of the accused's own acts of prostitution under G.S. 14-204.

(b) Any person who willfully performs any of the following acts commits the offense of promoting prostitution of a minor or mentally disabled person:

    (1)   Advances prostitution as defined in G.S. 14-203, where a minor or severely or profoundly mentally disabled person engaged in prostitution, or any person engaged in prostitution in the place of prostitution is a minor or is severely or profoundly mentally disabled at the time of the offense.

    (2)   Profits from prostitution by any means where the prostitute is a minor or is severely or profoundly mentally disabled at the time of the offense.

    (3)   Confines a minor or a severely or profoundly mentally disabled person against the person's will by the infliction or threat of imminent infliction of great bodily harm, permanent disability, or disfigurement or by administering to the minor or severely or profoundly mentally disabled person, without the person's consent or by threat or deception and for other than medical purposes, any alcoholic intoxicant or a drug as defined in Article 5 of Chapter 90 of the General Statutes (North Carolina Controlled Substances Act) and does any of the following:

        a.   Compels the minor or severely or profoundly mentally disabled person to engage in prostitution.

        b.   Arranges a situation in which the minor or severely or profoundly mentally disabled person may practice prostitution.

        c.   Profits from prostitution by the minor or severely or profoundly mentally disabled person.

For purposes of this subsection, administering drugs or an alcoholic intoxicant to a minor or a severely or profoundly mentally disabled person, as described in subdivision (3) of this subsection, shall be deemed to be without consent if the administering is done without the consent of the parents or legal guardian or if the administering is performed or permitted by the parents or legal guardian for other than medical purposes. Mistake of age is not a defense to a prosecution under this subsection.

(c) Unless a higher penalty applies, a violation of subsection (a) of this section is a Class F felony. A violation of subsection (a) of this section by a person with a prior conviction for a violation of this section or a violation of G.S. 14-204 (prostitution), G.S. 14-204.1 (solicitation of prostitution), or G.S. 14-204.2 (patronizing a prostitute) is a Class E felony.

(d) Unless a higher penalty applies, a violation of subdivision (1) or (2) of subsection (b) of this section is a Class D felony. A violation of subdivision (3) of subsection (b) of this section is a Class C felony. Any violation of subsection (b) of this section by a person with a prior conviction for a violation of this section or a violation of G.S. 14-204 (prostitution), G.S. 14-204.1 (solicitation of prostitution), G.S. 14-204.2 (patronizing a prostitute) is a Class C felony.

Elements

A person guilty of this offense

(1) willfully

(2) (a) advances prostitution *or*

(b) profits from prostitution.

Punishment

Class F felony. G.S. 14-205.3(c). Class E felony if the defendant has a prior conviction for this offense, for prostitution (G.S. 14-204), for solicitation of prostitution (G.S. 14-204.1), or for patronizing a prostitute (G.S. 14-204.2). G.S. 14-205.3(c). For special probation conditions, see G.S. 14-205.4.

Notes

Element (1). See "Willfully" in Chapter 1 (States of Mind) of the main volume.

Element (2)(a). A person advances prostitution when, acting as other than a prostitute or a patron of a prostitute, he or she:

- solicits another for prostitution,
- arranges or offers to arrange a meeting of people for prostitution,
- directs another to a place knowing the direction is for prostitution, or
- uses the Internet, including social media, to solicit another for prostitution.

G.S. 14-203(1)(a). A person also advances prostitution by keeping a place of prostitution. This means controlling or exercising control over the use of a place that could offer seclusion or shelter for prostitution and performing any of the following acts, when acting as other than a prostitute or a prostitute's patron:

- knowingly granting or permitting the use of the place for prostitution,
- granting or permitting the use of the place under circumstances from which the person should reasonably know that the place is used or is to be used for prostitution, or
- permitting the continued use of the place when the person should know that the place is being used for prostitution.

G.S. 14-203(1)(b).

Element (2)(b). To profit from prostitution means "[w]hen acting as other than a prostitute, to receive anything of value for personally rendered prostitution services or to receive anything of value from a prostitute, if the thing received is not for lawful consideration and the person knows it was earned in whole or in part from the practice of prostitution." G.S. 14-203(3). The profiting may occur by compelling a person to become a prostitute; by receiving a portion of the earnings from a prostitute for arranging or offering to arrange a situation in which the person may practice prostitution; or by any other means. G.S. 14-205.3(a)(2). However, profiting from prostitution "by any other means" does not apply to a minor engaged in prostitution or when the practice of prostitution underlying the offense consists exclusively of the defendant's own acts of prostitution under G.S. 14-204. G.S. 14-205.3(a)(2)c.

Evidence issues. See this note to "Prostitution," above in this supplement.

Related Offenses Not in This Chapter

See the offenses listed under "Prostitution," above in this supplement.

Promoting Prostitution of a Minor or Mentally Disabled Person

Statute

See G.S. 14-205.3(b), reproduced above in this supplement under "Promoting Prostitution."

Elements

A person guilty of this offense

   (1) willfully
   (2) (a) (i) advances prostitution *and*
           (ii) a minor or severely or profoundly mentally disabled person engaged in prostitution, *or*
           (iii) any person engaged in prostitution in the place of prostitution is a minor or severely or profoundly mentally disabled person, *or*
       (b) (i) profits from prostitution *and*
           (ii) the prostitute is
               1. a minor *or*
               2. a severely or profoundly mentally disabled person, *or*
       (c) (i) confines
           (ii) a minor or a severely or profoundly mentally disabled person
           (iii) against the person's will
           (iv) by
               1. the infliction or threat of imminent infliction of great bodily harm, permanent disability, or disfigurement *or*
               2. administering an alcoholic intoxicant or controlled substance, without consent or by threat or deception and for non-medical purposes, *and*
           (v) does any of the following:
               1. compels the minor or severely or profoundly mentally disabled person to engage in prostitution,
               2. arranges a situation for the minor or severely or profoundly mentally disabled person to practice prostitution, *or*
               3. profits from the minor or severely or profoundly mentally disabled person's prostitution.

Punishment

If Elements (2)(a) or (b) are involved, Class D felony. G.S. 14-205.3(d). If Element (2)(c) is involved, Class C felony. *Id.* Additionally, if the person has a prior conviction for violating this statute, G.S. 14-204 (prostitution), G.S. 14-204.1 (solicitation of prostitution), or G.S. 14-204.2 (patronizing a prostitute), punishment is as a Class C felony. G.S. 14-205.3(d). For special probation conditions, see G.S. 14-205.4.

Notes

Element (1). See "Willfully" in Chapter 1 (States of Mind) of the main volume.

Element (2) generally. A minor is a person under 18 years old. G.S. 14-203(2). The statute does not define the term "severely or profoundly mentally disabled."

Element (2)(a). "Advances prostitution" is defined under "Promoting Prostitution," above in this supplement.

Element (2)(c)(iii). Administering drugs or alcoholic intoxicants is deemed to be without consent if it is done without the consent of the parents or legal guardian or is performed or permitted by the parents or legal guardian for non-medical purposes. G.S. 14-205.3(b).

Mistake of age. Mistake of age is not a defense. G.S. 14-205.3(b).

Evidence issues. See this note to "Prostitution," above in this supplement.

Sex offender registration. A conviction of this offense triggers sex offender registration requirements. G.S. 14-190.13(5) (as amended by S.L. 2013-368, sec. 18).

Related Offenses Not in This Chapter

See the offenses listed under "Prostitution," above in this supplement.

24

Obscenity, Exploitation of a Minor, and Adult Establishment Offenses

---

Sexual Exploitation of a Minor (page 633)

Second-Degree Sexual Exploitation of a Minor (page 635)
Notes (page 636)

Element (1) (new note)
There was sufficient evidence that the defendant was aware of the contents of pornographic files found on his computer where, among other things, the files' titles clearly indicated that they contained pornographic images of children. State v. Jones, ___ N.C. App. ___, 789 S.E. 2d 651, 658 (2016).

Element (2) (new note)
A defendant's act of downloading images from the Internet onto his computer constituted a "duplication" within the meaning of the statute. State v. Williams, 232 N.C. App. 152, 157–58 (2014) (deciding this issue of first impression).

Multiple convictions and punishments (page 636)
In *State v. Williams*, 232 N.C. App. 152, 158–60 (2014), the court rejected the defendant's argument that the General Assembly did not intend to punish defendants for both receiving and possessing the same images.

Disclosure of Private Images (new crime)

This offense was enacted in 2015. S.L. 2015-250.

Statute

§ 14-190.5A. Disclosure of private images.
(a) Definitions.—The following definitions apply in this section:
(1) Disclose.—Transfer, publish, distribute, or reproduce.
(2) Image.—A photograph, film, videotape, recording, digital, or other reproduction.

(3) Intimate parts.—Any of the following naked human parts: (i) male or female genitals, (ii) male or female pubic area, (iii) male or female anus, or (iv) the nipple of a female over the age of 12.

(4) Personal relationship.—As defined in G.S. 50-B-1(b).

(5) Reasonable expectation of privacy.—When a depicted person has consented to the disclosure of an image within the context of a personal relationship and the depicted person reasonably believes that the disclosure will not go beyond that relationship.

(6) Sexual conduct.—Includes any of the following:

    a. Vaginal, anal, or oral intercourse, whether actual or simulated, normal or perverted.

    b. Masturbation, excretory functions, or lewd exhibition of uncovered genitals.

    c. An act or condition that depicts torture, physical restraint by being fettered or bound, or flagellation of or by a nude person or a person clad in undergarments or in revealing or bizarre costume.

(b) Offense.—A person is guilty of disclosure of private images if all of the following apply:

(1) The person knowingly discloses an image of another person with the intent to do either of the following:

    a. Coerce, harass, intimidate, demean, humiliate, or cause financial loss to the depicted person.

    b. Cause others to coerce, harass, intimidate, demean, humiliate, or cause financial loss to the depicted person.

(2) The depicted person is identifiable from the disclosed image itself or information offered in connection with the image.

(3) The depicted person's intimate parts are exposed or the depicted person is engaged in sexual conduct in the disclosed image.

(4) The person discloses the image without the affirmative consent of the depicted person.

(5) The person discloses the image under circumstances such that the person knew or should have known that the depicted person had a reasonable expectation of privacy.

(c) Penalty.—A violation of this section shall be punishable as follows:

(1) For an offense by a person who is 18 years of age or older at the time of the offense, the violation is a Class H felony.

(2) For a first offense by a person who is under 18 years of age at the time of the offense, the violation is a Class 1 misdemeanor.

(3) For a second or subsequent offense by a person who is under the age of 18 at the time of the offense, the violation is a Class H felony.

(d) Exceptions.—This section does not apply to any of the following:

(1) Images involving voluntary exposure in public or commercial settings.

(2) Disclosures made in the public interest, including, but not limited to, the reporting of unlawful conduct or the lawful and common practices of law enforcement, criminal reporting, legal proceedings, medical treatment, or scientific or educational activities.

(3) Providers of an interactive computer service, as defined in 47 U.S.C. § 230(f), for images provided by another person.

(e) Destruction of Image.—In addition to any penalty or other damages, the court may award the destruction of any image made in violation of this section.

(f) Other Sanctions or Remedies Not Precluded.—A violation of this section is an offense additional to other civil and criminal provisions and is not intended to repeal or preclude any other sanctions or remedies.

(g) Civil Action.—In addition to any other remedies at law or in equity, including an order by the court to destroy any image disclosed in violation of this section, any person whose image is disclosed, or used, as described in subsection (b) of this section, has a civil cause of action against any person who discloses or uses the image and is entitled to recover from the other person any of the following:

(1) Actual damages, but not less than liquidated damages, to be computed at the rate of one thousand dollars ($1,000) per day for each day of the violation or in the amount of ten thousand dollars ($10,000), whichever is higher.

(2) Punitive damages.

(3) A reasonable attorneys' fee and other litigation costs reasonably incurred.

The civil cause of action may be brought no more than one year after the initial discovery of the disclosure, but in no event may the action be commenced more than seven years from the most recent disclosure of the private image.

Elements

A person guilty of this offense:

(1) knowingly

(2) discloses an image of another person

(3) with the intent to

    (a) coerce, harass, intimidate, demean, humiliate, or cause financial loss to the depicted person, or

    (b) cause others to coerce, harass, intimidate, demean, humiliate, or cause financial loss to the depicted person, and

(4) the depicted person is identifiable from the disclosed image or from information offered in connection with it,

(5) the depicted person's intimate parts are exposed or the depicted person is engaged in sexual conduct in the disclosed image,

(6) the person discloses the image without the affirmative consent of the depicted person, and

(7) the person discloses the image under circumstances such that he or she knew or should have known that the depicted person had a reasonable expectation of privacy.

Punishment

If the defendant is 18 or older at the time of the offense, Class H felony. G.S. 14-190.5A(c)(1). If the defendant is less than 18 years old at the time of the offense, a first offense is a Class 1 misdemeanor and a second or subsequent offense is a Class H felony. G.S. 14-190.5A(c)(2) & (3).

Notes

Element (1). See "Knowingly" in Chapter 1 (States of Mind) of the main volume.

Element (2). To "disclose" means to transfer, publish, distribute, or reproduce. G.S. 14-190.5A(a)(1). The term "image" includes a photograph, film, videotape, recording, digital, or other reproduction. *Id.* at (a)(2).

Element (5). The term "intimate parts" means any of the following naked human parts: genitals, pubic area, anus, or the nipple of a female over the age of 12. G.S. 14-190.5A(a)(3). The term "sexual conduct" means any of the following:

- vaginal, anal, or oral intercourse, whether actual or simulated, normal or perverted;
- masturbation, excretory functions, or lewd exhibition of uncovered genitals;
- an act or condition that depicts torture, physical restraint by being fettered or bound, or flagellation of or by a nude person or a person clad in undergarments or in revealing or bizarre costume.

G.S. 14-190.5A(a)(6). This is the same definition of sexual conduct that applies with respect to obscenity. G.S. 14-190.1(c).

Element (7). The term "reasonable expectation of privacy" is defined as follows: "When a depicted person has consented to the disclosure of an image within the context of a personal relationship and the depicted person reasonably believes that the disclosure will not go beyond that relationship." G.S. 14-190.5A(a)(5). "Personal relationship" is defined by reference to G.S. 50B-1(b); it thus means a relationship where the parties

- are current or former spouses;
- are persons of opposite sex who live or have lived together;
- are related as parents and children, including others acting in loco parentis to a minor child or as grandparents and grandchildren;
- have a child in common;
- are current or former household members;
- are persons of opposite sex who are in a dating relationship or have been in a dating relationship.

G.S. 50B-1(b). A dating relationship "is one wherein the parties are romantically involved over time and on a continuous basis during the course of the relationship. A casual acquaintance or ordinary fraternization between persons in a business or social context is not a dating relationship." *Id.*

Exceptions. The statute carves out exceptions for

- images involving voluntary exposure in public or commercial settings and
- disclosures made in the public interest, including, but not limited to, the reporting of unlawful conduct or the lawful and common practices of law enforcement, criminal reporting, legal proceedings, medical treatment, or scientific or educational activities.

G.S. 14-190.5A(d)(1) & (2). The statute also provides an exception for "[p]roviders of an interactive computer service, as defined in 47 U.S.C. § 230(f), for images provided by another person." *Id.* at (d)(3).

Destruction of images. The court may order the destruction of images made in violation of the statute. G.S. 14-190.5A(e).

Multiple convictions and punishments. Punishment for this offense does not preclude punishment for some other criminal offense that might apply to the conduct at issue. G.S. 14-190.5A(f).

Civil action. Prosecution for this offense does not preclude civil sanctions or remedies. *Id.* In fact, the statute sets out a civil cause of action. G.S. 14-190.5A(g).

25
Lotteries, Gambling, and Related Offenses

Lottery Offenses (page 645)

Advertising a Lottery (page 645)
Related Offenses Not in This Chapter (page 646)

Replace the related offense that reads "Unlawful bingo. G.S. 14-309.5; 14-309.12" with the following:

Unlawful bingo. G.S. 14-309.5; 14-309.12; 14-309.14.

Gambling (page 650)
Notes (page 651)
Exceptions (page 651)
2012 legislation, S.L. 2012-6, enacted G.S. 14-292.2, making lawful certain Class III gaming on Indian lands.

Possession of a Slot Machine (page 651)
Notes (page 653)
Exceptions (page 653)
2012 legislation, S.L. 2012-6, enacted G.S. 14-292.2, making lawful certain Class III gaming on Indian lands.

Operation, etc. of a Video Gaming Machine (page 654)

Statute (page 654)

G.S. 14-306.1A(e) was repealed by 2012 legislation, S.L. 2012-6, sec. 3.

Notes (page 655)

Exceptions (page 655)

Delete the first sentence (and related citations) of this note and replace it with the following:

2012 legislation, S.L. 2012-6, enacted G.S. 14-292.2, making lawful certain Class III gaming on Indian lands.

Electronic Sweepstakes (page 657)

Notes (page 659)

Element (3) (page 659)

A sweepstakes can be conducted through the use of an entertaining display even if the prize is revealed to the patron before he or she plays the game. State v. Spruill, 237 N.C. App. 383, 386–87 (2014).

Constitutionality (new note)

In *Hest Technologies, Inc. v. North Carolina*, 366 N.C. 289 (2012), the court held that G.S. 14-306.4 does not violate the First Amendment. *See also* Sandhill Amusements v. North Carolina, 366 N.C. 323 (2012) (per curiam) (same).

26
Abandonment and Nonsupport

Abandonment and Nonsupport—Children (page 666)

Nonsupport of an Illegitimate Child (page 667)

2013 legislation, S.L. 2013-198, sec. 17, amended G.S. 49-2 to substitute the term "child born out of wedlock" for the term "illegitimate child."

27
Drug Offenses

Statute (page 673)

As a result of 2015 and 2016 legislation, S.L. 2015-299, sec. 2; S.L. 2016-93, sec. 6, add the following sentence at the end of subsection G.S. 90-87(16):

> The term does not include industrial hemp as defined in G.S. 106-568.51, when the industrial hemp is produced and used in compliance with rules issued by the North Carolina Industrial Hemp Commission.

2015 legislation, S.L. 2015-162, sec. 1, amended G.S. 90-89, adding new controlled substances to Schedule I as follows:

(1) eee. Acetyl Fentanyl.

(3) ff. Methoxetamine (other names: MXE, 3-MeO-2-Oxo-PCE).

(6) NBOMe Compounds.—Any material compound, mixture, or preparation which contains any quantity of the following substances, including its salts, isomers, and salts of isomers whenever the existence of such salts, isomers, and salts of isomers is possible within the specific chemical designation unless specifically excepted or unless listed in another schedule:

a. 25B-NBOMe (2C-B-NBOMe)—2-(4-Bromo-2,5-dimethoxyphenyl)-N-(2-methoxybenzyl)ethanamine.

b. 25C-NBOMe (2C-C-NBOMe)—2-(4-Chloro-2,5-dimethoxyphenyl)-N-(2-methoxybenzyl)ethanamine.

c. 25D-NBOMe (2C-D-NBOMe)—2-(2,5-dimethoxy-4-methylphenyl)-N-(2-methoxybenzyl)ethanamine.

d. 25E-NBOMe (2C-E-NBOMe)—2-(4-Ethyl-2,5-dimethoxyphenyl)-N-(2-methoxybenzyl)ethanamine.

e. 25G-NBOMe (2C-G-NBOMe)—2-(2,5-dimethoxy-3,4-dimethylphenyl)-N-(2-methoxybenzyl)ethanamine.

f. 25H-NBOMe (2C-H-NBOMe)—2-(2,5-dimethoxyphenyl)-N-(2-methoxybenzyl)ethanamine.

g. 25I-NBOMe (2C-I-NBOMe)—2-(4-Iodo-2,5-dimethoxyphenyl)-N-(2-methoxybenzyl)ethanamine.

h. 25N-NBOMe (2C-N-NBOMe)—2-(2,5-dimethoxy-4-nitrophenyl)-N-(2-methoxybenzyl)ethanamine.

i. 25P-NBOMe (2C-P-NBOMe)—2-(4-Propyl-2,5-dimethoxyphenyl)-N-(2-methoxybenzyl)ethanamine.

j. 25T2-NBOMe (2C-T2-NBOMe)—2,5-dimethoxy-N-[(2-methoxyphenyl)methyl]-4-(methylthio)-benzeneethanamine.

k. 25T4-NBOMe (2C-T4-NBOMe)—2,5-dimethoxy-N-[(2-methoxyphenyl)methyl]-4-[(1-methylethyl)thio]-benzeneethanamine.

l. 25T7-NBOMe (2C-T7-NBOMe)—2,5-dimethoxy-N-[(2-methoxyphenyl)methyl]-4-(propylthio)-benzeneethanamine.

That same legislation, sec. 2, amended G.S. 90-90(3)d. to now read as follows:

    d.   Methylphenidate, including its salts, isomers, and salts of its isomers.

2016 legislation, S.L. 2016-113, sec. 9, amended subsection (32) of G.S. 90-91(k) (definition of anabolic steroid) to read as follows:

32.   Any salt, ester, or isomer of a drug or substance described or listed in this subsection, if that salt, ester, or isomer promotes muscle growth. Except such term does not include (i) an anabolic steroid which is expressly intended for administration through implants to cattle or other nonhuman species and which has been approved by the Secretary of Health and Human Services for such administration or (ii) chorionic gonadotropin when administered by injection for veterinary use by a licensed veterinarian or the veterinarian's designated agent. If any person prescribes, dispenses, or distributes such steroid for human use, such person shall be considered to have prescribed, dispensed, or distributed an anabolic steroid within the meaning of this subsection.

2013 legislation, S.L. 2013-109, and 2015 legislation, S.L. 2015-162, sec. 3, amended G.S. 90-94(3) to read as follows:

(3)   Synthetic cannabinoids.—Any quantity of any synthetic chemical compound that (i) is a cannabinoid receptor agonist and mimics the pharmacological effect of naturally occurring substances or (ii) has a stimulant, depressant, or hallucinogenic effect on the central nervous system that is not listed as a controlled substance in Schedule I through V, and is not an FDA-approved drug. Synthetic cannabinoids include, but are not limited to, the substances listed in sub-subdivisions a. through j. of this subdivision and any substance that contains any quantity of their salts, isomers (whether optical, positional, or geometric), homologues, and salts of isomers and homologues, unless specifically excepted, whenever the existence of these salts, isomers, homologues, and salts of isomers and homologues is possible within the specific chemical designation. The following substances are examples of synthetic cannabinoids and are not intended to be inclusive of the substances included in this Schedule:

    a.   Naphthoylindoles. Any compound containing a 3-(1-naphthoyl)indole structure with substitution at the nitrogen atom of the indole ring by an alkyl, haloalkyl, alkenyl, cycloalkylmethyl, cycloalkylethyl, 1-(N-methyl-2-piperidinyl)methyl, or 2-(4-morpholinyl)ethyl group, whether or not further substituted in the indole ring to any extent and whether or not substituted in the naphthyl ring to any extent. Some trade or other names: JWH-015, JWH-018, JWH-019, JWH-073, JWH-081, JWH-122, JWH-200, JWH-210, JWH-398, AM-2201, WIN 55-212.

    b.   Naphthylmethylindoles. Any compound containing a 1H-indol-3-yl-(1-naphthyl)methane structure with substitution at the nitrogen atom of the indole ring by an alkyl, haloalkyl, alkenyl, cycloalkylmethyl, cycloalkylethyl, 1-(N-methyl-2-piperidinyl)methyl, or 2-(4-morpholinyl) ethyl group, whether or not further substituted in the indole ring to any extent and whether or not substituted in the naphthyl ring to any extent.

    c.   Naphthoylpyrroles. Any compound containing a 3-(1-naphthoyl) pyrrole structure with substitution at the nitrogen atom of the pyrrole ring by an alkyl, haloalkyl, alkenyl, cycloalkylmethyl, cycloalkylethyl, 1-(N-methyl-2-piperidinyl)methyl, or 2-(4-morpholinyl)ethyl group, whether or not further substituted in the pyrrole ring to any extent and whether or not substituted in the naphthyl ring to any extent. Another name: JWH-307.

    d.   Naphthylmethylindenes. Any compound containing a naphthylideneindene structure with substitution at the 3-position of the indene ring by an alkyl, haloalkyl, alkenyl, cycloalkylmethyl, cycloalkylethyl, 1-(N-methyl-2-piperidinyl)methyl, or 2-(4-morpholinyl)ethyl group, whether or not further substituted in the indene ring to any extent and whether or not substituted in the naphthyl ring to any extent.

e. Phenylacetylindoles. Any compound containing a 3-phenylacetylindole structure with substitution at the nitrogen atom of the indole ring by an alkyl, haloalkyl, alkenyl, cycloalkylmethyl, cycloalkylethyl, 1-(N-methyl-2-piperidinyl)methyl, or 2-(4-morpholinyl)ethyl group, whether or not further substituted in the indole ring to any extent and whether or not substituted in the phenyl ring to any extent. Some trade or other names: SR-18, RCS-8, JWH-250, JWH-203.

f. Cyclohexylphenols. Any compound containing a 2-(3-hydroxycyclohexyl)phenol structure with substitution at the 5-position of the phenolic ring by an alkyl, haloalkyl, alkenyl, cycloalkylmethyl, cycloalkylethyl, 1-(N-methyl-2-piperidinyl)methyl, or 2-(4-morpholinyl)ethyl group, whether or not substituted in the cyclohexyl ring to any extent. Some trade or other names: CP 47,497 (and homologues), cannabicyclohexanol.

g. Benzoylindoles. Any compound containing a 3-(benzoyl)indole structure with substitution at the nitrogen atom of the indole ring by an alkyl, haloalkyl, alkenyl, cycloalkylmethyl, cycloalkylethyl, 1-(N-methyl-2-piperidinyl)methyl, or 2-(4-morpholinyl)ethyl group, whether or not further substituted in the indole ring to any extent and whether or not substituted in the phenyl ring to any extent. Some trade or other names: AM-694, Pravadoline (WIN 48,098), RCS-4.

h. 2,3-Dihydro-5-methyl-3-(4-morpholinylmethyl)pyrrolo[1,2,3-de]-1, 4-benzoxazin-6-yl]-1-napthalenylmethanone. Some trade or other names: WIN 55,212-2.

i. (6aR,10aR)-9-(hydroxymethyl)-6, 6-dimethyl-3-(2-methyloctan-2-yl)-6a,7,10,10a-tetrahydrobenzo[c]chromen-1-ol 7370. Some trade or other names: HU-210.

j. 3-(cyclopropylmethanone) indole or 3-(cyclobutylmethanone) indole or 3-(cyclopentylmethanone) indole by substitution at the nitrogen atom of the indole ring, whether or not further substituted in the indole ring to any extent, whether or not further substituted on the cyclopropyl, cyclobutyl, or cyclopentyl rings to any extent. Substances in this class include, but are not limited to: UR-144, fluoro-UR-144, XLR-11, A-796,260 and A-834,735.

k. Indole carboxaldehydes. Any compound structurally derived from 1H-indole-3-carboxaldehyde or 1H-indole-2-carboxaldehyde substituted in both of the following ways:

1. At the nitrogen atom of the indole ring by an alkyl, haloalkyl, cyanoalkyl, alkenyl, cycloalkylmethyl, cycloalkylethyl, 1-(N-methyl-2-piperidinyl)methyl, 2-(4-morpholinyl)ethyl, 1-(N-methyl-2-pyrrolidinyl)methyl, 1-(N-methyl-3-morpholinyl) methyl, tetrahydropyranylmethyl, benzyl, or halo benzyl group; and

2. At the carbon of the carboxaldehyde by a phenyl, benzyl, naphthyl, adamantyl, cyclopropyl, or propionaldehyde group.

Whether or not the compound is further modified to any extent in the following ways: (i) substitution to the indole ring to any extent, (ii) substitution to the phenyl, benzyl, naphthyl, adamantyl, cyclopropyl, or propionaldehyde group to any extent, (iii) a nitrogen heterocyclic analog of the indole ring, or (iv) a nitrogen heterocyclic analog of the phenyl, benzyl, naphthyl, adamantyl, or cyclopropyl ring. Substances in this class include but are not limited to: AB-001.

l.   Indole carboxamides. Any compound structurally derived from 1H-indole-3-carboxamide or 1H-indole-2-carboxamide substituted in both of the following ways:

1.   At the nitrogen atom of the indole ring by an alkyl, haloalkyl, cyanoalkyl, alkenyl, cycloalkylmethyl, cycloalkylethyl, 1-(N-methyl-2-piperidinyl)methyl, 2-(4-morpholinyl)ethyl, 1-(N-methyl-2-pyrrolidinyl)methyl, 1-(N-methyl-3-morpholinyl) methyl, tetrahydropyranylmethyl, benzyl, or halo benzyl group; and

2.   At the nitrogen of the carboxamide by a phenyl, benzyl, naphthyl, adamantyl, cyclopropyl, or propionaldehyde group.

Whether or not the compound is further modified to any extent in the following ways: (i) substitution to the indole ring to any extent, (ii) substitution to the phenyl, benzyl, naphthyl, adamantyl, cyclopropyl, or propionaldehyde group to any extent, (iii) a nitrogen heterocyclic analog of the indole ring, or (iv) a nitrogen heterocyclic analog of the phenyl, benzyl, naphthyl, adamantyl, or cyclopropyl ring. Substances in this class include, but are not limited to: SDB-001 and STS-135.

m.   Indole carboxylic acids. Any compound structurally derived from 1H-indole-3-carboxylic acid or 1H-indole-2-carboxylic acid substituted in both of the following ways:

1.   At the nitrogen atom of the indole ring by an alkyl, haloalkyl, cyanoalkyl, alkenyl, cycloalkylmethyl, cycloalkylethyl, 1-(N-methyl-2-piperidinyl)methyl, 2-(4-morpholinyl)ethyl, 1-(N-methyl-2-pyrrolidinyl)methyl, 1-(N-methyl-3-morpholinyl) methyl, tetrahydropyranylmethyl, benzyl, or halo benzyl group; and

2.   At the hydroxyl group of the carboxylic acid by a phenyl, benzyl, naphthyl, adamantyl, cyclopropyl, or propionaldehyde group.

Whether or not the compound is further modified to any extent in the following ways: (i) substitution to the indole ring to any extent, (ii) substitution to the phenyl, benzyl, naphthyl, adamantyl, cyclopropyl, or propionaldehyde group to any extent, (iii) a nitrogen heterocyclic analog of the indole ring, or (iv) a nitrogen heterocyclic analog of the phenyl, benzyl, naphthyl, adamantyl, or cyclopropyl ring. Substances in this class include, but are not limited to: PB-22 and fluoro-PB-22.

n.   Indazole carboxaldehydes. Any compound structurally derived from 1H-indazole-3-carboxaldehyde or 1H-indazole-2-carboxaldehyde substituted in both of the following ways:

1.   At the nitrogen atom of the indazole ring by an alkyl, haloalkyl, cyanoalkyl, alkenyl, cycloalkylmethyl, cycloalkylethyl, 1-(N-methyl-2-piperidinyl)methyl, 2-(4-morpholinyl)ethyl, 1-(N-methyl-2-pyrrolidinyl)methyl, 1-(N-methyl-3-morpholinyl) methyl, tetrahydropyranylmethyl, benzyl, or halo benzyl group; and

2.   At the carbon of the carboxaldehyde by a phenyl, benzyl, naphthyl, adamantyl, cyclopropyl, or propionaldehyde group.

Whether or not the compound is further modified to any extent in the following ways: (i) substitution to the indazole ring to any extent, (ii) substitution to the phenyl, benzyl, naphthyl, adamantyl, cyclopropyl, or propionaldehyde group to any extent, (iii) a nitrogen heterocyclic analog of the indazole ring, or (iv) a nitrogen heterocyclic analog of the phenyl, benzyl, naphthyl, adamantyl, or cyclopropyl ring.

o. Indazole carboxamides. Any compound structurally derived from 1H-indazole-3-carboxamide or 1H-indazole-2-carboxamide substituted in both of the following ways:
   1. At the nitrogen atom of the indazole ring by an alkyl, halo-alkyl, cyanoalkyl, alkenyl, cycloalkylmethyl, cycloalkylethyl, 1-(N-methyl-2-piperidinyl)methyl, 2-(4-morpholinyl)ethyl, 1-(N-methyl-2-pyrrolidinyl)methyl, 1-(N-methyl-3-morpholinyl) methyl, tetrahydropyranylmethyl, benzyl, or halo benzyl group; and
   2. At the nitrogen of the carboxamide by a phenyl, benzyl, naphthyl, adamantyl, cyclopropyl, or propionaldehyde group.

   Whether or not the compound is further modified to any extent in the following ways: (i) substitution to the indazole ring to any extent, (ii) substitution to the phenyl, benzyl, naphthyl, adamantyl, cyclopropyl, or propionaldehyde group to any extent, (iii) a nitrogen heterocyclic analog of the indazole ring, or (iv) a nitrogen heterocyclic analog of the phenyl, benzyl, naphthyl, adamantyl, or cyclopropyl ring. Substances in this class include, but are not limited to: AKB-48, fluoro-AKB-48, APIN-CACA, AB-PINACA, AB-FUBINACA, ADB-FUBINACA, and ADB-PINACA.

p. Indazole carboxylic acids. Any compound structurally derived from 1H-indazole-3-carboxylic acid or 1H-indazole-2-carboxylic acid substi-tuted in both of the following ways:
   1. At the nitrogen atom of the indazole ring by an alkyl, halo-alkyl, cyanoalkyl, alkenyl, cycloalkylmethyl, cycloalkylethyl, 1-(N-methyl-2-piperidinyl)methyl, 2-(4-morpholinyl)ethyl, 1-(N-methyl-2-pyrrolidinyl)methyl, 1-(N-methyl-3-morpholinyl) methyl, tetrahydropyranylmethyl, benzyl, or halo benzyl group; and
   2. At the hydroxyl group of the carboxylic acid by a phenyl, benzyl, naphthyl, adamantyl, cyclopropyl, or propionaldehyde group.

   Whether or not the compound is further modified to any extent in the following ways: (i) substitution to the indazole ring to any extent, (ii) substitution to the phenyl, benzyl, naphthyl, adamantyl, cyclopropyl, or propionaldehyde group to any extent, (iii) a nitrogen heterocyclic analog of the indazole ring, or (iv) a nitrogen heterocyclic analog of the phenyl, benzyl, naphthyl, adamantyl, or cyclopropyl ring.

As a result of recent legislation, S.L. 2013-124; S.L. 2014-115, sec. 41(a); S.L. 2015-32, sec. 1, G.S. 90-95(d1) should read as follows:

(d1) (1) Except as authorized by this Article, it is unlawful for any person to:
   a. Possess an immediate precursor chemical with intent to manufacture a controlled substance; or
   b. Possess or distribute an immediate precursor chemical knowing, or hav-ing reasonable cause to believe, that the immediate precursor chemical will be used to manufacture a controlled substance; or
   c. Possess a pseudoephedrine product if the person has a prior conviction for the possession of methamphetamine, possession with the intent to sell or deliver methamphetamine, sell or deliver methamphetamine, trafficking methamphetamine, possession of an immediate precursor chemical, or manufacture of methamphetamine. The prior conviction may be from any jurisdiction within the United States.

   Except where the conduct is covered under subdivision (2) of this subsection, any person who violates this subdivision shall be punished as a Class H felon.

As a result of 2015 legislation, S.L. 2015-32, sec. 1, G.S. 90-95(d2) now reads as follows:

(d2) The immediate precursor chemicals to which subsection (d1) of this section applies are those immediate precursor chemicals designated by the Commission pursuant to its authority under G.S. 90-88, and the following (until otherwise specified by the Commission):

  (1) Acetic anhydride.
  (2) Acetone.
(2a) Ammonium nitrate.
(2b) Ammonium sulfate.
  (3) Anhydrous ammonia.
  (4) Anthranilic acid.
  (5) Benzyl chloride.
  (6) Benzyl cyanide.
  (7) 2 Butanone (Methyl Ethyl Ketone).
  (8) Chloroephedrine.
  (9) Chloropseudoephedrine.
(10) D lysergic acid.
(11) Ephedrine.
(12) Ergonovine maleate.
(13) Ergotamine tartrate.
(13a) Ether based starting fluids.
(14) Ethyl ether.
(15) Ethyl Malonate.
(16) Ethylamine.
(17) Gamma butyrolactone.
(18) Hydrochloric Acid. (Muriatic Acid).
(19) Iodine.
(20) Isosafrole.
(21) Sources of lithium metal.
(22) Malonic acid.
(23) Methylamine.
(24) Methyl Isobutyl Ketone.
(25) N acetylanthranilic acid.
(26) N ethylephedrine.
(27) N ethylpseudoephedrine.
(28) N methylephedrine.
(29) N methylpseudoephedrine.
(30) Norpseudoephedrine.
(30a) Petroleum based organic solvents such as camping fuels and lighter fluids.
(31) Phenyl 2 propane.
(32) Phenylacetic acid.
(33) Phenylpropanolamine.
(34) Piperidine.
(35) Piperonal.
(36) Propionic anhydride.
(37) Pseudoephedrine.
(38) Pyrrolidine.
(39) Red phosphorous.
(40) Safrole.
(40a) Sodium hydroxide (Lye).
(41) Sources of sodium metal.
(42) Sulfuric Acid.
(43) Tetrachloroethylene.
(44) Thionylchloride.
(45) Toluene.

Sale or Delivery and Related Offenses (page 694)

Sale or Delivery of a Controlled Substance (page 694)

Punishment (page 694)

Delete the third paragraph of this note and replace it with the following:

> The delivery of a Schedule III, IV, V, or VI substance is a Class I felony; the sale of a Schedule III, IV, V, or VI substance is a Class H felony. G.S. 90-95(b)(2).

Notes (page 694)

Element (2)(b) (page 694)

The State need not show that the defendant personally received compensation in exchange for the delivery. State v. Land, 223 N.C. App. 305, 313 (2012), *aff'd per curiam*, 366 N.C. 550 (2013).

> A synthetic cannabinoid is defined by G.S. 90-94(3).

Attempt and conspiracy (page 695)

Insert the following after the second sentence of this note:

> *See also* State v. Warren, ___ N.C. App. ___, 780 S.E.2d 835, 845 (2015) (applying G.S. 90-98 and holding that conspiracy to manufacture methamphetamine was properly punished as a Class C felony).

Jury instructions (new note)

Where the evidence showed that the defendant transferred less than 5 grams of marijuana, the trial court erred by not instructing the jury that in order to prove delivery, the State was required to prove that the defendant transferred the marijuana for remuneration. *Land*, 223 N.C. App. at 315.

Multiple convictions and punishments (page 696)

For another case standing for the proposition stated in this note that a defendant may not be separately convicted of both the sale and delivery of a controlled substance arising from a single transaction, see *State v. Fleig*, 232 N.C. App. 647, 650–51 (2014) (purchaser gave the defendant $20 for a bag of marijuana; purchaser then asked for another bag in light of the payment made and the defendant provided it).

Related Offenses Not in This Chapter (page 696)

As a result of 2016 legislation, S.L. 2016-93, sec. 5, add the following to this section:

> Distributing, dispensing, delivering, or purchasing marijuana on property used for industrial hemp production or in a manner intended to disguise the marijuana due to its proximity to industrial hemp. G.S. 106-568.57(a).

Furnishing a Controlled Substance to an Inmate (page 697)

Related Offenses Not in This Chapter (page 698)

As a result of 2015 legislation, S.L. 2015-47, delete the third offense listed here and replace it with the following:

> Furnishing alcoholic beverages, tobacco products, or mobile phones to an inmate or a delinquent juvenile. G.S. 14-258.1(b)–(d).

As a result of a 2014 legislative change, S.L. 2014-119, sec. 5(a), delete the last offense listed here and replace it with the following:

> Inmate's possession of a tobacco product. G.S. 14-258.1(e).
>
> Inmate's possession of a mobile phone or wireless communication device or component. G.S. 14-258.1(f).

Manufacture of a Controlled Substance (page 698)

Notes (page 699)

Element (2) (page 699)

Where officers find a controlled substance and an array of items used to package and distribute that substance, the evidence suffices to support a manufacturing conviction. State v. Miranda, 235 N.C. App. 601, 612 (2014) (evidence was sufficient where more than 28 grams of cocaine and several items that are commonly used to weigh, separate, and package cocaine for sale were seized from the defendant's bedroom). There was sufficient evidence of manufacturing methamphetamine where an officer observed the defendant and another person at the scene for approximately 40 minutes and among the items recovered there were a handbag containing a syringe and methamphetamine, a duffle bag containing a clear two liter bottle containing methamphetamine, empty boxes and blister packs of pseudoephedrine, a full pseudoephedrine blister pack, an empty pack of lithium batteries, a lithium battery from which the lithium had been removed, iodized salt, sodium hydroxide, drain opener, funnels, tubing, coffee filters, syringes, various items of clothing, and a plastic bottle containing white and pink granular material; the defendant's presence at the scene, the evidence recovered, the officer's testimony that the defendant and his accomplice were going back and forth in the area moving bottles, and testimony that the defendant gave instructions to his accomplice to keep the smoke out of her eyes was sufficient evidence of manufacturing. State v. Davis, 236 N.C. App. 376, 382–83 (2014).

Element (4) (page 699)

For additional cases supporting the proposition that in a manufacturing case based on preparing or compounding the State must prove intent to distribute, see *Miranda*, 235 N.C. App. at 610 (stating this requirement but finding no plain error where the trial court allowed the jury to find the defendant guilty of manufacturing by packaging as well as compounding and the undisputed evidence showed that he packed the controlled substance), and *State v. Simpson*, 230 N.C. App. 119, 124–25 (2013) (reiterating this requirement but finding no plain error where a jury instruction on this issue was lacking).

Multiple convictions and punishments (new note)

No double jeopardy violation occurs when a defendant is convicted of trafficking in methamphetamine, manufacturing methamphetamine, and possession of methamphetamine based on the same illegal substance. *Simpson*, 230 N.C. App. at 126–27.

Related Offenses Not in This Chapter (page 698)

As a result of 2016 legislation, S.L. 2016-93, sec. 5, add the following to this section:

> Manufacture of marijuana on property used for industrial hemp production or in a manner intended to disguise the marijuana due to its proximity to industrial hemp. G.S. 106-568.57(a).

Possession Offenses (page 700)

Possession of a Controlled Substance (page 700)

Punishment (page 701)

A synthetic cannabinoid is defined by G.S. 90-94(3).

In the first bulleted list in this section, replace the word "cocoa" with "coca."

This note states that for all misdemeanor controlled substance offenses, several provisions—including G.S. 90-95(e)(3) —elevate punishment based on the defendant's prior conviction record. Because G.S. 90-95(e)(3) operates as sentence enhancement and does not proscribe a separate offense, a misdemeanor enhanced under this provision is not subject to habitual felon status. State v. Howell, ___ N.C. App. ___, 792 S.E.2d 898, 900–01 (2016), *temporary stay allowed*, ___ N.C. App. ___, 794 S.E.2d 345 (Dec. 20, 2016).

Notes (page 702)

Element (1) (page 702)

A presumption that the defendant has the required guilty knowledge is created when the State makes a prima facie case that the defendant has committed a crime, such as possession of a controlled substance, trafficking by possession, or trafficking by transportation, that lacks a specific intent element. State v. Galaviz-Torres, 368 N.C. 44 (2015). However, when the defendant denies or contests having knowledge of the controlled substance that he or she has been charged with possessing or transporting, the existence of the requisite guilty knowledge becomes an issue of fact that must be decided by the jury. *Id.*; State v. Coleman, 227 N.C. App. 354, 359–60 (2013) (trafficking by possession case; the trial court committed plain error by failing to instruct on this element; although the defendant did not testify or present evidence to raise the issue of knowledge as a disputed fact, the State presented evidence that the defendant told a detective that he did not know the container contained heroin; this constituted a contention that the defendant did not know the true identity of what he possessed). For example, when the defendant admits having possession of a box stored in his or her car but denies knowing that the box contained the controlled substance at issue, whether the defendant knowingly possessed the controlled substance is an issue for the jury. *Coleman*, 227 N.C. App. at 359. By contrast, the defendant's denial of any knowledge of having possessed any container or controlled substance does not defeat the presumption and likewise does not create an issue on which the jury must be instructed. *Galaviz-Torres*, 368 N.C. 44 (in this trafficking case the defendant did not deny knowledge of the contents of a gift bag in which the cocaine was found or admit that he possessed a particular substance while denying any knowledge of the substance's identity; rather, the defendant denied having had any knowledge that the van he was driving contained either the gift bag or cocaine).

For a trafficking and possession with intent case where the evidence was insufficient to establish that the defendant knowingly possessed or transported the controlled substance, see *State v. Velazquez-Perez*, 233 N.C. App. 585, 588–93 (2014) (drugs were found in secret compartments of a truck driven by the defendant Villalvavo but owned by a passenger, Velazquez-Perez, who hired Villalvavo to drive the truck; while evidence regarding the truck's log books may have been incriminating as to Velazquez-Perez, it did not apply to Villalvavo, who had not been working for Velazquez-Perez long and had no stake in the company or control over Velazquez-Perez; Villalvavo's nervousness during the stop did not constitute adequate incriminating circumstances).

Element (2) (page 702)

For additional cases holding that the evidence was sufficient to establish constructive possession, see *State v. Lindsey*, 366 N.C. 325 (2012) (reversing 219 N.C. App. 249 (2012) for the reasons stated in the dissenting opinion, which found sufficient evidence of constructive possession where, after the defendant fled from his crashed van, officers found a bag containing marijuana near trash receptacles in the parking lot; detailed evidence concerning the distance of the bag from the defendant's van, the condition of the bag, and the fact that the van's passenger window was open supported the inference that the defendant discarded the bag while fleeing); *State v. Bradshaw*, 366 N.C. 90, 96–97 (2012) (sufficient evidence of constructive possession of drugs and a rifle when those items were found in a bedroom that was not under the defendant's exclusive control but several documents linked him to the contraband and placed him in the room within two days of when the contraband was found); *State v. Davis*, 236 N.C. App. 376, 383–84 (2014) (there was sufficient evidence that the defendant constructively possessed methamphetamine found in a duffle bag where, among other things, the defendant and his accomplice were the only people at the scene of the "one pot" outdoor meth lab and for approximately 40 minutes both moved freely about the site where all of the items were laid out on a blanket); *State v. Rodelo*, 231 N.C. App. 660, 665–66 (2014) (in a trafficking by possession case, there was sufficient evidence of constructive possession where the defendant was found hiding alone in a tractor-trailer where money was secreted; cocaine was found in a car parked, with its doors open, in close proximity to the tractor-trailer; the cash and the cocaine were packaged similarly; wrappings were all over the tractor-trailer and in the open area of a car parked close by; the defendant admitted knowing where the money was hidden; and the entire warehouse where the vehicles were had a chemical smell of cocaine); *State v. Torres-Gonzalez*, 227 N.C. App. 188, 195 (2013) (sufficient evidence in a trafficking by possession case involving an undercover sale); *State v. Hazel*, 226 N.C. App. 336, 344 (2013) (sufficient evidence that the defendant constructively possessed heroin found in an apartment that was not owned or rented by him); *State v. Chisholm*, 225 N.C. App. 592, 597 (2013) (sufficient evidence of constructive possession even though the defendant did not have exclusive possession of the bedroom where the drugs were found); *State v. Huerta*, 221 N.C. App. 436, 448–49 (2012) (sufficient evidence of constructive possession where the defendant admitted living for three years at the home where the drugs were found; where an illegally purchased pistol, ammunition, and more than $9,000 in cash were in his closet; and where he had more than $2,000 in cash on his person); and *State v. Adams*, 218 N.C. App. 589, 594–95 (2012) (sufficient evidence of constructive possession where the defendant drove a drug provider to a location that the defendant had arranged for a drug sale, knowing that the provider had the drugs).

For cases where there was insufficient evidence of constructive possession, see *State v. Holloway*, ___ N.C. App. ___, 793 S.E.2d 766, 772 (2016) (the only evidence tying the defendant to the residence or the contraband was his presence at the residence on the afternoon in question and a single photograph of him found face down in a plastic storage bin in a bedroom of the residence), *temporary stay allowed*, ___ N.C. App. ___, ___ S.E.2d ___ (Dec. 20, 2016); *State v. Dulin*, ___ N.C. App. ___, 786 S.E.2d 803, 810–11 (2016) (there was insufficient evidence that the defendant constructively possessed marijuana found in an uncovered fishing boat located in the yard of a home occupied by multiple people, including the defendant; the boat was roughly 70 feet from the house in an unfenced area; there was no evidence that the defendant had any ownership interest in or possession of the boat; and the defendant was never seen near the boat); and *State v. Garrett*, ___ N.C. App. ___, 783 S.E.2d 780, 784 (2016) (there was insufficient evidence of constructive possession of methamphetamine in a case that arose out of a controlled drug buy where, although the defendant led individuals to a trailer to buy drugs and entered the trailer with their money, the other individuals were the only ones who actually possessed the drugs).

Exceptions (new note)

Before searching a person or his or her premises or vehicle, an officer may ask the person whether a hypodermic needle or other sharp object that may cut or puncture the officer is on the defendant's person or in the premises or vehicle to be searched. If such an object is present and the person alerts the officer of that fact before the search, the person may not be charged with or prosecuted for possession of drug paraphernalia for the needle or sharp object or for possession of residual amounts of a controlled substance contained in the needle or sharp object. G.S. 90-113.22(c), as amended by S.L. 2015-284, sec 2.

Greater and lesser-included offenses (page 706)

Simple possession is a lesser-included offense of possession of a controlled substance on the premises of a local confinement facility, and a defendant may not be convicted of both when they stem from the same act of possession. State v. Barnes, 229 N.C. App. 556, 568–69 (2013), *aff'd*, 367 N.C. 453 (2014) (per curiam).

Multiple convictions and punishments (page 706)

No double jeopardy violation occurs when a defendant is convicted of trafficking in methamphetamine, manufacturing methamphetamine, and possession of methamphetamine based on the same illegal substance. State v. Simpson, 230 N.C. App. 119, 126–27 (2013).

Limited immunity from prosecution (new note)

A 2013 law, S.L. 2013-23, provides limited immunity from prosecution for persons seeking medical assistance for themselves or others in the event of a drug-related overdose. The law enacts G.S. 90-96.2, providing that a person who experiences a drug-related overdose or who seeks medical assistance for someone experiencing a drug-related overdose shall not be prosecuted for

- a misdemeanor offense under G.S. 90-95(a)(3) or
- a felony offense under G.S. 90-95(a)(3) involving less than 1 gram of cocaine or heroin

if the evidence of the crime was obtained as a result of the person seeking medical assistance. G.S. 90-96.2(b), (c). The term "drug-related overdose" means "an acute condition, including mania, hysteria, extreme physical illness, coma, or death resulting from the consumption or use of a controlled substance, or another substance with which a controlled substance was combined, and that a layperson would reasonably believe to be a drug overdose that requires medical assistance." G.S. 90-96.2(a).

2016 legislation, S.L. 2016-88, sec. 4, enacted G.S. 90-113.27(c), providing limited immunity for employees, volunteers, and participants in authorized needle and hypodermic syringe exchange programs when those persons possess residual amounts of a controlled substance contained in a used needle, hypodermic syringe, or injection supplies obtained from or returned to a program.

Possession of a Controlled Substance at a Prison or Local Confinement Facility (page 707)

Notes (page 707)

Element (1) (new note)

This offense is a general intent crime, and there is no requirement that a defendant specifically intended to possess the controlled substance on the premises of a local confinement facility. State v. Barnes, 229 N.C. App. 556, 561–66 (2013), *aff'd*, 367 N.C. 453 (2014) (per curiam) (rejecting the defendant's argument that he did not voluntarily enter the premises but was brought to the facility by officers against his wishes; the fact that the officers failed to warn the defendant that taking a controlled substance into the jail would constitute a separate offense was of no consequence).

Element (2) (new note)

The defendant's own testimony that he had a "piece of dope . . . in the jail" was sufficient evidence that he possessed a controlled substance on the premises. State v. Poole, 223 N.C. App. 185, 194 (2012).

Greater and lesser-included offenses (new note)

Simple possession is a lesser-included offense of possession of a controlled substance on the premises of a local confinement facility, and a defendant may not be convicted of both when they stem from the same act of possession. *Barnes*, 229 N.C. App. at 568–69.

Possession of a Controlled Substance with Intent to Manufacture, Sell, or Deliver (page 708)

Notes (page 708)

Element (4) (page 708)

There was sufficient evidence of the requisite intent with respect to 84.8 grams of marijuana found in the defendant's car where the marijuana was in multiple containers, including four dime bags, and a box of sandwich bags, digital scales, and a large quantity of cash in small denominations also were found. State v. Blakney, 233 N.C. App. 516, 520 (2014).

Related Offenses Not in This Chapter (page 710)

As a result of 2016 legislation, S.L. 2016-93, sec. 5, add the following to this section:

> Possession with intent to manufacture, distribute, dispense, deliver, or purchase marijuana on property used for industrial hemp production or in a manner intended to disguise the marijuana due to its proximity to industrial hemp. G.S. 106-568.57(a).

Possession of an Immediate Precursor with Intent to Manufacture a Controlled Substance (page 710)

Statute (page 710)

As noted above in this supplement, the list of immediate precursor chemicals in G.S. 90-95(d2) was amended by 2015 legislation. S.L. 2015-32, sec.1.

Notes (page 711)

Element (3) (page 711)

As noted above in this supplement, the list of immediate precursor chemicals in G.S. 90-95(d2) was amended by 2015 legislation. S.L. 2015-32, sec.1.

> In a case involving possession of pseudoephedrine with intent to manufacture methamphetamine, the court held that the evidence was sufficient even though the pseudoephedrine had not been identified through a chemical analysis. State v. Hooks, ___ N.C. App. ___, 777 S.E.2d 133, 140–41 (2015) (reasoning that chemical analysis is required only for a "controlled substance" and that pseudoephedrine is not such a substance).

Possession of Pseudoephedrine after Methamphetamine Conviction (new crime)

This offense was enacted by 2013 legislation, S.L. 2013-124, sec. 1, and amended by S.L. 2015-32, sec.1.

Statute

See G.S. 90-95(d1)(1)c., reproduced above in this supplement.

Elements

A person guilty of this offense

(1) possesses

(2) a pseudoephedrine product *and*

(3) has a prior conviction for

    (a) possession of methamphetamine

    (b) possession with the intent to sell or deliver methamphetamine,

    (c) sale or delivery of methamphetamine,

    (d) trafficking in methamphetamine,

    (e) possession of an immediate precursor chemical, *or*

    (f) manufacture of methamphetamine.

Punishment

Class H felony. G.S. 90-95(d1).

Notes

Element (1). See the note on Element (2) to "Possession of a Controlled Substance" in the main volume.

Element (3). The prior conviction may be from any jurisdiction within the United States. G.S. 90-95(d1)(1)c.

Strict liability (new note)

This is a strict liability offense. State v. Miller, ___ N.C. App. ___, 783 S.E.2d 512, 516, *review allowed*, ___ N.C. ___, 787 S.E.2d 21 (2016).

Constitutionality (new note)

In *State v. Miller*, ___ N.C. App. ___, 783 S.E.2d 512, *review allowed*, ___ N.C. ___, 787 S.E.2d 21 (2016), the court held that the defendant's due process rights were violated by his conviction of this "strict liability offense criminalizing otherwise innocuous and lawful behavior without providing him notice that a previously lawful act had been transformed into a felony for the subset of convicted felons to which he belonged." The court found that "the absence of any notice to [the defendant] that he was subject to serious criminal penalties for an act legal for most people, most convicted felons, and indeed, for [the defendant] himself only a few weeks previously [before the new law went into effect], renders the new subsection unconstitutional as applied to him." *Id.* at 518.

Related Offenses Not in This Chapter

See the offenses listed under "Possession of an Immediate Precursor with Intent to Manufacture a Controlled Substance." in the main volume.

Counterfeit Controlled Substance Offenses (page 711)

Creating a Counterfeit Controlled Substance (page 711)

Notes (page 712)

Element (3) (page 712)

For another case supporting the statement in this note that the State need not prove all of the factors in G.S. 90-87(6)b. to prove that the substance was intentionally misrepresented, see *State v. Chisholm*, 225 N.C. App. 592, 595 (2013).

Trafficking (page 721)

Statute (page 721)

2012 legislation, S.L. 2012-188, sec. 5, amended G.S. 90-95(h), adding time to the maximum sentences for drug trafficking to cover early release onto post-release supervision. The act adds three months to the maximum sentences for Class C, D, and E trafficking and nine months to the maximum sentences for Class F, G, and H trafficking.

Trafficking in Marijuana (page 725)

Punishment (page 725)

For 2012 legislative changes to the punishment provision, see "Statute," above in this supplement under "Trafficking."

Notes (page 726)

Element (1) (page 726)

See this note to "Possession of a Controlled Substance," above in this supplement.

In a trafficking by possession and transportation case there was sufficient evidence of knowing possession and transportation where the defendant drove the vehicle that contained the cocaine. State v. Lopez, 219 N.C. App. 139, 149–50 (2012).

For a case where the evidence was insufficient to establish that the defendant knowingly possessed or transported the controlled substance, see *State v. Velazquez-Perez*, 233 N.C. App. 585, 588–93 (2014) (drugs were found in secret compartments of a truck driven by the defendant Villalvavo but owned by a passenger, Velazquez-Perez, who hired Villalvavo to drive the truck; while evidence regarding the truck's log books may have been incriminating as to Velazquez-Perez, it did not apply to Villalvavo, who had not been working for Velazquez-Perez long and had no stake in the company or control over Velazquez-Perez; Villalvavo's nervousness during the stop did not constitute adequate incriminating circumstances).

Element (3) (page 727)

As a result of 2015 and 2016 legislation, S.L. 2015-299, sec. 2; S.L. 2016-93, sec. 6, add the following at the end of this note, before the ending quotation mark:

The term does not include industrial hemp as defined in G.S. 106-568.51, when the industrial hemp is produced and used in compliance with rules issued by the North Carolina Industrial Hemp Commission.

Element (5) (page 727)

When a defendant simultaneously possesses more than one cache of controlled substances, the amounts of each cache may—in certain circumstances—be combined to reach the trafficking amount. State v. Hazel, 226 N.C. App. 336, 347 (2013) (trafficking in heroin by possession case; amount of heroin recovered from the defendant's person outside the apartment was combined with heroin recovered from the apartment).

Greater and lesser-included offenses (page 728)

Conspiracy to traffic in cocaine is not a lesser-included offense of trafficking in cocaine. State v. Rodelo, 231 N.C. App. 660, 667 (2014).

Multiple convictions and punishments (page 728)

No double jeopardy violation occurs when a defendant is convicted of trafficking in methamphetamine, manufacturing methamphetamine, and possession of methamphetamine based on the same illegal substance. State v. Simpson, 230 N.C. App. 119, 126–27 (2013).

Relation to other offenses (page 729)

Delete this note.

Trafficking in Synthetic Cannabinoids (page 729)

Punishment (page 729)

For 2012 legislative changes to the punishment provision, see "Statute," above in this supplement under "Trafficking."

Notes (page 730)

Elements (3) and (5) (new note)

A synthetic cannabinoid is defined in G.S. 90-94(3), reproduced at the beginning of this chapter in this supplement.

Element (5) (page 730)

When a defendant simultaneously possesses more than one cache of controlled substances, the amounts of each cache may—in certain circumstances—be combined to reach the trafficking amount. State v. Hazel, 226 N.C. App. 336, 347 (2013) (trafficking in heroin by possession case; amount of heroin recovered from the defendant's person outside the apartment was combined with heroin recovered from the apartment).

The entire weight of a mixture containing a controlled substance covered by the trafficking statutes can be used to support trafficking charges; the fact that the mixture is at an intermediate stage in the manufacturing process and is not ingestible, is unstable, and is not ready for distribution is irrelevant. State v. Davis, 236 N.C. App. 376, 386–87 (2014).

For purposes of the trafficking statutes, a mixture includes a combination of a controlled substance and rice, added to remove moisture. State v. Miranda, 235 N.C. App. 601, 608–09 (2014) (rejecting the defendant's argument that a combination of cocaine and rice did not constitute a mixture within the meaning of the trafficking statute).

Constitutionality (new note)

This trafficking offense and the ones listed below cover trafficking in the specified controlled substance and in mixtures containing that substance. The North Carolina Court of Appeals has rejected constitutional challenges grounded in the statute's coverage of mixtures. State v. Ellison, 213 N.C. App. 300, 309–12 (2011) (rejecting the defendant's due process and cruel and unusual punishment arguments in a trafficking in opium case), *aff'd on other grounds*, 366 N.C. 439 (2013).

Relation to other offenses (new note)

The listing of a particular controlled substance on the drug schedules does not limit the State's ability to prosecute a defendant for trafficking in a substance when a trafficking statute otherwise applies. *Ellison*, 213 N.C. App. at 323 ("the controlled substance schedule to which a particular opiate derivative is assigned has nothing to do with the extent to which activities involving that substance are subject to punishment under the trafficking statutes").

Trafficking in Methaqualone (page 730)

The section on "Punishment" and the new notes listed above in this supplement under "Trafficking in Synthetic Cannabinoids" apply to this offense as well.

Trafficking in Cocaine (page 731)

The section on "Punishment" and the new notes listed above in this supplement under "Trafficking in Synthetic Cannabinoids" apply to this offense as well.

Trafficking in Methamphetamine (page 732)

The section on "Punishment" and the new notes listed above in this supplement under "Trafficking in Synthetic Cannabinoids" apply to this offense as well.

Trafficking in Amphetamine (page 733)

The section on "Punishment" and the new notes listed above in this supplement under "Trafficking in Synthetic Cannabinoids" apply to this offense as well.

Trafficking in MDPV (page 734)

The section on "Punishment" and the new notes listed above in this supplement under "Trafficking in Synthetic Cannabinoids" apply to this offense as well.

Trafficking in Mephedrone (page 735)

The section on "Punishment" and the new notes listed above in this supplement under "Trafficking in Synthetic Cannabinoids" apply to this offense as well.

Trafficking in Opium or Heroin (page 736)

The section on "Punishment" and the new notes listed above in this supplement under "Trafficking in Synthetic Cannabinoids" apply to this offense as well.

Notes (page 736)

Element (3) (page 736)

Trafficking in opium bases criminal liability on the total weight of the mixture involved; tablets and pills are mixtures covered by that provision, including prescription pharmaceuticals. State v. Ellison, 366 N.C. 439, 443–44 (2013).

Immunity for treatment with opioid antagonist (new note)

G.S. 90-12.7 provides immunity for treating an overdose with the opioid antagonist naloxone hydrochloride. S.L. 2013-23; S.L. 2016-17, secs. 1–2.

Trafficking in LSD (page 737)

The section on "Punishment" and the new notes listed above in this supplement under "Trafficking in Synthetic Cannabinoids" apply to this offense as well.

Trafficking in MDA and MDMA (page 738)

The section on "Punishment" and the new notes listed above in this supplement under "Trafficking in Synthetic Cannabinoids" apply to this offense as well.

Controlled Substance Offenses Involving Fraud, Misrepresentation, or Similar Activities (page 740)

Obtaining a Controlled Substance by Misrepresenting Oneself as a Licensed Practitioner (page 740)

Statute (page 740)

2013 legislation, S.L. 2013-90, amended subsection (b) of G.S. 90-108 to read as follows:

> (b) Any person who violates this section shall be guilty of a Class 1 misdemeanor. Provided, that if the criminal pleading alleges that the violation was committed intentionally, and upon trial it is specifically found that the violation was committed intentionally, such violations shall be a Class I felony unless one of the following applies:
> (1) A person who violates subdivision (7) of subsection (a) of this section and also fortifies the structure, with the intent to impede law enforcement entry, (by barricading windows and doors) shall be punished as a Class I felon.
> (2) A person who violates subdivision (14) of subsection (a) of this section shall be punished as a Class G felon.

This statutory change does not affect the offenses covered in the main volume.

Maintaining a Store, Dwelling, Vehicle, Boat, or Other Place for Use, Storage, or Sale of Controlled Substances (page 743)

Notes (page 744)

Element (1) (page 744)

For a case where this Element was satisfied, see *State v. Huerta*, 221 N.C. App. 436, 450 (2012).

Element (2) (page 744)

For a case where the evidence was sufficient to establish this element, see *State v. Williams*, ___ N.C. App. ___, 774 S.E.2d 880, 888 (2015) (the defendant received mail addressed to him at the residence, his probation officer visited him there to conduct routine home contacts, the defendant's personal effects were at the residence, including a pay stub and work gear, and he identified the house to a third party as being his; the court rejected the defendant's argument that the evidence was insufficient because it failed to show he was financially or otherwise responsible for the dwelling or its upkeep, noting that residency standing alone can establish this element).

For another case where the evidence was insufficient to establish this element, see *State v. Holloway*, ___ N.C. App. ___, 793 S.E.2d 766, 774 (2016) (there was no evidence that the defendant was the owner or lessee of the residence, paid for its utilities or upkeep, had been seen in or around the dwelling, or lived there), *temporary stay allowed*, ___ N.C. App. ___, ___ S.E.2d ___ (Dec. 20, 2016).

Element (4)(a) (new note)

A defendant cannot be convicted under this prong on the basis of his or her own use of drugs in his or her vehicle. State v. Simpson, 230 N.C. App. 119, 121–22 (2013).

Element (4)(b) (page 745)

For a case where the evidence was held to be sufficient to establish this element, see *State v. Williams*, ___ N.C. App. ___, 774 S.E.2d 880, 889 (2015) (officers found a bag containing 39.7 grams of 4-methylethcathinone and methylone, a plastic bag containing "numerous little corner baggies," a set of digital scales, and $460 in twenty dollar bills).

Drug Paraphernalia Offenses (revised title)

Possession of Drug Paraphernalia (page 747)

Statute (page 747)

2014 legislation, S.L. 2014-119, sec. 3(a), amended G.S. 90-113.22(a) to read as follows:

> (a) It is unlawful for any person to knowingly use, or to possess with intent to use, drug paraphernalia to plant, propagate, cultivate, grow, harvest, manufacture, compound, convert, produce, process, prepare, test, analyze, package, repackage, store, contain, or conceal a controlled substance other than marijuana which it would be unlawful to possess, or to inject, ingest, inhale, or otherwise introduce into the body a controlled substance other than marijuana which it would be unlawful to possess.

2013 legislation, S.L. 2013-147, added a new subsection (c) to the statute, which subsequently was amended by 2015 legislation, S.L. 2015-284, sec. 2, to read as follows:

> (c) Prior to searching a person, a person's premises, or a person's vehicle, an officer may ask the person whether the person is in possession of a hypodermic needle or other sharp object that may cut or puncture the officer or whether such a hypodermic needle or other sharp object is on the premises or in the vehicle to be searched. If there is a hypodermic needle or other sharp object on the person, on the person's premises, or in the person's vehicle and the person alerts the officer of that fact prior to the search, the person shall not be charged with or prosecuted for possession of drug paraphernalia for the needle or sharp object, or for residual amounts of a controlled substance contained in the needle or sharp object. The exemption under this subsection does not apply to any other drug paraphernalia that may be present and found during the search. For purposes of this subsection, the term "officer" includes "criminal justice officers" as defined in G.S. 17C-2(3) and a "justice officer" as defined in G.S. 17E-2(3).

Notes (page 749)

Element (2) (new note)

For a discussion of actual and constructive possession in the context of drug possession offenses, see the note on Element (2) to "Possession of a Controlled Substance." For a case where the evidence was sufficient to establish that the defendant possessed drug paraphernalia, see *State v. Dulin*, ___ N.C. App. ___, 786 S.E.2d 803, 807–09 (2016) (paraphernalia (including, among other items, a digital scale and a marijuana grinder) was in plain view in a common living area of a home over which the defendant exercised nonexclusive control; the defendant spent hours at the house on the day in question and admitted that a blunt was in his truck parked out front; police found marijuana in the truck's console and in the house behind a photograph of the defendant; and several people visited the house while the defendant was there, including a man who shook hands with defendant as if they were passing an item back and forth).

Element (5) (new note)

As a result of 2014 legislation, this offense pertains to controlled substances other than marijuana. G.S. 90-113.22(a) (as amended by S.L. 2014-119, sec. 3(a)). If the controlled substance is marijuana, "Possession of Marijuana Paraphernalia," below, applies.

Exceptions (new note)

Before searching a person or his or her premises or vehicle, an officer may ask the person whether a hypodermic needle or other sharp object that may cut or puncture the officer is on the defendant's person or in the premises or vehicle to be searched. If such an object is present and the person alerts the officer of that fact before the search, the person may not be charged with or prosecuted for possession of drug paraphernalia for the needle or sharp object or for possession of residual amounts of a controlled substance contained in the needle or sharp object. G.S. 90-113.22(c). The exception does not apply to any other drug paraphernalia found during the search. *Id.*

Greater and lesser-included offenses (new note)

"Possession of Marijuana Paraphernalia," below, is a lesser-included offense of this one. G.S. 90-113.22A (enacted by S.L. 2014-119, sec. 3(b)).

Limited immunity from prosecution (new note)

A 2013 law, S.L. 2013-23, provides limited immunity from prosecution for persons seeking medical assistance for themselves or others in the event of a drug-related overdose. The law enacts G.S. 90-96.2, providing that a person who experiences a drug-related overdose or who seeks medical assistance for someone experiencing a drug-related overdose shall not be prosecuted for this offense if the evidence of the crime was obtained as a result of the person seeking medical assistance. G.S. 90-96.2(b), (c). The term "drug-related overdose" means "an acute condition, including mania, hysteria, extreme physical illness, coma, or death resulting from the consumption or use of a controlled substance, or another substance with which a controlled substance was combined, and that a layperson would reasonably believe to be a drug overdose that requires medical assistance." G.S. 90-96.2(a).

2016 legislation, S.L. 2016-88, sec. 4, enacted G.S. 90-113.27(c) providing limited immunity for employees, volunteers, and participants in authorized needle and hypodermic syringe exchange programs when those persons possess needles, hypodermic syringes, or other injection supplies obtained from or returned to an exchange program.

Possession of Marijuana Paraphernalia (new crime)

Statute

See G.S. 90-113.21, reproduced in the main volume under "Possession of Drug Paraphernalia."

§ 90-113.22A. Possession of marijuana drug paraphernalia.

(a) It is unlawful for any person to knowingly use, or to possess with intent to use, drug paraphernalia to plant, propagate, cultivate, grow, harvest, manufacture, compound, convert, produce, process, prepare, test, analyze, package, repackage, store, contain, or conceal marijuana or to inject, ingest, inhale, or otherwise introduce marijuana into the body.

(b) A violation of this section is a Class 3 misdemeanor. A violation of this section shall be a lesser included offense of G.S. 90-113.22.

Elements

A person guilty of this offense

(1) knowingly

(2) uses or possesses with the intent to use

(3) drug paraphernalia

(4) for any of the following purposes:

(a) to plant, propagate, cultivate, grow, harvest, manufacture, compound, convert, produce, process, prepare, test, analyze, package, repackage, store, contain, or conceal *or*

(b) to inject, ingest, inhale, or otherwise introduce into the body

(5) marijuana.

Punishment

Class 3 misdemeanor. G.S. 90-113.22A(b).

Notes

Generally. This offense was enacted in 2014. S.L. 2014-119, sec. 3(b). In terms of elements, it is the same as "Possession of Drug Paraphernalia" except that this offense pertains only to marijuana paraphernalia. Thus, the relevant notes to that offense apply here as well.

Greater and lesser-included offenses. This offense is a lesser-included offense of "Possession of Drug Paraphernalia." G.S. 90-113.22A(b).

Related Offenses Not in This Chapter

See the offenses listed under "Possession of Drug Paraphernalia."

28

Motor Vehicle Offenses

Driving While License Revoked or Disqualified (page 755)

Statute (page 755)

Recent legislation, S.L. 2012-146, sec. 8; S.L. 2013-360, sec. 18B.14(f); S.L. 2015-186, sec. 2; S.L. 2015-264, sec. 38(a), amended the statute so that subsections (a), (a1), (a2), and (a3) now read as follows:

(a) Driving While License Revoked.—Except as provided in subsections (a1) or (a2) of this section, any person whose drivers license has been revoked who drives any motor vehicle upon the highways of the State while the license is revoked is guilty of a Class 3 misdemeanor.

(a1) Driving While License Revoked for Impaired Driving.—Any person whose drivers license has been revoked for an impaired driving revocation as defined in G.S. 20-28.2(a) and who drives any motor vehicle upon the highways of the State is guilty of a Class 1 misdemeanor. Upon conviction, the person's license shall be revoked for an additional period of one year for the first offense, two years for the second offense, and permanently for a third or subsequent offense.

If the person's license was originally revoked for an impaired driving revocation, the court may order as a condition of probation that the offender abstain from alcohol consumption and verify compliance by use of a continuous alcohol monitoring system, of a type approved by the Division of Adult Correction of the Department of Public Safety, for a minimum period of 90 days.

The restoree of a revoked drivers license who operates a motor vehicle upon the highways of the State without maintaining financial responsibility as provided by law shall be punished as for driving without a license.

(a2) Driving Without Reclaiming License.—A person convicted under subsection (a) or (a1) of this section shall be punished as if the person had been convicted of driving without a license under G.S. 20-35 if the person demonstrates to the court that either of the following is true:

 (1) At the time of the offense, the person's license was revoked solely under G.S. 20-16.5 and one of the following applies:

  a. The offense occurred more than 45 days after the effective date of a revocation order issued under G.S. 20-16.5(f) and the period of revocation was 45 days as provided under subdivision (3) of that subsection; or

  b. The offense occurred more than 30 days after the effective date of the revocation order issued under any other provision of G.S. 20-16.5.

(2) At the time of the offense the person had met the requirements of G.S. 50-13.12, or G.S. 110-142.2 and was eligible for reinstatement of the person's drivers license privilege as provided therein.

In addition, a person punished under this subsection shall be treated for drivers license and insurance rating purposes as if the person had been convicted of driving without a license under G.S. 20-35, and the conviction report sent to the Division must indicate that the person is to be so treated.

(a3) Driving After Notification or Failure to Appear.—A person shall be guilty of a Class 1 misdemeanor if:

(1) The person operates a motor vehicle upon a highway while that person's license is revoked for an impaired drivers license revocation after the Division has sent notification in accordance with G.S. 20-48; or

(2) The person fails to appear for two years from the date of the charge after being charged with an implied consent offense.

Upon conviction, the person's drivers license shall be revoked for an additional period of one year for the first offense, two years for the second offense, and permanently for a third or subsequent offense. The restoree of a revoked drivers license who operates a motor vehicle upon the highways of the State without maintaining financial responsibility as provided by law shall be punished as for driving without a license.

2015 legislation, S.L. 2015-186, sec. 2, amended subsection (d) so that the first sentence of that subsection now reads as follows:

A person who was convicted of a violation that disqualified the person and required the person's drivers license to be revoked who drives a motor vehicle during the revocation period is punishable as provided in subsection (a1) of this section.

Driving While License Revoked (page 756)

Punishment (page 756)

As a result of the legislation noted above, delete the text of this section and replace it with the following:

Class 3 misdemeanor, except that if the circumstances listed in G.S. 20-28(a2) apply, the person will be punished as if he or she had been convicted of driving without a license under G.S. 20-35. G.S. 20-28(a2).

Notes (page 757)

Element (2) (page 757)

As a result of 2016 legislation, S.L. 2016-90, sec. 13(a), delete the text after the first sentence of this note and replace it with the following:

Neither mopeds nor electric assisted bicycles are motor vehicles. G.S. 20-4.01(7a) (definition of electric assisted bicycle); -4.01(23) (definition of motor vehicle); -4.01(27)(d1) (definition of moped).

Element (4) (page 757)

2016 legislation, S.L. 2016-90, sec. 10(c), amended G.S. 20-48, allowing the DMV to give notice by email or other electronic means under certain circumstances.

Related Offenses Not in This Chapter (page 758)

The statutory citation for the second offense in this section should be to G.S. 20-28.

Driving While License Revoked for an Impaired Driving Revocation (page 758)

Statute (page 758)

As a result of the 2015 legislation noted above, the statutory citation in this section should read as follows:

G.S. 20-28(a1).

Punishment (page 758)

As a result of the 2015 legislation noted above, delete the text of this section and replace it with the following:

Class 1 misdemeanor, G.S. 20-28(a1), except that if the circumstances listed in G.S. 20-28(a2) apply, the person will be punished as if he or she had been convicted of driving without a license under G.S. 20-35. G.S. 20-28(a2).

Failure to Appear after an Implied Consent Offense Charge (page 760)

Statute (page 760)

As a result of the 2015 legislation noted above, the statutory citation in this section should read as follows:

G.S. 20-28(a3).

Impaired Driving and Related Offenses (page 762)

Impaired Driving (page 762)

Punishment (page 762)

2012 legislation, S.L. 2012-146, sec. 9, amended G.S. 20-179(g) (Level One punishment) to provide that a judge may reduce the minimum term of imprisonment to a term of not less than 10 days if a condition of special probation is imposed requiring the defendant to abstain from alcohol consumption and be monitored by a continuous alcohol monitoring (CAM) system for a period of not less than 120 days. Pretrial CAM monitoring may be credited against the 120-day monitoring period, up to 60 days.

S.L. 2012-146 also amended G.S. 20-179(h) (Level Two punishment) to now provide that the term of imprisonment may be suspended only if a condition of special probation is imposed to require the defendant to serve a term of imprisonment of at least seven days or to abstain from consuming alcohol for at least 90 consecutive days, as verified by a CAM system. Up to 60 days of pretrial CAM monitoring may be credited against the 90-day monitoring period. 2013 legislation, S.L. 2013-348, made additional changes to G.S. 20-179(h), requiring the completion of 240 hours of community service in certain circumstances.

As amended by S.L. 2012-194, S.L. 2012-146 also added new subsections, (k2) and (k3), to G.S. 20-179 providing as follows:

- The judge may order as a condition of special probation for any level of offense under G.S. 20-179 that the defendant abstain from alcohol consumption as verified by a CAM system. G.S. 20-179(k2).
- The court may authorize probation officers to require defendants to submit to CAM for assessment purposes if the defendant has been required to abstain from alcohol

consumption during the term of probation and the probation officer believes the defendant is consuming alcohol. G.S. 20-179(k3). The defendant bears the cost of the CAM in these circumstances. *Id.*

Notes (page 764)

Element (1) (page 764)

There was sufficient evidence apart from the defendant's extrajudicial confession that he was driving the vehicle when the defendant was the only person in the vehicle and he was sitting in the driver's seat. State v. Reeves, 218 N.C. App. 570, 573–74 (2012).

Element (2) (page 765)

As a result of 2016 legislation, S.L. 2016-90, sec. 13(a), delete the last sentence of the first paragraph of this note and replace it with the following:

Mopeds and electric assisted bicycles are vehicles but are not motor vehicles. G.S. 20-4.01(7a) (definition of electric assisted bicycle), -4.01(23) (definition of motor vehicle), and -4.01(27)(d1) (definition of moped).

Element (3) (page 765)

In *State v. Ricks*, 237 N.C. App. 359, 364–66 (2014), the court held that a cut through on a vacant lot was not a public vehicular area and that when instructing the jury on this element, the court should give the entire statutory definition of that term.

Element (4)(a) (page 765)

In a felony death by vehicle case, the evidence was sufficient to establish that the defendant was impaired even without evidence of the defendant's blood-alcohol level where the defendant admitted to an officer drinking "at least a 12-pack" and admitted at trial that she drank at least seven or eight beers; a responding officer noticed the strong odor of alcohol and that the defendant slurred her words and opined that she seemed intoxicated; and a doctor who treated the defendant at the hospital diagnosed her with alcohol intoxication, largely based on her behavior. State v. Hawk, 236 N.C. App. 177, 180–81 (2014).

Related Offenses Not in This Chapter (page 768)

As a result of 2016 legislation, S.L. 2016-34, add the following to this section:

Impaired boating offenses. G.S. 75A-10.3.

Operating a School Bus, School Activity Bus, Child Care Vehicle, Ambulance, Other EMS Vehicle, Firefighting Vehicle, or Law Enforcement Vehicle after Consuming Alcohol (revised title) (page 772)

Statute (page 772)

2013 legislation, S.L. 2013-105, amended subsection (a) of G.S. 20-138.2B to read as follows:

(a) Offense.—A person commits the offense of operating a school bus, school activity bus, child care vehicle, ambulance, other emergency medical services vehicle, firefighting vehicle, or law enforcement vehicle after consuming alcohol if the person drives a school bus, school activity bus, child care vehicle, ambulance, other emergency medical services vehicle, firefighting vehicle, or law enforcement vehicle upon any highway, any street, or any public vehicular area within the State while consuming alcohol or while alcohol remains in the person's body. This section does not apply to law enforcement officers acting in the course of, and within the scope of, their official duties.

Elements (page 772)

As a result of 2013 legislation, S.L. 2013-105, Element (2) should read as follows:

(2) a school bus, school activity bus, child care vehicle, ambulance, other emergency medical services vehicle, firefighting vehicle, or law enforcement vehicle

Notes (page 773)

Exception (new note)

This offense does not apply to law enforcement officers acting in the course and scope of their official duties. G.S. 20-138.2B(a) (as amended by S.L. 2013-105).

Serious Injury by a Vehicle (page 777)

Felony Serious Injury by a Vehicle (page 778)
Related Offenses Not in This Chapter (page 779)

As a result of 2016 legislation, S.L. 2016-34, add the following to this section:

Injury by impaired boating offenses. G.S. 75A-10.3.

Reckless Driving (page 781)

Reckless Driving: Carelessly and Heedlessly (page 781)
Notes (page 781)

Multiple convictions and punishments (page 782)
Double jeopardy bars convicting a defendant of speeding and reckless driving when the defendant also is convicted of felony speeding to elude arrest, which was raised from a misdemeanor to a felony based on the aggravating factors of speeding and driving recklessly. State v. Mulder, 233 N.C. App. 82, 89–94 (2014) (going on to conclude that, additionally, the legislature did not intend for multiple punishments in this context).

Reckless Driving: Endangering Persons or Property (page 782)
Notes (page 783)

Generally (new note)
There was sufficient evidence of reckless driving where the defendant was intoxicated, all four tires of her vehicle went off the road, road marks indicated that she lost control of her vehicle, and the vehicle overturned twice and traveled 131 feet from where it went off the road before it flipped and another 108 feet after it flipped. State v. Geisslercrain, 233 N.C. App. 186, 189–90 (2014).

The mere fact that an unlicensed driver ran off the road and collided with a utility pole is insufficient to sustain a conviction. *In re* A.N.C., 225 N.C. App. 315, 325–26 (2013) (evidence showed only that the juvenile's vehicle collided with a utility pole; there was no evidence that the collision resulted from careless or reckless driving).

School Bus Offenses (page 796)

Statute (page 796)

As a result of 2013 legislation, S.L. 2013-293, subsection (e) of G.S. 20-217 is amended to read as follows:

> (e) Except as provided in subsection (g) of this section, any person violating this section shall be guilty of a Class 1 misdemeanor and shall pay a minimum fine of five hundred dollars ($500.00). A person who violates subsection (a) of this section shall not receive a prayer for judgment continued under any circumstances.

That legislation also amended subsection (g) and enacted subsections (g1) and (g2) to read as follows:

> (g) Any person who willfully violates subsection (a) of this section and strikes any person shall be guilty of a Class I felony and shall pay a minimum fine of one thousand two hundred fifty dollars ($1,250). Any person who willfully violates subsection (a) of this section and strikes any person, resulting in the death of that person, shall be guilty of a Class H felony and shall pay a minimum fine of two thousand five hundred dollars ($2,500).
>
> (g1) The Division shall revoke, for a period of one year, the drivers license of a person convicted of a second misdemeanor violation under this section within a three-year period. The Division shall revoke, for a period of two years, the drivers license of a person convicted of a Class I felony violation under this section. The Division shall revoke, for a period of three years, the drivers license of a person convicted of a Class H felony violation under this section. The Division shall permanently revoke the drivers license of (i) a person convicted of a second felony violation under this section within any period of time and (ii) a person convicted of a third misdemeanor violation under this section within any period of time.
>
> In the case of a first felony conviction under this section, the licensee may apply to the sentencing court for a limited driving privilege after a period of six months of revocation, provided the person's drivers license has not also been revoked or suspended under any other provision of law. A limited driving privilege issued under this subsection shall be valid for the period of revocation remaining in the same manner and under the terms and conditions prescribed in G.S. 20-16.1(b). If the person's drivers license is revoked or suspended under any other statute, the limited driving privilege issued pursuant to this subsection is invalid.
>
> In the case of a permanent revocation of a person's drivers license for committing a third misdemeanor violation under this section within any period of time, the person may apply for a drivers license after two years. The Division may, with or without a hearing, issue a new drivers license upon satisfactory proof that the former licensee has not been convicted of a moving violation under this Chapter or the laws of another state. The Division may impose any restrictions or conditions on the new drivers license that the Division considers appropriate. Any conditions or restrictions imposed by the Division shall not exceed two years.
>
> In the case of a permanent revocation of a person's drivers license for committing a second Class I felony violation under this section within any period of time, the person may apply for a drivers license after three years. The Division may, with or without a hearing, issue a new drivers license upon satisfactory proof that the former licensee has not been convicted of a moving violation under this Chapter or the laws of another state. The Division may impose any restrictions or conditions on the new drivers license that the Division considers appropriate. Any conditions or restrictions imposed by the Division shall not exceed three years.
>
> Any person whose drivers license is revoked under this section is disqualified pursuant to G.S. 20-17.4 from driving a commercial motor vehicle for the period of time in which the person's drivers license remains revoked under this section.
>
> (g2) Pursuant to G.S. 20-54, failure of a person to pay any fine or costs imposed pursuant to this section shall result in the Division withholding the registration renewal of a motor vehicle registered in that person's name. The clerk of superior court in the county in which the case was disposed shall notify the Division of any person who fails to pay a fine

or costs imposed pursuant to this section within 20 days of the date specified in the court's judgment, as required by G.S. 20-24.2(a)(2). The Division shall continue to withhold the registration renewal of a motor vehicle until the clerk of superior court notifies the Division that the person has satisfied the conditions of G.S. 20-24.1(b) applicable to the person's case. The provisions of this subsection shall be in addition to any other actions the Division may take to enforce the payment of any fine imposed pursuant to this section.

Passing or Failing to Stop for a Stopped School Bus (page 796)

Punishment (page 797)

As a result of 2013 legislation, S.L. 2013-293, delete the text of this section and replace it with the following:

Class 1 misdemeanor and mandatory minimum fine of $500. G.S. 20-217(e). A defendant may not receive a prayer for judgment continued for this offense. *Id.*

Notes (page 797)

License revocations and consequences for failure to pay fines (new note)
2013 legislation, S.L. 2013-293, enacted G.S. 20-217(g1) and (g2) pertaining to license revocations and consequences of failing to pay fines imposed upon conviction.

Felony Passing or Failing to Stop for a School Bus (page 797)

Punishment (page 798)

As a result of 2013 legislation, S.L. 2013-293, delete the text of this section and replace it with the following:

If Element (3)(a) is present, the offense is a Class I felony with a mandatory minimum fine of $1,250. G.S. 20-217(g). If Element (3)(b) is present, the offense is a Class H felony with a mandatory minimum fine of $2,500. *Id.*

Notes (page 798)

License revocations and consequences for failure to pay fines (new note)
See this note under "Passing or Failing to Stop for a Stopped School Bus," above in this supplement.

Failure to Stop, Move Over, or Slow Down for an Emergency Vehicle (page 801)

Statute (page 801)

2013 legislation, S.L. 2013-415, sec. 1(e), amended subsection (a) of G.S. 20-157 to read as follows:

(a) Upon the approach of any law enforcement or fire department vehicle or public or private ambulance or rescue squad emergency service vehicle, or a vehicle operated by the Division of Marine Fisheries, or the Division of Parks and Recreation of the Department of Environment and Natural Resources, or the North Carolina Forest Service of the Department of Agriculture and Consumer Services when traveling in response to a fire alarm or other emergency response purpose, giving warning signal by appropriate light and by audible bell, siren or exhaust whistle, audible under normal conditions from a distance not less than 1000 feet, the driver of every other vehicle shall immediately drive the same to a position as near as possible and parallel to the righthand edge or curb, clear of any intersection of streets or highways, and shall stop and remain in such position unless otherwise directed by a law enforcement or traffic officer until the law enforcement or fire department vehicle, or the vehicle operated by the Division of Marine Fisheries, or the Division of Parks and Recreation of the Department of Environment and Natural Resources, or the North Carolina Forest Service of the Department of Agriculture and Consumer Services, or the public or private ambulance or rescue squad emergency service vehicle shall have passed. Provided, however, this subsection shall not apply to vehicles traveling in the opposite direction of the vehicles herein enumerated when traveling on a four lane limited access highway with a median divider dividing the highway for vehicles traveling in opposite directions, and provided further that the violation of this subsection shall be negligence per se. Violation of this subsection is a Class 2 misdemeanor.

2012 legislation, S.L. 2012-14, and 2015 legislation, S.L. 2015-26, sec. 3, amended the definition of the term "public service vehicle" in G.S. 20-157(f). That term now includes:

a vehicle that (i) is being used to assist motorists or law enforcement officers with wrecked or disabled vehicles, (ii) is being used to install, maintain, or restore utility service, including electric, cable, telephone, communications, and gas, (iii) is being used in the collection of refuse, solid waste, or recycling, or (iv) is a highway maintenance vehicle owned and operated by or contracted by the State or a local government and is operating an amber colored flashing light authorized by G.S. 20-130.2.

Failure to Stop for an Emergency Vehicle (page 802)

Elements (page 802)

As a result of 2013 legislation, S.L. 2013-415, sec. 1(e), Element (3) should read as follows:

(3) upon the approach of a
    (a) law enforcement or fire department vehicle, ambulance, rescue squad vehicle, *or*
    (b) vehicle operated by the Division of Marine Fisheries, the Division of Parks and Recreation, or the North Carolina Forest Service when traveling in response to a fire alarm or other emergency response purpose

Aggravated Failure to Stop for an Emergency Vehicle (page 803)

Elements (page 803)

As a result of 2013 legislation, S.L. 2013-415, sec. 1(e), Element (3) should read as follows:

(3) upon the approach of a
    (a) law enforcement or fire department vehicle, ambulance, rescue squad vehicle, *or*
    (b) vehicle operated by the Division of Marine Fisheries, the Division of Parks and Recreation, or the North Carolina Forest Service when traveling in response to a fire alarm or other emergency response purpose

Notes (page 804)

Element (6) (page 804)

Delete the second paragraph of this note and replace it with the following:

The term "public service vehicle" means a vehicle that

- is being used to assist motorists or law enforcement officers with wrecked or disabled vehicles,
- is being used to install, maintain, or restore utility service, including electric, cable, telephone, communications, and gas,
- is being used in the collection of refuse, solid waste, or recycling, or

- is a highway maintenance vehicle owned and operated by or contracted by the State or a local government and is operating an amber colored flashing light authorized by G.S. 20-130.2.

G.S. 20-130.2. G.S. 20-157(f), as amended by S.L. 2012-14 and S.L. 2015-26, sec. 3.

Failure to Move Over or Slow Down for a Stopped Emergency or Public Service Vehicle
(page 804)

Elements (page 804)

As a result of 2013 legislation, S.L. 2013-415, sec. 1(e), Element (4)(a) should read as follows:

(4) (a) (i) law enforcement or fire department vehicle, ambulance, rescue squad vehicle, or public service vehicle, *or*

(ii) vehicle operated by the Division of Marine Fisheries, the Division of Parks and Recreation, or the North Carolina Forest Service when traveling in response to a fire alarm or other emergency response purpose

---

Speeding to Elude Arrest (page 806)

Statute (page 806)

As a result of 2013 legislation, S.L. 2013-243, secs. 6–7, the italicized note after G.S. 20-141.5 should read:

Subsections (d) through (k) are not reproduced here.

Felony Speeding to Elude Arrest (page 806)

Notes (page 807)

Element (1) (page 807)

For a case where there was sufficient evidence, even though the officer lost sight of the vehicle for a period of time, that the defendant was the driver of the vehicle, see *State v. Lindsey*, 366 N.C. 325 (2012) (per curiam) (reversing 219 N.C. App. 249 (2012) for the reasons stated in the dissenting opinion).

State of mind (new note)

The evidence established that the defendant intended to elude an officer notwithstanding her assertion that she drove away because she preferred to be arrested by a female officer rather than the male officer who stopped her; the defendant's preference was irrelevant to whether she intended to elude the officer. State v. Cameron, 223 N.C. App. 72, 74–75 (2012).

Multiple convictions and punishments (new note)

Double jeopardy bars convicting a defendant of speeding and reckless driving when the defendant also is convicted of felony speeding to elude arrest, which was raised from a misdemeanor to a felony based on the aggravating factors of speeding and driving recklessly. State v. Mulder, 233 N.C. App. 82, 89–94 (2014) (going on to conclude that, additionally, the legislature did not intend for multiple punishments in this context).

Forfeiture (new note)

2013 legislation, S.L. 2013-243, sec. 6, repealed existing forfeiture provisions and enacted G.S. 20-141.5(k), S.L. 2013-243, sec. 7, providing that if a person is convicted of felony speeding to elude arrest, the motor vehicle used is subject to forfeiture in accordance with the procedure set out in G.S. 20-28.2, -28.3, -28.4, and -28.5.

Aggravated Felony Speeding to Elude Arrest (page 808)

Notes (page 809)

Forfeiture (new note)
See this note under "Felony Speeding to Elude Arrest," above in this supplement.

Aggravated Misdemeanor Speeding to Elude Arrest (page 810)

Notes (page 810)

Forfeiture (new note)
See this note under "Felony Speeding to Elude Arrest," above in this supplement.

Case Index

Statute Index

North Carolina Session Laws